UP TO THE FRONT OF THE LINE

Robert P. Turner

UP TO THE FRONT
OF THE LINE

BLACKS IN THE
AMERICAN POLITICAL SYSTEM

National University Publications
KENNIKAT PRESS • 1975
Port Washington, N.Y. • London

Manufactured in the United States of America

Published by
Kennikat Press Corp.
Port Washington, N.Y./London

Library of Congress Cataloging in Publication Data

Turner, Robert P
    Up to the front of the line.

    (National university publications)
    Bibliography: p.
    Includes index.
    1. Negroes—Politics and suffrage. 2. Ne-
groes—Civil rights. 3. Negroes—History.
4. Slavery in the United States. I. Title.
E185.T88   320.9'73   75-15614
ISBN 0-8046-9097-9

CONTENTS

A note of gratitude is due Gwendolyn Turner for typing and correcting several drafts of the manuscript and for overall logistical management of the project. The author is also fortunate to have had available the facilities and staffs of Rush Rhees and Rundell Libraries.

UP TO THE FRONT OF THE LINE

CHARLIE SMITH

This is the story told by a man called Charlie Smith of his arrival in America. The incident and series of events described in the account stem from the curiosity of an African lad of twelve from Liberia who had never before seen a white man. Purported to be the oldest man in the world, the Bartow, Florida, resident, at 132 years old—an age verified by the Social Security Administration and the American Medical Association, is the oldest living man in the United States.

I asked my mumma if I could go down to the landing to see. Well this man—his name was Legree—fooled us onto the boat . . . and when we came back up on deck, we was right out in the Atlantic. I cried all the way over. . . .

They put us in a big square in New Orleans and strung rope like a fence all around. Every time they puts me on the block, no one bids 'cause I was small. So they take me off and put me back later but no one wants me.

Finally old man Charlie Smith, he steps over the rope and takes me. He carries me back to his ranch in Texas. . . . I never did find out how much he paid for me.

Charlie Smith

1

FROM THE BEGINNING

We came from Africa—some of us aboard ships with those men of Europe whose names lend romance and splendor to Western history.

We were brought from Africa—most of us by men whose names history rarely recounts but whose deeds shall never be forgotten.

From the beginning we were here, and from the beginning the political significance of our presence has dictated the organic framework of the new nation.

Black men such as Pedro Alonzo Niño piloted Columbus' fleet on the latter's exploration of the New World. Likewise, Balboa had a large number of negroes aboard his ship during the discovery of the Pacific Ocean. Cortez was accompanied by a negro who brought rice and wheat to the Western Hemisphere. Negroes accompanied Narváez and his successor, Cabeza de Vaca, through what is now the Southwestern United States.

Western history is replete with examples of the black man's presence in the New World prior to 1619. Furthermore, evidence[1] is beginning to accumulate which places the black man in the New World long before the European was to appear. And why not? After all, Africa is nearer to America than is Europe.

The majority of our ancestors arrived beginning in 1619 when the Dutch East India Company sold twenty negroes to the colonists in Jamestown, Virginia, to fulfill conditions of servitude. At this time the colonies had no statutes respecting slavery, but the Virginians quickly invoked the law of Moses[2] authorizing the enslavement of "strangers." This article sanctioned the slave-trade and the holding of negroes and Indians in

3

bondage. Hereafter, *slaving* became a very profitable and organized business operated by specially chartered companies. As an indication of the venture, half way into the second half of the seventeenth century the trade became so profitable that, as a result of a general demand, it was thrown open to all vessels. This brought in vessels from America—from Newport and Boston. The slavers traveled between America and forts previously established on the coast of Guinea. The French operated out of a section of Senegal, the English on the Gambia Coast, and the English and Dutch on the Gold Coast. Their slave cargoes were composed of Africans of all descriptions: Senegalese, considered part Arabic; Coromantees, strong of mind and body; Iboes, psychologically unadaptable to slavery. A few Moors and some brown people from Madagascar were also imported.

Since there were no legislative precepts for slavery in the Colonies when the first Africans arrived in 1619, the latter were looked upon judicially in much the same way as white indentured servants. Oddly enough, it was in Massachusetts, not Virginia, that the earliest colonial legislation on the subject of slavery took place. The Massachusetts "Body of Liberties or Fundamentals" of 1641 contains the following statement taken from the Mosaic Law: "There shall never be any bond slavery, villeinage, nor captivity among us, unless it be lawful captives taken in just wars, and such strangers that willingly sell themselves, or are sold, unto us." This law, as one can see, sanctioned not only slavery but also slave-trade. Slavery as such was not legally recognized by Virginia until some twenty years later in 1662 when the negro was considered permanently in bondage to his master, "incapable of making satisfaction for the time lost in running away by addition of time."

Until near the end of the seventeenth century, the labor demands of the slowly expanding colonies could be met by indentured servants from Europe. Consequently, there were not many requests for Africans and the number of slaves grew slowly. In 1688 England ceased exporting indentured servants causing an instant increase in the number of slaves needed to replace those who died as well as the indentured servants who would no longer be forthcoming. Moreover, the British government looked upon slaves as essential to colonization. Likewise, other European nations trafficking in slaves supplied their colonies abundantly. Accordingly, the number of slaves in colonial America increased from approximately 58,850 in 1715 to 501,000 in 1775. The first United States Census taken in 1790 states that there were 697,897 slaves in the country out of a total population of 3.9 million inhabitants. By the year 1800 there were 893,041 slaves in America.

Politically speaking, the whole point would be missed if we were to allow, for even a moment, the notion that the importance of the negro lay in numbers alone. The slave, in fact, had no political voice; he could not even vote. The question, of a much more serious nature, was simply this: How was the black man to be looked upon vis-à-vis the white man? How was the black man to be looked upon with respect to the laws of mankind in light of the laws of God? If he was to be looked upon as a sub-human species not amenable to the civilized practices of white men, the slave was no different from any other property his owner might possess such as oxen or swine. On the other hand, if slaves were to be considered human beings, the question then became one of political representation. How, under a democratic form of government, were the slaves to be counted in order to determine the number of elected representatives at the various levels of government? How was justice to be administered? What would be the relationship of the slave to the political, economic, and civil policies of the nation?

Proponents on both sides of the issue—human versus sub-human status of negroes—were numerous and, beginning in 1621, heated debates ensued in every colonial legislature. The debate on the status of the slave went beyond mere political and economic considerations. Quite often the pros and cons of the matter were restated and justified on moral and religious grounds. Regardless of the form, the basic question always centered around such topics as: Should the slave be regarded as person or property? Should the slave be set free having converted to Christianity? Could the slave own land? What was the status of his offspring? How should intermarriage be viewed? What was the status of the offspring when one parent was black and the other white, or when one was free and the other slave? What was the relationship between master and slave?

Slavery was made hereditary in 1662. Virginia was the first to initiate such a system. Following the lead of Virginia all of the other colonial assemblies over the next seventy-three years enacted similar legislation: Maryland, 1663; Massachusetts, 1698; Connecticut and New Jersey, 1704; Pennsylvania and New York, 1706; South Carolina, 1712; Rhode Island, 1728; and North Carolina, 1741.

It is a fact that the black man had no politcal voice during the early colonial days. He had no political voice because he could not vote. However, it would be a grave mistake to think that the negro was politically insignificant. From the moment in 1619 when those twenty Africans arrived in Jamestown, Virginia, until 1741 when North Carolina settled the question of hereditary slavery within its boundaries, more laws were enacted in the legislative chambers of the colonies dealing with the status of the black man than on any other subject. It was during this pre-Revolutionary period that the highly politicized significance of the black man's presence transformed the African into a slave.

Although powerless and without voice, the political significance of the black man's presence became evident during the early stages of the Revolution. The entire question of the status of the negro sent out philosophical reverberations to the very foundation and *raison d'être* of the new nation. Was not the Declaration of Independence based upon the "rights-of-man" theory which justified universal liberty? Granted there were some who argued that the Declaration of Independence did not apply to negroes. Nevertheless, in 1774, a speaker before the Provincial Congress of Massachusetts brought the substance of the issue into proper focus when he cautioned of the "propriety, that while we are attempting to free ourselves from slavery, our present embarrassments, and preserve ourselves from slavery, that we also take into consideration the state and circumstances of the negro slaves in this province."

Finding it impossible to reconcile their holding of men to bondage while simultaneously asserting the right of all men to freedom, the leaders of the Revolution met the issue head-on. James Otis, when arguing the case of the Writs of Assistance, also argued that the slave should be freed. Patrick Henry, based upon his denunciation of royalist agents within the country, analogized and later expressed himself on the right of the negro to freedom.

The Philosopher of the Revolution, Thomas Jefferson, justified the revolt against England on the grounds that the King had promoted the slave trade. Incorporated into the original draft of the Declaration of Independence appeared an indictment against George III. The King was charged by Jefferson with having violated the "most sacred rights of life and liberty of a distant people, who never offended him, captivating them into slavery into another hemisphere or to incur miserable death in their transportation thither." Alongside Jefferson stood other makers of the Revolution including Henry Laurens of South Carolina and George Washington of Virginia. These men supported Jefferson in 1776 when he declared "that all men are created equal, that they are endowed by their Creator with certain inalienable Rights, that among these are Life, Liberty and the pursuit of Happiness."

As beautiful as these words are and as clear as was their meaning, they had little effect in abating the voices of those who considered the negro a savage and therefore unfit to fight in a gentlemen's war. In the beginning their sentiment prevailed. The fact that negroes had numbered among the first to die (Crispus Attucks) and had served meritoriously at Bunker Hill (Peter Salem) in defense of the new nation was not considered in this matter. Consequently, the early attempts to enlist negroes on a larger scale to fight in the war failed. As Washington was soon to learn, when he took command of the Army at Cambridge, this ban applied not only to slaves but to free men of color as well.

Despite relentless debate, the prohibition on negroes serving in the Army continued as standard operating procedure for some time. It was not until the colonists realized that the British were successfully deploying negro troops in North Carolina and Georgia that the colonial leaders began receding from their stance of denying the enlistment of negroes. The actual enlistment practices, however, were matters to be decided by the individual members of the Commonwealth. Historical evidence indicates that the negro served with valor during the Revolutionary War.

During this period all of the colonies except South Carolina and Georgia made a general effort toward wiping out slavery; in addition, the Continental Congress began prohibiting the importation of slaves. At the close of the war attempts led by Thomas Jefferson before the Congress to enact rules that would comprehensively exclude slavery from vast dominions of Federal territory failed. Through passage of the Ordinance of 1787,[3] the last Continental Congress, meeting in New York simultaneously with the Constitutional Convention in Philadelphia, slavery was excluded from the Northwest Territory.

Attempts to change the status of the negro, so evident during the Revolution, fizzled at the end of the war. Slavery existed in every state with the exception of Massachusetts. The majority of slaves resided in the South. In those states having small black populations, emancipation proceeded smoothly. Where negroes were in large numbers a reaction against their being set free developed.

When the Constitutional Convention met in 1787 to revise the Articles of Confederation (1777), the product of their efforts was the Constitution of the United States. To insure their being well represented at the proceedings the states sent their most highly informed and knowledgeable men. The main problem that had to be settled by these men was that having to do with the rule of apportionment. How many members should serve in the first branch of the government? Should the number from each state be fixed or should it change as the state population changed? Should property be taken into account when deciding apportionment, or should population be the sole criterion?

The South called for representation based on total number, bond and free. The North demanded representation according to the number of free persons only. The South wanted the negroes to be counted in order to obtain greater representation but not when it came to the apportionment of Federal taxes. Obviously, the North disagreed. A representative from New Jersey, who regarded slaves only as property, reminded the South that since it did not allow for representation of slaves in the state, it had no basis for seeking their representation in the Federal government. One of Pennsylvania's delegates could not see why the slaves should be represented when they were not allowed to vote. If they were to be admitted as citizens, he questioned, why not on an equal basis with other citizens? If they were to be admitted as property why shouldn't all property be considered in the determination?

A compromise solution was finally reached when it was agreed, on a suggestion of Benjamin Franklin, that representation be based on taxation, the latter being estimated by counting all whites and multiplying the total number of blacks by three-fifths. This formulation was agreed upon for determining representation in the House by a pro-slavery South seeking greater political power and an anti-slavery North now more concerned with good government than with the "rights-of-man." It was also decided that each state should have two senators.

Monday, May 14, 1787, was the day established for the meeting of the delegates in convention, the sole purpose of which was to revise the "Federal System of Government." No business was transacted on this date.

The actual business of the Convention began on Friday, May 25, 1787, when delegations from nine states met and unanimously elected George Washington, former Commander-in-Chief, President of the Convention. Major William Jackson was chosen Secretary and a committee to prepare standing rules and order was appointed.

On May 29, the subject of representation was broached when a delegate from Virginia, Randolph, introduced a resolution stating that "the rights of suffrage in the National Legislature ought to be proportional to the Quotas of contribution, or to the number of free inhabitants." No action was taken on the resolution and when it was again introduced on the following day it was postponed by agreement. With respect to the question of representation, the presence of the negro was beginning to make itself felt. When the Committee of the Whole met on June 11, it was agreed that in the House of Representatives representation ought to be based on some "equitable ratio of representation in proportion to the whole number of white and other free citizens and inhabitants of every age, sex and condition, including those bound to servitude for a term of years and three-fifths of all other persons not comprehended in the foregoing description, except Indians not paying taxes, in each state." The effect of this resolution was to politically emasculate and reduce blacks to the status of property. Or as one delegate who was opposed to basing representation upon property put it, "Why should the blacks, who were property in the South, be in the rule of representation any more than the cattle and horses of the North?"

The value of the negro to the Southern region of the country lay in his economic worth as a laborer, a producer of wealth. White indentured servants, as well as Indians, were not physically suited to the climate and rigors of toil that the several economies demanded—tobacco in Maryland, Virginia, and North Carolina; indigo and rice in South Carolina and Georgia. Northern delegates reasoned that since large profits accrued to the South as a result of slave labor—in one year South Carolina's exports totaled 600,000 pounds sterling—some sort of export tax ought to be considered when apportioning taxes to the states. The South would hear none of this. Its argument was based upon the fact that this constituted a special tax for which it could not receive proportional representation. This line of reasoning prevailed. On a motion by Gouverneur Morris of New York agreement was reached on July 12 stating that "direct" taxation ought to be in proportion to representation. The following day the whole question of "proportioning representation to direct taxation, and to the white and three-fifths of the black inhabitants, and requiring a census within six years, and within every ten years afterwards" carried. Prior to this time, a motion to consider blacks as equal to whites had failed while a subsequent motion to consider the former equivalent to three-fifths of the latter had passed.

The basic questions of taxation and representation and the political status of the negro having been settled for the House of Representatives, agreement came shortly thereafter with regards to the Senate. Agreement was reached July 24 for allowing two senators from each state.

Compromise had been the name of the game up to this point. Both sides had won. The black man was the loser. Northern interests were being realized through the progress toward union achieved during the proceedings. The price they had to pay was large. Southerners had maintained their cheap labor supply. They were the big winners. Because the "rights-of-man" doctrine did not apply to foreigners, more than 700,000 Africans had been enslaved.

Prospects toward nationhood had never looked better—the question of taxation and representation having been resolved. As to the matter of slavery, this was a question left entirely to the individual states. The national government had laid the foundation and would therefore offer no interference. But what about the future of slavery? What would be its effect upon the new nation? Feeble attempts were made to place the

9

blame on those states that would profit directly from the venture. Efforts were initiated to put a limiting date after which importation of slaves might be prohibited. James Madison emphasized that "twenty years will produce all the mischief that can be apprehended from the liberty to import slaves." He feared the effects of such a "dishonorable" institution upon the American character. It was agreed, finally following several compromises dealing with the omission of the term "slave" and avoidance of references to specific states, that the "migration or importation of such persons as the several states now existing shall think proper to admit, shall not be prohibited by the Legislature prior to the year 1808, but a tax or duty may be imposed on such importations not exceeding ten dollars per person." This provision did nothing to affect slavery. It simply provided for a small revenue to be collected by the Federal Government on each slave brought into the country and allowed for the issue to remain settled—at least, until the year 1808. The slave interest had won another battle but in so doing they were forced to yield their demand requiring two-thirds of each house to pass a navigation act. The two-thirds requirement was replaced by that of a simple majority.

Due to a gentlemen's agreement, the status of the negro was now firmly established in the country. Certainly implicitly understood among the delegates from the several states, if not explicitly stated, the black man was a slave. All parties were obliged to honor the code. Furthermore, to avoid misunderstanding, legislation was required on the national level that would subject all parties to this recognition. This was accomplished on August 29, 1787, when a motion carried which stated that if "any person bound to service or labor in any of the United States shall escape into another State, he or she shall not be discharged from such service or labor, in consequence of any regulations subsisting in the State to which they escape, but shall be delivered up to the person justly claiming their service or labor."

The end of the Convention was now in sight. On Monday, September 10, just seven days prior to adjournment, the last major debate, made inevitable by the presence of the negro, occurred. It took place over the several methods proposed for changing the Constitution. A motion by Roger Sherman of Connecticut, amended by James Wilson of Pennsylvania, requiring three-fourths of the state legislatures to ratify any proposed constitutional amendment had been agreed to *nemine contradicente*. James Madison was not satisfied with the wording of the resolution and moved to postpone its consideration so that the Convention might take up his proposal. Alexander Hamilton seconded the motion. However, John Rutledge, the delegate from South Carolina, would not cede authority for altering those articles relating to slavery to "states not interested in that property and prejudiced against it." The South Carolina delegate's objection was obviated when the Convention passed an amended version of Mr. Madison's motion.[4]

The gentlemen's agreement on the status of the negro was confirmed and the gap between the two races made permanent on September 13 when the Convention unanimously consented to strike out the word "servitude" in Article I Section 2 and in its place substitute "service." They agreed that the former applied only to slaves, whereas the latter expressed the "obligation of free persons." Since the Constitution was a document prepared by free people to protect the rights of free people— yes, even criminals—no inferences as to the political rights of "all others" were to be remotely implied.

On September 17, 1787, 127 days after its tremulous beginning, the Convention adjourned sine die—the framers of the Constitution having achieved their goal.

From the beginning we were there. We were there on the tongues of and in the minds of every delegate, and the exigencies of the moment required that action be taken regarding our presence. And so it happened: thirty-eight men from Europe with the stroke of a pen—a singular, consummate, political act—surreptitiously declared that three-quarters of a million people from Africa were to be slaves.

2

GROWING PAINS

The struggle was over. Union had been forged. The crucible of American democracy had been hammered out on the anvil of duplicity. What was once a loosely organized fraternity of states under the old Articles of Confederation had now been converted into a nation under the Constitution. The Federal bargain had been struck.

Congress was to hold its first session in New York City in 1789. On April 6 of that year, Congress got down to the nuts and bolts business of making laws to govern the new nation. Immediately those political questions engendered by the black man's presence came to the fore when a House member from the state of Virginia moved to amend a pending tariff bill so as to impose a duty of ten dollars on every slave imported. The representative from Virginia later commented wryly that it was shameful that the "Constitution prevented Congress from prohibiting the importation altogether" since it was contrary to the principles of the Revolution. As was to be expected, considering the make-up of the Congress, the amendment was received with alternate skepticism and delight. Whereas congressional members from the deep South accused fellow southerners of attempting to deny them those comforts Virginia had enjoyed which naturally accrued from slave labor, northern delegates agreed wholeheartedly with the object of the amendment. Eventually, after substantial debate, the motion was withdrawn based upon a suggestion by James Madison that the intent of the amendment could best be realized if brought forth as a separate bill. A committee to achieve this purpose was appointed but was never heard from.

GROWING PAINS

When the second session of Congress convened in 1790, there existed 697,897 slaves in the United States. Slavery was to be found in every state of the Union except Massachusetts where, in 1783, judicial decree had stated that a clause in its constitution, declaring all men to be born free and equal, abolished slavery. The Pennsylvania legislature passed an act in 1780 which was designed to gradually emancipate and prohibit the further importation of slaves. This act also eliminated hereditary servitude. Several other states—Connecticut, Rhode Island, New Hampshire—followed Pennsylvania's lead. Attempts in New York to do likewise failed in 1785. Nevertheless, the legislatures of Delaware, Maryland, New Jersey, New York, and Virginia were able to repeal restrictive laws on emancipation which dated back to Colonial days. In 1787, Rhode Island forbade its citizens to engage in the slave trade. Similar prohibitionary legislation was soon to be enacted in Massachusetts, Connecticut, and Pennsylvania.

At this point, it is noteworthy to recall, although it is not the intent of the book to deal with the subject at length, that the political consequences of the black man's presence in America was very early seen in many non-political (*sensu stricto*) organizations, namely, the church. Indeed much of the early clamor in opposition to slavery began in the church.[1] Outside of the church, societies promoting the abolition of slavery sprang up and developed active memberships in all states north of Virginia. The Philadelphia Organization founded in 1787 listed Benjamin Franklin as its President and under his leadership was one of the first groups to petition Congress relating to the subject of abolishing slavery.

The petition presented by Dr. Franklin's organization, though ostensibly related solely to the question of slavery, was, in fact, much broader in its impact. Congressional enactment resulting from this petition struck right at the quick of the new nation, at the federal-state relationship. As we shall see in many instances throughout this chapter, the political and constitutional issues occasioned by the black man's presence will become the arena in which the powers of Congress relative to the states shall be ultimately decided.

America, positioned to embark upon a rapid expansion, was ill prepared to do so for sectional interest based upon political power and economics—both of which were related to the overriding question of slavery—had to be dealt with. The South, well aware of the benefits of slave labor, was not about to yield to the dabbling abolitionists. The North, prosperous without slave labor, wishing only not to be outmaneuvered politically or economically by the South, opted in favor of balance. Consequently, during the era of expansion, many political compromises were reached. Simply stated, the object of each territorial compromise was to hold the

13

nation together and to prove to European skeptics that the American experiment in democracy could work. Justification for the Revolution was required and both parties knew it.

In December 1789 the North Carolina Legislature ceded all of her western territory to the United States. The cession was built around the understanding that Congress would not enact any laws intended to emancipate the slaves. Congress agreed to this stipulation on April 2, 1790, and the Tennessee Territory came in "slave."

Vermont came into the Union on February 18, 1791, as a "free" state. As in the case of North Carolina, Congress acquiesced to the wishes of the state constitution (1777) which had been altered in 1785 under the first article of the Bill of Rights to read: "No male person born in this country, or brought from overseas, ought to be bound by law to serve any person as a servant, slave or apprentice after he arrives at the age of twenty-one years, nor female, in like manner, after she arrives at the age of twenty-one years, unless they are bound by their own consent after they arrive at such age, or are bound by law for the payment of debts, damages, fines, costs, or the like." Vermont was the first state to prohibit and abolish slavery.

The two cases are politically significant for they indicate that at this point the entire Congress of the United States was willing to be guided by the congressional resolution stemming from Dr. Franklin's organization's petition which read in part "that Congress have no right to interfere in the emancipation of slaves, or in the treatment of them, in any of the states, it remaining with the several states alone to provide any regulations therein which humanity and true policy require." Briefly stated, this resolution when coupled with Article I, Section Nine of the Constitution prohibited Congress from tampering with slavery, at least until 1808.

By an act of Congress, Kentucky entered the Union in 1791. However, it did not frame a state constitution until 1792. Its constitution was unlike those of Vermont and North Carolina in the sense that it left the question of slave emancipation entirely up to the owners. The Kentucky Constitution, in addition to reserving the right to pass laws prohibiting the introduction of slaves for the purpose of sale, also required humane treatment of slaves under penalty of equitable forfeiture—to some other slave master.

In the years following 1792 the nation witnessed very little congressional debate on the subject of slavery. With the exception of a fugitive slave law passed by Congress in 1793 and an act passed in 1794 prohibiting the fitting out of vessels in the United States for supplying any foreign countries with slaves, no legislation was forthcoming. Nevertheless, based on the question of slavery, the right of individuals and groups to petition the House for redress of grievances, and the duty of the House to consider such petitions were firmly established. As time will prove, this right was of great benefit to both those congressional members as well as those extra-legislative organizations, such as churches and abolitionist societies who wished to have the question of slavery aired before the country. In adapting this measure, the House had provided a major weapon to be used by the then infant abolitionist societies in their fight against slavery. Also of inestimable value in the abolitionist movement would be a number of black newspapers (Table 1).*

Any number of reasons can be given for the decline in congressional debate caused by the black man's presence. However, it should be realized that the slave's value lay in his worth as a source of free labor and as a person to be enumerated for purposes of congressional apportionment. Such factors were important to northern and southern politicians alike only when questions of territorial expansion were before the National Legislature. It should also be realized that the political aspects of government had changed since the days of the Founding Fathers. What had originally been a country with no political parties provided for in either the Declaration of Independence or in the Constitution had now evolved, since the second term of George Washington, into one with two major parties having their appeal based on issues such as class, economics, reform, tariff, and expansion. Political leaders such as Hamilton and Jefferson, who had at an earlier date been in the forefront of the struggle for the "rights-of-man" were preoccupied with and to be found on opposite sides in the struggle to build and maintain political parties representing their respective philosophies of federal government.

The political debate engendered by the issue of slavery was to reappear full-bloom on the congressional floor in the session of 1797. Advocates requested that the United States take over jurisdictional rights from Britain in West Florida and form a government to be called the Mississippi Territory.

In all respects, excluding the prohibition of slavery, this territory was to be administered similarly to that northwest of the Ohio River. That portion of the bill which excluded the prohibition on slavery drew immediate opposition. Northern delegates claimed that not to prohibit slavery in the proposed territory would be a direct violation of the pact proposed by Thomas Jefferson and agreed to at the Continental Congress. The South was adamant in its opposition. An attempt to appease the South by amending the bill to exempt current slaveholders from the

* All tables located in Appendix

15

prohibition failed. Finally, an amendment offered by a southern delegate prohibiting the introduction of slaves from outside the limits of the United States was carried without opposition. This amendment is interesting for it amounts to another action taken on the part of a southern delegate which would eventually lead to an outlawing of the African slave trade. Similar action had previously been taken by the legislative bodies of North and South Carolina. The State of Georgia outlawed the African slave trade in 1798 and the State of New York, after three unsuccessful attempts in the Legislature, passed a law in 1799 permitting the gradual abolition of slavery.

These apparently paradoxical political acts on the part of southern legislative assemblies and congressional delegates should not be construed as having emanated from any new humanity. Rather, they were due to several simple economic facts of life. In Virginia, due to the embargo and the exhaustion of the land, slavery had become a burden upon the masters. Although Georgia, South Carolina, and North Carolina produced two varieties of cotton, their products, long-staple and short-staple, could not compete with Britain's whose production rose from 5 million pounds in 1775 to 56 million in 1800. In 1794 the South could produce only 2 million pounds of cotton. The British product came mostly from Brazil, the West Indies, and the Middle East. Slavery was a dying institution but when Eli Whitney patented the cotton gin in 1794 the Industrial Revolution came to the South and so did the need for greater numbers of slaves. The opposition to the African slave trade evidenced among the Virginia representatives came in part from the fact that the state was too far north to grow cotton. Consequently, it could not prosper directly from the new invention but it would be able to develop and profit from the domestic slave trade with the added advantage of being able to extricate itself from the slave system.[2]

January 2, 1800 saw a new twist in the political debate ensuing from the black man's presence. Occasioned by the firmly established right of individuals and groups to petition Congress, the free negroes of Philadelphia did exactly that in behalf of their enslaved brothers. The request was submitted by their city representative and called for action on the part of Congress regarding a more stringent enforcement of the laws against the African slave trade and the eventual abolition of slavery. As was to be expected the slaveholding interest objected to the petition on the grounds that congressional powers did not extend into areas concerned with abolishing slavery. It is also to be expected that much of the clamor against the petition arose when southern congressmen considered the temerity of negroes appealing to that august body. The petition was eventually withdrawn before a vote could be taken. However, at a later date Congress did enact a law calling for more stringent provisions relative to United States ships supplying foreign countries with slaves. The importance of the petition lies in the fact that it represented the first time that negroes had appealed to the National Legislature for a redress of grievances on the question of slavery.

Georgia ceded her western territory to the United States in 1802 on conditions provided for in the Congressional Ordinance of 1787 with the exception of the article forbidding slavery. Out of this territory the states of Alabama and Mississippi were formed. These two new members entered the Union as slave states. Ohio came in as a free state in 1803 and the remainder of the territory resulting from the Ordinance of 1787 was called the Indiana Territory. William Henry Harrison was appointed Governor. Congress opposed introducing slavery into the new territory although the inhabitants were pro-slavery. In the end, as was to be expected, the will of Congress prevailed. Eventually the two states carved out of this territory, Indiana and Illinois, entered the Union free.

On April 30, 1803, the United States, under the Presidency of Thomas Jefferson, purchased the province of Louisiana from the French for 15 million dollars. Land involved in the purchase extended from the Canadian border to the Gulf of Mexico and took in twelve states. The political events leading up to this historic occasion demonstrate the overwhelming political importance, both nationally and internationally, of the black man's presence.

Having reached an accord with Spain in 1801 for the retrocession of Louisiana, and having signed preliminary articles of peace with Britain, France now had designs on America. The reestablishment of the glorious French empire in North America had long been the dream of Napoleon's Foreign Minister, Charles Talleyrand. This would mean eventual war with the United States. The leaders in both countries were well aware of this. It was also a certainty that in any such conflagration France would be the ultimate victor.

To prepare the way for the North American venture, Napoleon sent his brother-in-law, General Charles Leclerc, to retake the island of Haiti from the black Governor, Toussaint L'Ouverture, and to reestablish slavery in the French colony. From this base, the assault on America was to be launched. The French expedition set sail for the island near the end of 1801. But all did not go as anticipated for the French Army; it was soon to be confronted by Toussaint's well-disciplined army of 51,000 warriors who had earlier freed themselves and their people from the yoke of slavery through constant uprisings during the French Revolution.

17

Contrary to Napoleon's wishes, these men were not about to be reenslaved. And, as Hannibal had needed Sicily, Napoleon now needed Santo Domingo. Toussaint had to be destroyed, for without the island, Napoleon could not support his troops on the continent. The scene was set for the brutal struggle between the well-equipped army of Napoleon and the warrior "savages" of Toussaint. On the outcome of this battle rested the entire fate of the United States. Henry Adams, a noted historian of the period, stated, when speaking of the significance of the struggle, that "if he (Toussaint) and his blacks should succumb easily to their fate, the wave of French empire would roll on to Louisiana and sweep far up the Mississippi, if Santo Domingo should resist, and succeed in resistance, the recoil would spend its force in Europe, while America would be left to pursue her democratic destiny in peace."[3]

The French troops landed on the third of February. In addition to the French citizens, their army was composed of Spanish, German, and Polish rabble, many of whom had only recently been manumitted. They were met by the black general, Christophe, who ordered part of the city set on fire. This was a tactic quite often employed by the natives to deprive the enemy of resources. The blacks were not afraid to fight. They had learned during their struggle for freedom that whites were no superior species and therefore possessed no superior power. In attempts to subdue the blacks, whites committed atrocious acts by throwing blacks by the hundreds into the ocean. The sight of their brothers' bodies being washed ashore drove the blacks to massacre still greater numbers of whites. General Leclerc, on orders from Paris, began using mulattoes in his struggle against Toussaint. He promised them that after the war they would be better off than the blacks. But having once sided with France against Toussaint and lost, they too were weary of the white man's trickery.

After three months of bitter fighting and the destruction of one French army, Toussaint was taken prisoner in a vicious plot and sent to Europe to die in the cold Jura Mountains. Napoleon, thinking that he had triumphed, gave orders to reenslave the negroes and to prepare an expedition, indirectly bound via Santo Domingo, for Louisiana. Through the capture of Toussaint, the way had been cleared for France to become the greatest power in the world.

Perceiving the course of events, Thomas Jefferson, who had long been a friend of the French, made a 180-degree turn. The President of the United States was prepared to side with Louis Pichon, French chargé d'affaires, in order to halt French aggression in North America. He stated this position in strong words in his correspondence of April 1802 with Robert Livingston, the American minister in Paris. But strong words were useless for the outcome depended on nothing the President could do. The course of events lay entirely in the hands of the blacks of Santo Domingo.

Both white men were wrong. In thinking that the capture of Toussaint had ended the war, Napoleon made a grave mistake. For as Henry Adams states, "The idea that leaders were everything, and masses without leaders nothing, was a military view of society which led Napoleon into all his worst speculations." The President of the United States in his premature conclusion concerning the outcome of the war erred in not understanding what freedom means to the black man and, consequently, what price he is willing to pay to be free.

Napoleon's army was to have sailed for Louisiana in September 1802. It never did. For "as fast as regiments could be named they were consumed in the fiery furnace of Santo Domingo." In addition to the defeats rendered the French by the Santo Domingoans, the yellow fever epidemic of 1802 destroyed many thousands of Europeans. General Leclerc, consumed by the fever at the age of thirty, cursed the ill-fated expedition.

The death of the young general did not end the war. He was replaced by Rochambeau of Revolutionary War fame, a Bacchus-like figure who wore big boots and believed that slavery should be restored to the island and that the master should have the right of life and death over the slave. In order to bring the island under control he immediately instituted an unparalleled "Reign of Terror." He drowned so many natives that the negroes refused to eat fish "for fear they would eat their own relatives." However, he did not stop at drownings; he sent negroes before the firing squad, to the gallows, and buried them alive. Asphyxiation with sulfur fumes and starvation were common stock in his sadistic repertoire. His desire and lengths to which he was prepared to go to subdue the blacks is best attested to in his own words in a letter he sent to General Ramel, Commander of Tortuga, dated May 6, 1803:

I am sending you, my Dear Commandant, a detachment of fifty men of the National Guard of Le Cap, commanded by Monsieur Bari. The detachment is followed by twenty-eight bulldogs. These reinforcements should enable you to bring your operations to a successful close. I must not fail to inform you that no ration or allowance of any kind will be allowed for the maintenance of the dogs. You are to feed negroes to them.

These were futile acts of desperate men. The blacks were determined to be free. For as of January 1803, fifty thousand French troops, thousands of white civilians, and huge quantities of supplies had been consumed in a year of war. What had been the richest of all France's possessions was now destroyed. Frenchmen feared settling on the island. After several more months of vicious battle, Napoleon realized that his army had been defeated. And with this defeat, his dream of Empire in North America was eclipsed.

Talleyrand was ordered to sell Louisiana. The same week that the purchase was made, Toussaint L'Ouverture died in the cold mountain dungeon unaware that his humble people in Santo Domingo had defeated the army of Napoleon. Later, Henry Adams was to write that "the prejudice of race alone blinded the American people to the debt they owed to the desperate courage of five hundred thousand Haytian Negroes who would not be enslaved."[4]

In retrospect, Napoleon's greatest error was in not recognizing the offer made by Toussaint who was willing to have "the sovereign dominion of the island restored to France, the soil, buildings, and other immovable property, to the old proprietors." He simply wanted France to recognize "liberty to the slaves, who are to labor for wages." Had Napoleon been wise he would have enlisted Toussaint in his army thus assuring the success of his proposed venture in North America. In that event, the history of North America and these United States would have been altered drastically. Napoleon's insensitivity to the fires of freedom that burn in the black man's soul was one of the things that cost France her historic dream of Empire. This same fire of freedom led to the defeat of Napoleon's army, doubled the area of the United States, and took America one step closer to its "manifest destiny."

America was expanding. And irreconcilably fixed to every new land acquisition was the question of the black man's status. So it is not surprising that upon acquiring the Louisiana Territory, Congress, in the early stages of its session of 1804-5, was brought face-to-face with the question of slavery in the area. An abolitionist society then in session in Philadelphia presented Congress with a petition requesting that noble body to prohibit the further importation of slaves in the newly acquired region of Louisiana. As a result of the abolitionist activity, Congress wrote into the act organizing the territory of Orleans—a section of land between the Pearl and Mississippi Rivers which later became the State of Louisiana—the stipulation that no slaves could be carried there except from some other portion of the United States. To this was added a second qualification requiring that no domestic slaves could be brought into the region who had not been in the country prior to 1798. The insertion of this added qualification in the eyes of Congress was warranted by the South Carolina Legislature's action to revive the African slave trade after a quiescent interval of fifteen years.

During the next two-year period, maneuverings before Congress, both on behalf of and against the institution of slavery, were prevalent but very little was accomplished. Attempts to place a ten-dollar tax on every slave imported and to free "all children born of slaves" within the District of Columbia failed. On the other hand, several attempts by the Legislature of the Indiana Territory reinforced by their Governor, William Henry Harrison, to allow for slavery in that region were rejected by Congress. The State of New Jersey, the last of the old Confederation to do so, passed an act unanimously securing freedom to all persons born in the state after July 4, 1806.

Up to this point in the history of the American Federal System, national debate on the question of slavery had taken place in the Congress of the United States. It was before this body that abolitionist societies, church groups, and, indeed, negroes themselves had presented petitions imploring the United States Government for a wide redress of grievances related to the entire question of the black man's status. Among the congressmen themselves, in spite of vigorous debate pro and con, there existed a working agreement based upon constitutional interpretation that Congress had no power to enact laws respecting slavery. The whole subject of slavery came under the jurisdiction of the "several states," i.e., states rights. In the aggregate congressional mind, preservation of the rapidly expanding Union required such an arrangement. No one was about to rock the boat. For the moment, both sides opted in favor of a unity ratio with respect to slave versus non-slave status of newly-entering states and territories.

The political arena in which the battles over slavery were being waged was suddenly enlarged. For the first time since the founding of the Federation, the Executive Branch of the Government entered the picture. In his message at the beginning of the session of 1806-7, President Thomas Jefferson suggested that Congress use its authority to abolish the African slave trade. He stated: "I congratulate you, fellow citizens, on the approach of the period at which you may interpose your authority, constitutionally to withdraw the citizens of the United States from all further participation in those violations of human rights which have so long been continued on the unoffending inhabitants of Africa, and which the morality, the reputation and the best interests of our country have long been eager to proscribe."

A House committee of seven—three southerners, four northerners—was selected whose task it was to report out a bill containing provisions realizing the President's wishes. The committee headed by Congressman Early of Georgia presented a bill to the House which would "prohibit the importation or bringing of slaves into the United States or territories thereof after the 31st day of December 1807." According to the measure:

A fine of 20,000 dollars would be imposed upon all persons concerned in fitting out of any vessel for the slave trade, with the forfeiture of the vessel; likewise a fine of 5,000 dollars, with forfeiture also of vessel, for taking on board any negro, mulatto, or person of color in any foreign country with the purpose of selling such a person within the jurisdiction of the United States as a slave. For a person actually transporting said persons from any foreign country and selling such as a slave within the United States, the penalty was imprisonment for not less than five years nor more than ten with a fine not exceeding 10,000 nor less than 1,000 dollars. No vessel of less than forty tons was to take any slaves on board except for transportation on the inland bays and rivers of the United States. . . .[5]

Amidst heated debate and overt threats of non-compliance, the bill finally passed the House 63 to 49. Representative John Randolph of Virginia, a friend, party leader, and formidable ally of Jefferson, opposed the measure violently. He went so far as to declare that "if disunion should ever take place, the line of disseverance would not be between east and west, lately the topic of so much alarm, but between the slaveholding and non-slaveholding states."

What about Thomas Jefferson, himself a slave holder, the third President of the United States, a member of the Virginia Dynasty, author of the Declaration of Independence and the Statutes of Virginia, and a man who intuitively knew the whereabouts of every dot and comma placed in the United States Constitution? What prompted him to take such unprecedented Executive action? What role was he playing? Was he motivated by moral, economic, or political reasons? It seems, on close inspection, that it was the last factor which elicited this unexpected response. The titular head of the Democratic party[6] was well aware of the close alliance of the free negroes in the North with the Federalist party and the growing anti-slavery movement taking place in the "free states." Jefferson remembered that in the election of 1800[7] Hamilton and the Federalist party had nominated John Adams and C. C. Pinckney of South Carolina, a slaveholder, to run for the two top offices with the intent of actually electing the latter. Jefferson knew that the Federalist party was not sincere in its anti-slavery pronouncements; rather, it was politically motivated and planned to use the emotionally pregnant slavery issue as a means of reviving the dying organization.

Thomas Jefferson, with an eye toward future enfranchisement of the white working class, was able to capture the middle ground away from his opponents in the Federalist party on the question of slavery by a simple executive pronouncement that offended neither section of the country. Likewise, it did little to change the political and economic status of the black man.

GROWING PAINS

The third President of the United States, well aware of the political significance of the black man, was out to build the Democratic party. To accomplish this required time uninterrupted by the violent upheavals that would accompany national political debate on the subject. By calming the political waters Jefferson was able to build a strong Democratic party which led ultimately to the dissolution of the Federalists. The management of the party after 1800 was entirely in the hands of the South for it was the thirty-seven electoral votes from Virginia, South Carolina, Georgia, and Kentucky that insured him his margin of victory over Adams. Ten of those votes derived from the three-fifths rule. As we shall see later, enfranchisement of working-class whites meant disenfranchisement of free negroes. This process was in line with Jefferson's proposal to recolonize some part of Africa with slaves from Virginia and, in their place, import from Europe a peasant class of whites to be used as laborers. Through this means the state of Virginia would eventually rid itself of all its slaves.

Thomas Jefferson, the Squire from Albemarle County, scientist, scholar, civil libertarian, the third President of the United States, a revolutionary who had invoked the "rights-of-man" doctrine to free himself and his people from the yoke of colonial oppression, acquiesced to Anglo-Saxon folly when it came to the moral and political rights of the black man. The statesman who took pride in the authorship of the Declaration of Independence and who died fifty years to the day of its enactment could not rise to the great task before him. He could only play politics with it and would ultimately succeed in his game which "limboized" the negro. Just as it had led to the death of Alexander Hamilton in a gun duel with Aaron Burr, it would lead ultimately to the destruction of the Federalist party based on their opposition to the War of 1812. The Democratic party, controlled by slaveholders, would reign supreme but it carried the Jeffersonian ideals and principles of American democracy in a direction opposite to that of their original intent. In New York where free negroes were allowed to exercise their franchise, the Democratic leaders made an issue of the negro vote. The intent of the party leaders was to discredit the Federalists, who received the black vote en masse, as the party of the negro. This appeal struck a sonorous note on the ears of the white working class. In the election of 1808, the Democrats put their anti-negro sentiment into a song which commenced "Federalists with blacks Unite." They further disheartened the negro by challenging each vote that he cast at the polls. When the Democrats finally gained control of the state legislature they enacted legislation requiring negroes to obtain special passes in order to vote in state-wide elections. Later they amended the state constitution to increase the property qualifications for negroes from 100 to 250 dollars. At the same time, they abolished it altogether for whites.

During the two-term administration of James Madison, the political energy of the country was dissipated by the War of 1812—the war that no one wanted and furthermore no one understood. The slaveholder-dominated Democratic party of Jefferson was elated over the outcome of the war. For in addition to having their Federalist opposition silenced as a result of the war, they were to receive indemnification for their slaves as provided for in an agreement reached between America and Britain and arbitrated by the Emperor of Russia.

In his message to Congress on December 5, 1814, President Madison recommended a Hamiltonian program to his Democratic Congress. His program called for spending large sums of money—27 million—for the Army, Navy, and military academies. It also called for the establishment of a national bank and the protective tariff. Congress responded positively. Congressional members of the slaveholding aristocracy had begun to sense that the future lay with industrialization and not with agrarianism. But Madison made one mistake which was to have a devastating economic effect upon the South—an effect similar to that of the Embargo Act of the Jefferson Administration. In a bill sponsored by John C. Calhoun that would provide for internal improvements at the expense of the Federal Government, the President reverted to his anti-Hamiltonian type and vetoed the measure. The veto affected the South only, for the northern states such as New York, Pennsylvania, and Massachusetts were able to finance roads and canals through private capital. However, without the benefit of new roads and internal waterways, the South could not expect to compete against the North in the fast-moving westward expansion. How ironic that through the action of a southern President, the South was predestined to second-class economic status and doomed to become dependent upon slavery, the forced labor of the black man, for its economic survival.

James Monroe, the last of the Virginia Dynasty, entered the White House in 1817. Due to the demise of the Federalist party and a strong upsurge of nationalism that swept the country following the War of 1812, the country now entered into an "Era of Good Feelings," that lasted between 1817 and 1824. On the issue of the black man's status, feelings were no less inflamed than before. In Congress the lines were drawn more tightly and heated debate was to recur. The westward expansion resumed. Cotton was king and the African slave trade, in spite of prohibitory laws, was kept alive. Similarly, the domestic slave trade increased dramatically with Washington becoming the vortex of the trading

whirlwind. Kidnapping of free negroes to be sold into bondage became a profitable business. The South, having unwittingly relegated itself to an inferior economic status, was not about to yield to northern anti-slavery sentiment and dismantle the odious institution, the jugular vein through which the economic life blood of the region ran. A southern attempt providing for the administration of the old Fugitive Slave Act similar to the fugitive-from-justice laws almost passed Congress. Mississippi was admitted to the Union on December 10, 1817. According to the provisions of its constitution, grand juries were to be dispensed with in the indictment of slaves and slaves were not allowed jury trials except in capital cases.

The Democratic party of Jefferson had succeeded too well in eliminating its political competition. But a new dynamic peculiar to the two-party system was to set in and produce factionalism and young aggressive leadership within the ranks of the party. It seems that an undeniable political law was at work. This law requires that when one of the major political parties attains an overwhelming majority or excessive and unwieldy power and/or when the opposition party goes out of existence, factionalism will occur producing rival groups within the party vying for personal power. Under these conditions, the internecine struggle becomes the equilibrating force which leads ultimately to the reestablishment of a second party. Within the Democratic party, two obvious factions began to emerge. The states rights group, headed by William H. Crawford of Georgia, Secretary of the Treasury, favored a strict constructionist interpretation of the Constitution as to the question of the negro's status. This group was endorsed by President Monroe and had most of its support in the deep South. The second faction headed by Henry Clay, a westerner from the State of Kentucky, favored a more centralized government. Clay was the Speaker of the House. Allied with the Speaker were John Quincy Adams, Secretary of State, an easterner from Massachusetts, and John C. Calhoun, Secretary of War, from South Carolina. This latter group would eventually find a new home in a party called the National Republicans. Thus, the merits and the political viability of the two-party system would be reaffirmed.

The opinion of the slaveholding states on the question of slavery had held sway for, in spite of feeble northern and upper-southern attempts at solution of the problem, things remained virtually the same. In March of 1818 a delegation from Missouri presented Congress with petitions asking for admission to the Union as a state. A select committee, to which the petition was sent, reported out a bill authorizing the people of the territory to form a constitution and state government, and for such state to be admitted into the Union with all rights and privileges of the original states. The bill was read the required number of times before a committee of the whole but no action was taken. On February 13, 1819 of the next session, the House dissolved into a committee of the whole under the chairmanship of General Smith of Maryland to consider the Missouri bill which was also taken up the following Monday.

In the minds of the northern representatives there were many vexatious problems associated with the Missouri question. And as many realized, both North and South, future governmental policies of territorial and industrial expansion depended upon the nature of its resolution. Currently, there were eleven northern and eleven southern states in the Senate. An admission of a new one would upset the balance of power, but more importantly, it raised the fundamental question of whether slavery would eventually be permitted throughout the entire Louisiana Purchase. The old west was about to give way to the new west. Whereas the Ohio had once been the divide between freedom and slavery, there would now be none beyond the Mississippi. Since Missouri lay too far north to be considered a slave state did it necessarily follow that if she were entered as a slave state, slavery would be permitted throughout the entire Louisiana Purchase? And would this foretell of southern economic and political expansion at the expense of the North? Questions such as these had to be answered and delegates had to feel reassured that no matter what the outcome they and their constituencies were not being shortchanged. Irrespective of the consequences, neither side could afford to lose.

General Talmadge of New York set the stage for the protracted debate on the subject that would eventually witness overt threats of secession on the part of southern representatives. A virtual watershed of debate ensued occasioned by the New Yorker's motion to amend the bill so as to provide "that the introduction of slavery, or involuntary servitude, be prohibited and that all children born within the said state after the admission thereof into the Union, shall be declared free at the age of twenty-five years."

Mr. Fuller from Massachusetts reasoned that Article IV, Section III of the Constitution gave the Congress discretionary power authorizing them to prescribe the exact conditions under which any new states would enter the Union. He also argued that the existence of slavery in *any* state was a broad departure from the Republican principles upon which the country was founded. Quoting the Declaration of Independence which states "We hold these truths to be self-evident—*that all men are created equal*—that they are endowed by their maker with certain inalienable rights; that among these are life, liberty and the pursuit of happiness," he stated that since slaves are men it follows that in a purely Republican form of government they, having been created by God, are born free and entitled to life, liberty, and the pursuit of happiness. Attempts at recolonization of slaves in Africa by southerners he referred to as hypocritical. How could men profiteering in slaves be sincere in their desire to rid themselves of the wicked institution by shipping their burdens across thousands of miles of sea while at the same time arguing to extend it to every new land acquisition?

In expressing a contrary point of view, Mr. Scott, the congressional delegate from Missouri, warned the committee to "beware of the fate of Caesar and Rome." Georgia's Representative Cobb, in a highly impassioned speech, added that if such debate persisted, the Union would be dissolved; he further stated the hassle over this issue had "kindled a fire which all the waters of the ocean cannot put out, which seas of blood can only extinguish." The gauntlet of slavery which warmed the hand of oppression had been flung down. It was to be retrieved immediately, without hesitation, by the aging representative from New York who replied that:

If a dissolution of the Union must take place, let it be so! If a civil war, which gentlemen so much threaten, must come, I can only say let it come! My hold on life is probably as frail as that of any man who now hears me; but while that hold lasts, it shall be devoted to the service of my country— to the freedom of man. If blood is necessary to extinguish any fire which I have assisted to kindle, I can assure gentlemen, while I regret the necessity, I shall not forebear to contribute my mite—if I am doomed to fall I shall, at least, have the painful consolation to believe that I fall, as a fragment in the ruins of my country.[8]

The debate proceeded in this manner for several days. Each interval widened the gulf between the camps. Finally, when the vote came, the Talmadge amendment carried in the committee of the whole 82 to 78. The House sustained the committee action. Over on the Senate side the bill was in for tougher sledding. On February 27, 1819, the Senate voted in the affirmative to strike out all provisions regarding the question of slavery in the Missouri petition. The bill went back to the House where a vote of concurrence failed. Eventually the bill fell between the two houses and was lost. For the moment, Missouri would not be allowed into the Union. Congress adjourned in March and the question was not taken up until the next session.

The Missouri question was hotly debated outside Congress during the recess and when a new Congress reassembled on December 6, 1819, the issue of slavery in the territory came to the fore. Henry Clay of Kentucky was elected Speaker of the House and on a motion by a delegate from Missouri, regarding that territory's petition, the matter was referred to a select committee of five which included Scott of Missouri. The handwriting on the wall became unabashedly evident when several attempts by anti-slavery representatives to have committees formed representing their point of view failed. Excluding Scott of Missouri, three of the other four committee members came from slaveholding states. In the Senate, as in the House, the pro-slavery adherents were determined to have their way. While the select House committee was considering the petition, a bill came down from the Senate calling for admission of the state of Maine into the Union with a rider authorizing the people of Missouri to form a state constitution placing no restrictions on slavery. This bill was sent back to the Senate which voted not to recede from the attachment of Missouri from the Maine bill and not to recede from its amendment prohibiting slavery west of Missouri, and north of 36° 30' north latitude.

Following several days of frantic parliamentary maneuvering in both houses, during which time no agreement could be reached, a Senate-House Conference was formed. The conference committee recommended that the following report be adopted: 1) The Senate should give up the combination of Missouri in the same bill with Maine; 2) The House should abandon the attempt to restrict slavery in Missouri; 3) Both houses should agree to pass the Senate's separate Missouri bill, with restriction or compromising proviso, excluding slavery from all territory north and west of Missouri. The report was accepted by the House with Clay getting credit for the compromise. President Monroe who had taken no part in the controversy put his signature to the bill on March 6, 1820.

Thus the Missouri Territory was accorded the privilege of entering the Union as a state bound by no provisions regarding slavery. Immediately thereupon, the bill admitting Maine as a state passed both houses without controversy. A tenuous deal had been made. Civil war had been averted. The unity ratio was maintained. Slavery was not to be permitted in any other part of the Louisiana Purchase north of 36° 30'—the southern boundary of Missouri. Supposedly this left only the southern territories of Arkansas and Florida open to slavery. But John Quincy Adams realized that "the present question is a mere preamble—a title page to a great tragic volume" and if the Union must be dissolved, slavery is the precise question on which it ought to break.

Between 1810 and 1820 there appeared an increase in the slave population of approximately 30 per cent. Whereas previously there had been 1.2 million there were now some 1.5 million slaves within the United States boundaries. With the exception of Illinois, the institution had decreased markedly in the free states. Slavery had also decreased in Maryland with Virginia showing only a slight increase—8 per cent. North Carolina and South Carolina combined showed an average increase of 26 per cent. In the deep South—Tennessee, Mississippi, and Louisiana—slavery had risen 79, 92, and 99 per cent respectively. Slavery, for a number of reasons, had become the basis for southern society. In the deep South, in spite of increased production, the price of cotton had remained steady. The economic base of the upper South was stabilized and maintained through slave trading. Therefore, it is not surprising that to the southern politicians, the vast majority of whom were slaveholders, it was simply a matter of enlightened self-interest to defy any attempts which might threaten the existence of the "peculiar institution." Past events, namely the death of the Federalist party, had placed the slaveholding interest, which also had control of Democratic party patronage, in control of the Congress.

While the Adams-Clay faction of the party was preoccupied with the task of organizing their forces—following the disputed election of 1824 which eventually placed John Quincy Adams in the White House and landed the Secretary of State office for Henry Clay—the slaveholding interests in Congress were busy at work buttressing the institution of slavery—the pillar upon which their economic and social existence depended. In response to an opinion of the Attorney General declaring the South Carolina law authorizing the imprisonment of colored mariners unconstitutional, Governor Troup of Georgia labeled the action as "officious and impertinent intermeddling with our domestic concerns" and entreated all to be prepared "to stand by your arms." A select committee of the House to which the whole subject had been referred reported out a resolution concurring in sentiment with the Governor and further pledging their lives, their fortune, and their sacred honor. On June 7, 1825, in condemnation of the Attorney General's argument before the Supreme Court that slavery was inconsistent with the laws of God and nature and therefore ought not to exist, the Governor of Georgia wrote concerning the United States Government that "they have adopted a conceit; and if they love that more than they love us, they will cling to it and throw us off; but it will be written in your history, that you did not separate from your household without adopting the fraternal language: choose ye this day between our friendship and that worthless idol you have set up and worshipped." The South had become adamant and no longer would hide its enmity toward those high-minded northerners, intent on destroying its way of life by abolishing the very institution on which its existence depended. If this meant disunion, so be it! For if the compact had become too heavy and could no longer be borne, let each "find peace among themselves." Superficial attempts at appeasement by President Adams which called for an arrangement with Great Britain affecting the surrender of fugitive slaves taking refuge in Canada failed.

Resulting from the events surrounding the election of 1824, the split in the Democratic party became permanent. The Adams-Clay wing assumed the name National Republicans. Under this banner, they emphasized nation building as their main theme in preference to states' rights. They favored strengthening the government in Washington through enactment of high protective tariffs for manufacturers and constructing roads and canals from revenue derived therefrom. Because their program favored manufacturers and a loose construction of the Constitution they were particularly attractive to many who had earlier espoused a Hamiltonian ideology. Although united on many issues, the party was not completely homogeneous, for numbered among their ranks were many wealthy southern slaveholders. Later—1834—as a reaction to Jackson's ill-fated banking policies and in a move calculated to produce a psychological rejection of "King Andrew I," the name of the party was changed to Whig.

The southern faction of the Democratic party began uniting in a deal coordinated by Martin Van Buren of New York, behind Andrew Jackson the Hero of New Orleans. Jackson's appeal was due in part to his states' rights advocacy and his strict constructionist tendencies. Allied with Jackson was William Crawford of Georgia and John C. Calhoun of South Carolina. Martin Van Buren who was the leader of the Crawford faction in New York later became Jackson's political advisor. Accusing the National Republicans of a "corrupt bargain," the Democratic party firmly united behind "Old Hickory," began a campaign amidst cries of "Jackson and Reform" calling for the ouster of corrupt office-holders and sweeping in of honest ones. In turn, the "Adams men" accused General Jackson of having lived in adultery with the woman he eventually married. They campaigned behind the slogan, "Do you want a whore in the White House?"

When it was all over, John Quincy Adams who polled a respectable 43.9 per cent of the popular vote was thoroughly trounced by Jackson in the Electoral College by a vote of 178 to 83. Andrew Jackson became the seventh President of the United States as the result of the first election in which the so-called doctrine of "universal manhood suffrage" was approached. In all states, with the exception of South Carolina and Maryland, the electors were chosen by a statewide vote. Maryland chose its electors by district whereas South Carolina left the selection to the State Legislature. The election of 1828 which some referred to as a revolution of the uncultured masses saw 1.2 million persons exercise their franchise in contrast to only 352,062 in 1824. The Democratic party of Thomas Jefferson, founded on the floor of the United States House of Representatives, had indeed, in the mind of Andrew Jackson, become the party of the people. Except for eight years under the Whig Administration, the Democrats remained in power until 1861. During their entire twenty-four-year regime, their political stance remained unstintingly pro-slavery—an important factor relative to the black man's role in the development of the two-party system.

Frightened and incensed by periodic attempts on the part of negroes to gain their freedom by revolt (Denmark Vessey, 1822, South Carolina, and Nat Turner, 1831, Virginia), the southern power bloc in Congress was able to rescind earlier legislation and enact rules preventing a formal reception of any anti-slavery resolutions before that body.[9] The National Anti-Slavery Society formed in 1833 was under constant attack. In Boston, William Lloyd Garrison, publisher of the *Liberator,* was dragged through the streets at the end of a rope by a lynch mob. Abolitionists' newspaper offices were destroyed. In Illinois, Elijah Lovejoy, an abolitionist editor, was killed. Negroes in New York and Philadelphia were beaten and their homes burned under tacit approval of northern Democratic party politicians. The anti-abolitionist sentiment in Congress cried out for national censorship of anti-slavery literature and President Jackson acquiesced urging Congress to act accordingly. When the bill to achieve this, introduced by John C. Calhoun, was voted down on the basis of its unconstitutionality, the Postmaster General intimated before Congress that certain states might use their own discretion in this matter. With the whole question of the black man's status so vividly before the public it certainly would not be long before it was to appear full bloom in a national election.

3

THE ISSUE

For the first time, during the election of 1836, the question of slavery became an issue in a presidential campaign. The *Richmond Whig* accused Martin Van Buren, the Democratic party candidate, of having supported negro suffrage in New York and of having been in opposition to Missouri's admission as a slave state. The southern Whigs referred to him as a "tricky Yankee" who would sell them out over the issue of slavery. Martin Van Buren, "The Little Magician," was able to assuage his southern supporters' feelings by personally reassuring them by letter that he would do nothing to interfere with their constitutional rights. He later chided the abolitionists for recklessly disregarding the "consequences of their conduct." His Whig opponent, William Henry Harrison, was charged with having remarked that he envisioned the day "when a North American sun would not look down upon a slave." In denial of this, Harrison's supporters referred to a speech in which he labeled the actions of the abolitionists "weak, injudicious, presumptuous and unconstitutional."

Time and events had conspired to make slavery a national political issue. The same technology that had produced the great pyramids of Egypt had been called upon to build the South's political economy. In terms of cotton alone, the South would prosper over a ten-year period between 1839 and 1849 to the tune of 798 million dollars per year on an investment of 800 million dollars. The black man was the *sine qua non* of its economy. Politically speaking, according to the census of 1850, more than 20 per cent of the South's representation in the House of Representatives was derived from its black population based on the three-fifths clause of the

THE ISSUE

Constitution. It is therefore quite understandable that on the question of slavery the South had become paranoid and any man seeking national office had better not forget it.

Martin Van Buren defeated William Henry Harrison by an electoral vote of 170 to 113 to become the eighth President of the United States. He was able to carry all but three southern states.[1] Acknowledging his debt of gratitude, he stated in his inaugural address that having assumed office he would become an "inflexible and uncompromising opponent of every attempt on the part of Congress to abolish slavery in the District of Columbia against the wishes of the slave-holding states, and also with a determination equally decided to resist the slightest interference with it in the States where it exists."

The pragmatism of American politics which had impelled Thomas Jefferson, the third President of the United States, to address himself to the question of the black man's status, now declared that Martin Van Buren do likewise. Unbeknownst to him and those in his presence, every Chief Executive thereafter would be faced with the same dilemma—"the very hinge upon which the fate of the nation shall turn." In order for the country to stand, every President of the United States would be required to address himself to the domestic racial question.

In Congress, the slaveholding interests served early notice that the Missouri Compromise was not worth the paper on which it was written. Via an extremely circuitous route, Senators Linn and Benton from the state of Missouri were able to engineer through Congress during the session of 1835–36 a bill providing for the annexation of Indian reservation land located on free soil west of the Missouri Line. This action, in direct contravention of the Compromise, for some reason attracted little attention. The territory, about the size of seven counties, became one of the state's most populous and wealthy sections. Hemp and tobacco were its main products. Slaves were its main source of labor. This region was to become the most pro-slavery section of the state.

During Martin Van Buren's term of office the Republic of Texas first applied for annexation to the United States. In Congress, resolutions passed by state legislatures for and against annexation evoked heated debate and led to continued threats of secession from all sides. The underlying cause for discord was the question dealing with its admission as a slave or free state. Mr. Preston, the senator from South Carolina who supported its admission as a slave state, argued that if the South were not allowed to extend its system of slavery into the territory that "we neither can nor ought to continue in political union on such terms." President Van Buren who realized the danger of war with Mexico over the Texas question, also recognized the potential for internal discord over the extension and, for these reasons, aided somewhat by his own personal aversion to slavery, discouraged the project.

The Presidential election of 1840 paired the same candidates as the previous one. William Henry Harrison, the Whig candidate, ultimately triumphed based largely upon his supporters having made issue of the fact that Van Buren had approved the issue of a court-martial containing the testimony of a negro. This alone may or may not have been enough to cause the southern faction of the Democratic party to turn against their own candidate. Other factors, however, tended to complicate the situation and to exacerbate the paranoia of the South. Paramount among these was the formation of the nation's first anti-slavery political organization, the Liberty Party. This "New Organization" formed by abolitionists who had disagreed with Harrison over his disapproval of taking part in *any* activities of a government supporting slavery nominated James G. Birney of Kentucky, an ex-slaveholder, as its Presidential candidate. Of the over 2.3 million votes cast the Liberty party garnered a paltry 7,069. But this of itself is not the whole story. Interestingly enough, with the exception of Indiana, which had sought admission as a slave state while Harrison was Governor, the Party received some support in every free state and showed greatest strength in New York, Massachusetts, and Ohio.

During the election of 1840, the Democratic party in their first national platform introduced a plank which was to remain a regular portion of all their pre-war platforms. This plank allowed that Congress had no power to interfere with the institution of slavery, that this was entirely a matter for the "several states." William Henry Harrison, in his Inaugural Address, stated that the efforts promoted by abolitionists would lead only to "disunion, violence and civil war" and that they were basically counterproductive in terms of their stated objective.

On the floor of Congress political controversy over the question of slavery continued unabated and was substantially heightened when John Quincy Adams presented a petition to the House on January 24, 1842, calling for a peaceable dissolution of the Union. The petition was signed by forty-six citizens of Haverhill, Massachusetts, and was based upon their unwillingness to continue to suffer an inequality of economic and political benefits placed upon their shoulders so that the South might continue to prosper. The motion of Mr. Adams to send it to a select committee with instructions to show why the request of the petitioners should not be granted evoked heated debate. Representative Gilmer of Virginia called for the previous question, obtained the floor, and moved that the representative from Massachusetts be censured for having presented such a petition. Mr. Marshall of Kentucky submitted resolutions labeling Mr. Adams' actions "a high breach of privilege, a contempt offered to the House, a direct proposition to each member to commit perjury and involving necessarily in its consequences the destruction of the country, and the crime of high treason." The debate over the petition continued with little letup until February 7 during which time Mr. Wise from Virginia charged Adams with being an ally of British philanthropists and American abolitionists intent on overthrowing slavery and wrecking the southern economy. He also implied that the gentleman from Massachusetts suffered from hereditary monomania—a state of mind which left him "astute to design, obstinate and zealous in power and terrible in action, and an instrument well fitted to dissolve the Union."

Rising in his own defense Mr. Adams offered the opinion that the charges of Mr. Marshall were outside the jurisdiction of the House and for that body to entertain them would be a direct abrogation of his constitutional rights. He did agree that the House was within its rights to censure him as called for by Mr. Gilmer and it was to this point that he addressed himself unequivocally in a speech which bears repeating for it contains the unmitigated feelings of the northern interests in Congress over the question of slavery:

There was a trial in this house, about four or five years ago, of a member of the house for crime. (Mr. Wise had had connection with the duel between Messrs. Graves and Cilley, in which the latter was killed.) There came into this house then a man with his hands and face dripping with the blood of murder, the blotches of which were yet hanging upon him; and the question was put, upon the proposition of those very democrats to whom he has this day rendered the tribute and homage of his thanks, that he should be tried by this house for that crime, the crime of murder. I opposed the trial of that crime by this house. I was willing that the parties to that atrocious crime should be sent to their natural judges, to have an impartial trial; and it is very probable that I saved that blood-stained man from the censure of the house at the time. . . .

I wish to speak of the slaveholders of this house and of the Union with respect. There are three classes of persons included in the slave interest as representatives here. As to the slaveholder, I have nothing to say against him, except if I am to be tried by him, I shall not have an impartial trial. I challenge him for partiality—for preadjudication upon this question, as a question of contempt, which I repeat, is the only charge on which I can be made to answer here, I say he is not impartial. Every slaveholder has not only an interest, but the most sordid of interests—a personal, pecuniary interest—which will govern him. I come from a portion of the country where slavery is known only by name; I come from a soil that bears not the foot of a slave upon it. I represent here the descendants of Bedford, and Winslow, and Carver, and Alden—the first who alighted on the rock of Plymouth. And am I, the representative of the descendants of these men—of the *free* people of the state of Massachusetts, that bears not a slave upon it—am I to come here and be tried for high treason because I presented a petition—*a petition*—to this house, and because the fancy or imagination of the gentleman from Kentucky supposes that there was anti-slavery or the abolition of slavery in it? The gentleman charges me with subornation of perjury and of high treason, and he calls upon this house, *as a matter of mercy and grace,* not to expel me for these crimes, but to inflict upon me the severest censure they can; and to decide upon that, there are one hundred members of this house who are slaveholders. Is any one of them impartial? No. I trust they will not consider themselves as impartial men; I trust that many of them will have those qualms of conscience which the gentleman from Accomac (Mr. Wise) assigns as his reason for being excused, and that they will not vote upon a question on which their personal, pecuniary, and most sordid interests are at stake.[2]

The first to rise to the defense of Mr. Adams was Representative Underwood of Kentucky who defended the right of petition and agreed that the House was not the proper tribunal before which one should be arraigned for the alleged crimes. More importantly, he cautioned the House, lest it allow itself to be transformed into the very instrument through which political zeal and morality meld to become the *casus belli.* For the best way to insure martyrdom to the aging gentleman from Massachusetts would be to censure him. Next, Mr. Botts of Virginia took the floor in defense of the northern legislator. In his speech he stated that this was not the first time in which such a petition had been heard before this body. Congressman Rhett, three or four years ago, drew up a resolution calling for Congress to appoint a committee to report out means of dissolving the union. He also informed them that a high administrative official—Secretary of Navy, Upshur—openly favored immediate dissolution of the Union and that if any one was to be brought up on charges of high treason certainly it was the Secretary and not Mr. Adams.

After several days of additional testimony John Quincy Adams agreed to have the whole matter of his censure tabled, provided it never be taken up again. As to the reception of the petition it was refused by a vote of 40 to 106.

If the mood of Congress were opposed to disunion it was also necessarily hypersensitive concerning its position vis-à-vis the broader question of the black man's status. For as we shall see, it quite often involved other nations having no reciprocal treaty agreements. Representative Giddings of Ohio was censured for arguing, based upon the peculiar set of legal circumstances surrounding the brig, *Creole*,[3] that there did exist in fact a "positive municipal law" which was necessarily confined to the jurisdictional area of the power creating it. Once the *Creole* had left the territory under jurisdiction of a given state—in this case Virginia—the laws of that state no longer were applicable to the persons aboard the vessel. In short, the persons on board became liable only to the laws of the United States. He therefore argued that since the United States Constitution made no provisions respecting slavery and since no Federal slave laws were violated, any attempt on the part of the government to have said persons returned amounted to a recognition by the United States of a "commerce in human beings." In strong words, he considered this situation detestable, a denial of the rights of the free states, unconstitutional, and in conflict with the national interest. Without recourse to a hearing, and lacking the prestige of a John Quincy Adams, the vote for censure against the Ohioan carried 125 to 69. On March 22, 1842, the representative from Ohio resigned and returned home to be reelected in a special election April 26 by a majority of about 3,500 votes—an overwhelming vote of confidence. His censure, resignation, reelection, and subsequent return to Congress on May 5 further reflected the growing division in the country and the political potential inherent in the question of the black man's status.

The Texas question was yet unresolved. John Tyler who ascended to the Presidency following the death of Harrison after only thirty days in office attempted to "reannex" Texas via a treaty carrying his signature and negotiated through John C. Calhoun, Secretary of State, and Texas chargé d'affaires, Van Zandt, in Washington. The treaty ratification which required a two-thirds vote failed miserably. Benton of Missouri, who favored statehood for Texas, contended that the treaty proposed annexation of much more land than originally belonged to Texas. According to a treaty with Spain in 1819 the area included land between the Sabine River and Rio del Norte, and the Gulf of Mexico and the Red River. He labeled the "reannexation of Texas" scheme as envisaged by this treaty a fraud—his major objection being that it would mean war with Mexico. Later in the session of 1844 he introduced a bill for annexation which required Mexico's consent. However, before it could be taken up Congress adjourned.

Prior to their party's nominating convention, public sentiment had declared Clay (Whig) and Van Buren (Democrat) to be the Presidential candidates in the election of 1844. The leading issue was Texas. Accordingly, they were requested to state publicly their views on the annexation question. Assuredly, the topic of slavery would be a prominent part of any such discussion.

Henry Clay opposed the annexation of Texas under the circumstances then extant in the country's relationship with Mexico. He did not disapprove of it because of the slavery issue. In his mind this question would readily resolve itself as a natural consequence of the Texas geography. On the basis of information available to him, the new acquisition was amenable to division into five smaller states. In three of the states slave labor would prove unprofitable, hence these would be free states while the remaining two would be slave. The unity ratio would be maintained again. This position insured him the unanimous Whig party nomination at the Baltimore Convention of 1844.

Van Buren did not fare as well. His reasons for opposing annexation at that time were different from Clay's as relations with a foreign power were involved. However, on the question of slavery he differed widely. He and his New York supporters were firmly in opposition to its spread into the new territory. This cost him the nomination although he received a majority vote in the early balloting.[4] Through successful behind-the-scenes maneuvering, Robert Walker, a Mississippi delegate, was able to induce then President Tyler to withdraw and throw his support to James K. Polk, former Speaker of the House and ex-Governor of Tennessee, the country's first dark horse candidate. In order to retain his northern flank consisting of Tammany Hall Irish and New York and Ohio farmers (currently incensed over the British Corn Law which kept their grain out of England) he offered them the great Oregon Territory. His strategy worked and Polk received the party's presidential nomination on the ninth ballot at Baltimore in 1844.

According to Walker, "reannexation and reoccupation" was to be the Democratic campaign slogan. The words were carefully chosen to imply that both Texas and Oregon were American territory. Texas, by the Florida Treaty of 1819, and Oregon, via "manifest destiny."

Over in the State Department, Tyler's Secretary of State, John C. Calhoun, was at work preparing the international climate for the Administration's move on Texas. Realizing that American annexation of Texas would most certainly involve war with Mexico, the Secretary took necessary action stating the country's position to the French Government and disclaiming any British "philanthropy" relative to the American institution of slavery as being purely economically and politically inspired. In a letter to the American Minister in Paris, dated August 12, 1844, Mr. Calhoun, an ardent expansionist, laid out the American claim to Texas. He was well aware that it had been rumored that France would unite with Britain in some manner to protest the annexation of Texas and that American abolitionists figured in the scheme. His object in writing the letter was to insure France that her best interest lay in remaining neutral and not joining forces with England. As to America's natural right to Texas and its willingness to fight

THE ISSUE

to protect it, he stated:

> It is our destiny to occupy that vast region; to intersect it with roads and canals; to fill it with cities, towns, villages, and farms; to extend over it our religion, customs, constitution, and laws, and to present it as a peaceful and splendid addition to the domains of commerce and civilization. It is our policy to increase by growing and spreading out into unoccupied regions, assimilating all we incorporate: in a word, to increase by accretion, and not through conquest, by the addition of masses held together by the adhesion of force.
>
> No system can be more unsuited to the latter process, or better adapted to the former, than our admirable federal system. If it should not be resisted in its course, it will probably fulfill its destiny without disturbing our neighbors or putting in jeopardy the general peace; but if it be opposed by foreign interference, a new direction would be given to our energy, much less favorable to harmony with our neighbors, and to the general peace of the world.
>
> The change would be undesirable to us, and much less in accordance with what I have assumed to be primary objects of policy on the part of France, England, and Mexico.[5]

Evidently England's main objection, as stated by them, was based on their opposition to African slavery in the United States. Secretary of State Calhoun was prepared to risk war with England, Mexico, and France, if need be, to insure its continual spread westward. In his mind the scheme for the abolition of slavery began in the United States and received worldwide sanction in the abolitionist societies' international meeting in London in 1840. Here it was brought to the attention of the British Government who then began using its influence and diplomacy to effect a future course.

Calhoun viewed Britain's abolitionist sentiment as purely economic and political and was prepared to define it as such in no uncertain terms. Her abolishing slavery in the West Indies was based on the fallacious calculation that free labor would be more productive than slave labor and, since her political advantage depended upon her tropical production, an increase in the latter would automatically mean an increase in the former. This turned out not to be the case for under the system of free labor production had fallen off. In addition, the indemnification paid the slave owners—100 million dollars—had caused the price of sugar and other tropical products paid by the British people to rise 50 million dollars—the direct result being that she could no longer supply her own wants. Referring to 1808 when England had abolished slavery, he explained that the rest of the countries involved in production of tropical products and dependent upon slave labor of the negro had increased their annual production from 72 million dollars to 220 million with a current fixed capital investment of 4 billion dollars. On the other hand, Britain, with a fixed capital investment of only 830 million dollars could produce a paltry 50 million dollars annually. Figures such as these told the whole story. Slave labor was more productive than free labor. Great Britain had made a grave mistake and could no longer compete in the world market. She was therefore out to destroy her main competition, the United States. At least this was the way Secretary of State Calhoun saw it. If the successful British abolitionists' movement could be transported across the Atlantic and slavery abolished in the South and emerging West, Britain, based upon her new slave colonies in East and Central Africa, could again attain world political and economic superiority solely upon her production of cotton, sugar, and coffee.

Both European powers, new and old, knew too well the extent to which the political and economic survival of their system depended upon the toil of the black man. According to *Blackwood's Magazine* for June 1841, a leading British publication, free labor in the British East and West Indies and Mauritius produced only 4 million pounds of sugar while the United States, Cuba, and Brazil, taking advantage of slave labor, produced 9.6 million pounds during the same period. British production of coffee amounted to 27.4 million pounds while Cuba and Brazil produced 201.6 million pounds. As to cotton, the all-important American crop, the British possessions could produce only 137 million pounds compared to production in the United States alone which amounted to 790.5 million pounds. When it came to the annexation of Texas or any other new lands Secretary Calhoun and indeed all knowledgeable men were prepared to admit that "the vast increase of capital and production" derived from those parts of the world employing slave labor was due solely to those nations' "policy toward the negro race."

The cotton interests in Congress, well aware of the political and economic realities of their section of the country's existence, remained firmly resolved that Texas should be acquired and with no prohibition on slavery. In a very close election, their candidate, James K. Polk, was elected President in November of 1844. In an ironic twist of events that witnessed the increased political appeal of the anti-slavery issue, Clay, the Whig party candidate, lost the election by slightly over 33,000 votes. The fledgling Liberty party, with James Birney as its candidate, captured over 63,000 votes in the free states—an increase of some 900 per cent over the previous election. It was agreed that most of these votes were taken away from Clay. This fact proved fatal in New York which Polk took by a margin of 5,000 votes. Had the Liberty party not attracted 16,000 votes in that state, undoubtedly they would have fallen into the Clay column.

THE ISSUE

Clay, the Whig candidate, but for the zeal of the anti-slavery, anti-Texas Liberty party, could have become the eleventh President of the United States. As to what course he would have pursued once in office we can only speculate. Based on his pre-convention correspondence, it is safe to assume that his stance on the question of slavery in Texas would have been more moderate than that of Polk. The irony of the situation lay in the fact that the Liberty party in its fervor to oppose slavery in the Texas territory defeated the candidate from whom it was most likely to obtain an attentive ear.

On March 1, 1845, in the closing hours of the twenty-eighth Congress, the Senate amendment regarding Texas was agreed to by the House and the annexation of the new territory was decreed. On March 2, the last day of his administration, President Tyler put his signature to the joint resolution which held the possibility that four new states in addition to Texas could be formed out of the territory. Of those states lying south of the Missouri Compromise line (36° 30′ north latitude) their entry into the Union as slave or free depended solely upon the wishes of the inhabitants. In those states lying north of the compromise line, slavery or involuntary servitude would be prohibited except in the punishment for crime.

James K. Polk, an ardent champion of states' rights, assumed the Presidency on March 4, 1845. In his Inaugural Address, aware of the division in Congress and the growing secessionist move in the country, the President indicated that he realized that a protracted imbalance in the federal-state relationship over the issue of slavery would lead to disunion. Borrowing the words of Thomas Jefferson, he emphasized his "support of the state governments in all their rights, as the most competent administration for our domestic concerns and the surest bulwark against anti-republican tendencies," further acknowledging, "the preservation of the General Government in its whole constitutional vigor, as the sheet anchor of our peace at home and abroad." He went on to reaffirm his faith in the American system by declaring "Our Federal Union—it must be preserved." The abolitionists he reproached as "misguided persons" having occasionally engaged in "schemes and agitation" that if successful would lead to the dissolution of the Union.

Texas acquired statehood on December 29, 1845. A previous severing of diplomatic relations between Mexico and the United States had occurred and as predicted, war between the two was quick in coming. In the spring of 1846, the United States Army under command of General Zachary Taylor was ordered by President Polk to advance to the east bank of the Rio Grande del Norte. This was disputed territory. It was claimed by Texas—but never occupied—as her western boundary. Considering the land as part of their possession, Mexico did not recognize the claim. The Mexicans were goaded into attacking which led to a hostile collision between the two powers. President Polk publicly labeled the Mexicans aggressors declaring that they had shed "American blood on American soil."

Old Glory had been fired upon and the country rallied to her cause. But this was of short duration, for as the war was seen to last, Whig representatives in Congress heaped increasing criticism upon the Administration. A young awkward congressman known only in his home state of Illinois led the charge. He demanded on the congressional floor that the Administration disclose to the public the exact "spot" on which "American blood" had been shed on "American soil." The persistence of this young man, one Abraham Lincoln by name, in addition to earning the nickname "Spot," proved to be the undoing of the Democrats in Congress. For the first time since 1843, they lost control of the House during mid-term of the twenty-ninth Congress. The growing anti-slavery issue in the country had expressed itself politically in the Texas annexation question and the concerns of the period were everywhere producing new leadership.

Realizing the ill effects of a protracted war with Mexico on the morals of the country and the stability of the Democratic party, President Polk took immediate action aimed at inducing Mexico into ceding the land to the United States Government. On August 8, 1846, he submitted a message to Congress calling for immediate appropriations to be used in negotiating with Mexico. The provisions of the bill he submitted called for 30,000 dollars to be used in immediate efforts and an additional 2 million dollars to be placed at his disposal for future peace negotiations. Immediately, the incipient fractiousness in the Democratic party over the question of the black man's status vis-à-vis territorial expansion was seen to manifest itself. David Wilmot, the fledgling representative from Pennsylvania, after prior consultation with other northern Democrats, offered an amendment to the appropriation measure. According to his rider which later became known as the Wilmot Proviso, the monies put at the Executive's disposal could not be used to obtain land from the Republic of Mexico which would be open to slavery or involuntary servitude—except for the punishment of crime. The Proviso carried in the committee of the whole and was passed by the House on the basis of a sectional vote. In the Senate, before debate on a motion by Mr. Lewis from Alabama to strike out the petition could be fully concluded, the time fixed for adjournment came. On August 10, 1847, both houses adjourned sine die. The bill, having passed the House, received no Senate action. The thirtieth Congress convening on December 6, 1847, took no further action on the amendment as originally proposed. For all intents and purposes the Wilmot Proviso was dead and the question of

THE ISSUE

slavery in the Texas Territory laid to rest.

A bill for organizing the Oregon Territory was laid before the Senate early in the second session. The back-room political deals arranged by Robert Walker of Mississippi between pro-slavery and anti-slavery factions of the Democratic party during the 1844 nominating convention had been forgotten. On the Senate floor the power of Congress to legislate on the subject of slavery again came under attack. Former Secretary of State, John C. Calhoun, who was now representing South Carolina before that body, held that Federal interference on the subject of slavery would be disastrous to the cause of Union. By his standards, the Northwest Ordinance (1787), so dear to the heart of Jefferson, and the Missouri Compromise (1820) would be the first chapters in any historical presentation of doom. According to his controversions, the fundamental notion of the Declaration of Independence that "all men are created equal" was merely a "hypothetical truism." He asserted that there was not a word of real truth in it and supported this position by arguing that: "Men are not born free. While infants, they are incapable of freedom; they are subject to . . . their parents." It therefore followed that in no less manner were men born "equal." Alluding to Biblical reference, he reinforced his point concerning equality. "All men are not created. Only two, a man and a woman, were created, and one of these was pronounced subordinate to the other. All others have come into the world by being born, and in no sense, as I have shown, either free or equal." In concluding his argument, Calhoun insisted that freedom and equality were not guaranteed to all men by accident of birth and that, therefore, all classes were not entitled to them. The two being, as he considered them, high prizes to be won, should only be bestowed as rewards for high mental and moral development. The notion of equality and freedom of all men as envisioned by Thomas Jefferson in the Declaration of Independence was beginning to "germinate and produce its poisonous fruits." The third President of the United States, "the author of that document," had an "utterly false view of the subordinate relations of the black to the white race in the south," and in consequence of this, believed "that the former, though utterly unqualified to possess liberty, were as fully entitled to both liberty and equality as the latter; and that to deprive them of it was unjust and immoral."

Such were the thoughts of Senator Calhoun, arguing his point in behalf of the slave interests in Congress. Their aim was to rescind the Northwest Ordinance of 1787 by decrying its most venerated supporter. Should they be successful, the vast Oregon territory,[6] which at that time included Oregon, Washington, Idaho, and portions of Montana and Wyoming, would be open to slave labor and therefore to the extension of southern economic and political interests.

History records that they met with little success for on August 2, 1847, a House bill was passed providing for a territorial government and extending, thereto, the provisions of the Ordinance of 1787. Eleven days later the same bill passed the Senate.

The United States Government signed a peace treaty with Mexico on February 2, 1848. According to the terms of the treaty under which the United States paid the Mexican Government 15 million dollars, the American claim to Texas was recognized. The Mexican cession of Upper California and New Mexico was also part of the deal. It was from these territories, larger in size than France and Germany combined, that the present states of Arizona, California, Nevada, New Mexico, Utah, and parts of Colorado and Wyoming were carved.

The actions of Polk, the expansionist President, regarding the Mexican War came under attack in many quarters. The Whigs charged that he had forced the war in order to spread the institution of slavery. Americans throughout the country were momentarily nauseous at their country's dishonorable intentions. In Congress, Lincoln supported a resolution condemning the war as "unnecessarily and unconstitutionally begun by the President of the United States." But Polk remained unperturbed; he knew too well the power of his office. The size of the electorate had more than doubled since Jackson's first term.[7] The power of the Presidency lay in the hands of the electorate, at most, to be temporized by Congress. For, as he put it in his last annual message to Congress; "The President represents in the executive department the whole people of the United States as each representative of the legislature department represents portions of them." Similar statements by Jackson on the power of the executive had angered the Senate and drawn cries of outrage from Clay. But things were different now and a new relationship existed between the executive and legislative branches of government. Any popularly elected President with broad-based support throughout the electorate was free to push for enactment of his policies above and beyond those of the Congress. To avoid any potential breach in communication between politically compatible executive and legislative branches of government requires the invocation of a para-structure not mentioned in the Constitution. The paramount responsibility of this unit—on the national level, is to elect the President. It is through working with state and local party organizations that the national organization is able to transmit the executive policies to the nationwide electorate. And based on their reaction to a given set of policies, the people, through a given set of electors, choose their President. It was through this basic understanding of the American political system that Polk was able to assert the power

THE ISSUE

of his office and take the country into war with Mexico.

Nationally, the Whigs had learned from an earlier episode, the War of 1812, of the perils of opposing war. They also knew that military heroes, for some reason, have a hypnotic appeal to the American electorate. The desire to elect the President heightened by the discovery of gold in California led the Whig party to nominate General Zachary Taylor, the hero of Mexico, over Daniel Webster, Henry Clay, and General Winfield Scott for the Presidency in their Iowa convention of 1848. As a result of Taylor's having previously declared that he would leave all questions of policy to Congress, the Whig Convention adopted no platform. His Vice-Presidential running mate was Millard Fillmore of New York.

The fragile political alliances within the Democratic party had begun to deteriorate. The incipient fractiousness over the question of the extension of slavery into the western territories which Polk knew existed just beneath the suface began to appear on top. In New York State, the Party had split into two factions. One of these, the Barnburners, controlled the legislature and had elected the governor in 1844. This faction, composed of Van Buren men, supported the Wilmot Proviso and received no federal patronage from the Polk administration. Another Democratic group, the Hunkers, maintained control of the state party organization through the aid of federal patronage. They controlled the State Convention held in Syracuse in 1847 and rejected the Barnburner resolution which called for an "uncompromising hostility to the extension of slavery into the territory now free." As a result of the rejection, they held their own meeting in Herkimer, New York, and pledged not to support any presidential candidate at the National Convention favoring the extension of slavery. Meeting in Utica in 1848, prior to the National Democratic Convention, they reaffirmed their position that slavery was contradictory to Democratic party principles and to the American tradition. They, like the Hunkers, chose their own slate of delegates to the National Convention.

When presented with two sets of delegates from New York State, the National Democratic Convention held in Baltimore in May 1848 sought a compromise between the factions and offered to allow each to cast half the state's votes. Both rejected this offer. When the Barnburners withdrew, the Convention went on to nominate General Lewis Cass of Michigan, former Secretary of War under Jackson and the foremost exponent of "squatter sovereignty." He described this principle at length in a letter dated December 24, 1847, to A.O.P. Nicholson, Esq., of Nashville, Tennessee. The matter of slavery in the new territories, he said, he would: "Leave to the people, who will be affected by the question, to adjust it upon their own responsibility, and in their own manner. . . ."

45

Both major parties had chosen former generals as presidential candidates. In neither party convention of 1848 was the growing anti-slavery sentiment in the nation allowed to be expressed. While the Whig party had no platform, the Democratic party adopted one not incompatible to the slave interest. It seemed that, momentarily at least, both parties had put the lid on the tempest in the political pot by either ignoring the slavery issue or else by reading its main exponents out of the party.

Partisan exclusion of slavery as a political issue was not to be of any lengthy duration. In August 1848 a convention held in Buffalo brought together anti-slavery Whigs and Democrats and members of the old Liberty party in the formation of a new party uniting under a single banner as "the opponents of Slavery-extension." The new organization was called the Free Soil party. Included among its leaders were Martin Van Buren of New York and his son, John; Charles Francis Adams, son of John Quincy Adams; John P. Hale, the anti-slavery advocate from New Hampshire; Charles Sumner of Massachusetts; and Samuel J. Tilden of New York. These were not political dilettantes, as many of the earlier abolitionists had been; these were men of formidable political skill. The Free Soil party convention nominated Martin Van Buren, a former Democrat, as its presidential candidate, and Charles Francis Adams, a former Whig, for the Vice-Presidency. The extremist flank of the anti-slavery movement formed the Liberty League and chose Gerrit Smith from upstate New York, a philanthropist, as its prime national candidate. He also received support of organized labor (Industrial Congress) and ran on a platform espousing free land for settlers.

The outcome of the 1848 election placed "Old Rough and Ready" Zachary Taylor, a Louisiana slaveholder, in the White House. He narrowly defeated General Cass who had votes taken from him by the presence of Van Buren on the ticket. In New York State where the Free Soil party candidate outran the Democratic one, the state's electoral votes were cast in behalf of Taylor. Pennsylvania, in reaction to the Democratic Congress having lowered the tariff in 1846, also went Whig. In terms of the major party candidates, the outcome of the presidential election could not be viewed as a triumph for either anti-slavery or pro-slavery interests. On the contrary, it indicated that the popular vote in the country was rather evenly divided between the two military heroes (Taylor, 1.4 million, Cass, 1.2 million) with the Free Soil party playing the decisive role. The new anti-slavery party running its candidate on a ticket opposing the spread of slavery captured 261,263 votes from all the free states, including some from North Carolina. This vote total represented a fourfold increase over that of the Liberty party which garnered 62,300 votes in 1844. Clearly the issue of slavery had a broad political appeal that was on the increase.

THE ISSUE

Opposing this trend, witnessed by the Democratic takeover of Congress, would be a concomitant increase in sectionalism. The Cotton Kingdom, controlled by those who ruled the Democratic party, was in control of Congress and Congress was in control of the country.

By a confluence of circumstances, General Zachary Taylor had defeated General Lewis Cass, nothing had been settled by the outcome of the election. The issue of slavery, perpetually before the Chief Executive, remained unsettled. In the closing remarks of his inaugural address on March 5, 1849, Taylor broached the subject and alluded to the duty of Congress "to adopt such measures of conciliation as may harmonize conflicting interests and tend to perpetuate that Union which should be the paramount object of our hopes and affections." He then called upon the "goodness of Divine Providence . . . to assuage the bitterness which too often marks unavoidable difference of opinion."

Perhaps the President's prayers might have been answered, for it had been suggested, in the spirit of compromise, that California be divided into two states—one slave and one free. This would allow the unity ratio to be maintained. But the discovery of gold interdicted the usual course of events and compelled the inhabitants to seek statehood on somewhat extraordinary grounds.

Gold was discovered on land owned by Indians in California on January 24, 1848.[8] James W. Marshall, a New Jersey native, was erecting a sawmill for John A. Sutter, a Swiss emigrant, who was starting a lumber business on the American River, forty miles from New Helvetia. Hoping to obtain the right to work the gold for Marshall and himself from the Indian owners, Sutter attempted to keep the discovery a secret. He obtained agreement from his workers to keep their tongues quiet for six weeks in order to give him time to properly negotiate his claim. The attempt at secrecy failed when Sutter's emissary to Colonel Mason, the military governor, let word of the discovery out. Due to poor communications the word traveled slowly and a real gold rush did not develop for a few months. But when the fever came, it really came! According to the San Francisco *Californian* which had to suspend publication on May 29, 1848, because it had become entirely superfluous: "The whole country, from San Francisco to Los Angeles, and from the sea shore to the base of the Sierra Nevadas, resounds with the sordid cry of 'gold, Gold, GOLD!' while the field is left half planted, the house half built and everything neglected but the manufacture of shovels and pick-axes."

At the beginning only Californians were involved in the rush but, by June of 1848, word had reached the Hawaiian Islands and gold-seekers from across the Pacific had joined the rush. By October people from Oregon had begun the southward migration and, beginning in September,

Chile and Peru sent several thousand men northward. At this point the
rush was still a west coast phenomenon but on February 28, 1849, the
first delegation from the Atlantic seaboard arrived. By the end of 1849 a
considerable number of Europeans from England's penal colony in Aus-
tralia began to arrive. When the fever struck in the summer of 1848 there
were approximately 14,000 persons—excluding Indians. This population
had increased to slightly under 20,000 by the end of the year. Of this
figure, between six and eight thousand were Americans—the remainder
being Latin Americans, Pacific Islanders, etc. One year later, at the end
of 1849, the population exclusive of Indians had increased to just under
100,000. Americans formed one half to two thirds of the total.

Gold production for fiscal 1848 was recorded at 245,300 dollars. This
figure sky-rocketed to 10.2 million dollars in 1849 and to 41.3 million in
1850. The peak year was fiscal 1852 when gold production rose to 81.3
million dollars. In 1874 gold production was recorded at 17.3 million
dollars.

With the discovery of gold in 1848 and the subsequent in-migration of
people from all parts of the world there came many problems. Neither the
military nor the *alcaldes* established by the Treaty of Guadalupe Hidalgo
were equipped to cope with them. The situation required a more democratic form of governance which, for the present, Congress had not provided. So after an earlier futile attempt in January 1849 on the part of
the people to organize a constitutional convention, General Riley, Colonel
Mason's successor, issued a proclamation calling for the convening of such
a body. In September 1849 the constitutional convention began its proceedings. The overwhelming majority of its delegates were Americans
with only a sprinkling of native-born Californians and foreigners being represented. The greatest debate centered around the question of slavery.
The miners in the region and the convention delegates were unmistakably
opposed to slavery. Their opposition arose not out of any pains of conscience nor qualms of moral indignation. No. Simply stated, they were
opposed to having slave labor work the mines.

On October 13, 1849, the work of the convention was finished and
the delegates signed the state constitution. One month later, P.H. Burnett,
a gold rush immigrant from Oregon, was elected governor in an election
in which less than one-sixth of the American population voted. California
was now prepared to seek admission into the Union as the thirty-first
state. Her fate lay in the hands of Congress.

The thirty-first Congress was organized on December 23, 1849. On
the following day, President Taylor submitted his first annual message to
both houses of Congress. In it he called for the admission of California

THE ISSUE

as a state and for an avoidance of debate so often occasioned by "those exciting topics of a sectional character." In spite of all attempts, his hopes to avoid those rabid discussions which hitherto had accompanied every new land acquisition, were short-lived. On January 4, 1850, General Sam Houston of Texas introduced the issue of slavery into the California question. In a letter to the Senate he called for extending the terms of the Missouri Compromise all the way to the Pacific Ocean. This meant that slavery could be permitted in California south of the parallel $36° 30'$ if the inhabitants so deemed it worthwhile. In short, he wanted no stipulations prohibiting slavery in any congressional actions attending the admission of California as a state. In response to this proposal there were those who argued that the whole question of the black man's status in California was academic since the people through their petition had declared a prohibition against slavery. There was also the technical question, arising from the fact that California had not passed through territorial status, that had to be resolved. Likewise, the standard debate relative to the powers of Congress over the institution of slavery could be expected to reappear. But there was a deeper more serious mood in Congress. In the concluding phase of its struggle to reach its "manifest destiny" the ship of state was rife with dissent. The black man's status which had once been an issue over which honorable gentlemen would disagree but never part company, had become *the issue* that would threaten the existence of a nation. Frayed nerve endings brought about by the continuous hassle over this question had produced unmollified anxiety among the congressmen. The atmosphere was electric with paranoia and neither side was immune to it.

Calhoun declared that "the Union was in danger." The South was outraged at the shabby treatment it had received beginning in 1787 with the Northwest Ordinance right up to the Missouri Compromise of 1820. This latter document shortchanged the southern interests who received only 609,023 square miles compared to 1.2 million claimed by the North. He considered the plan submitted by the President to be an extension of the Wilmot Proviso and, therefore, a further encroachment upon the rights of the South. In his mind the equilibrium that had existed between the two sections at the adoption of the Constitution had been destroyed. The revenue system (tariff), unduly harsh upon the South since they were the major exporting states, only added to the outrage. If, as proposed by the President, California was to be admitted as a free state, another 526,078 square miles of American territory would be misappropriated in favor of the North. There was no way under such conditions that the South could honorably remain in the Union.

To further attest to the disquiet of the situation, Calhoun's secessionist forays were parried by Daniel Webster of Massachusetts, an individual who, like Henry Clay, had built a reputation as an able compromiser. Webster, incensed by the thought of secession, was quick to take the floor in response. He declared:

Secession! Peaceable secession! Sir, your eyes and mine are never destined to see that miracle. Who is so foolish—I beg everybody's pardon—as to expect to see any such thing? There could be no such thing as a peaceable secession—a concurrent agreement of the members of this republic to separate? Where is the flag of the republic to remain? What is to become of the army?—of the navy?—of the public lands? How is each of the states to defend itself? To break up this great government! to dismember this great country! to astonish Europe with an act of folly, such as Europe for two centuries has never beheld in any government! No, sir! no, sir! There will be no secession. Gentlemen are not serious when they talk of secession.

Strong words these were for a man heretofore known as a great conciliator, but relatively weak when compared to President Taylor's earlier announcement concerning secession that he would personally take to the field and hang anyone found guilty of rebellion.

Animated debate continued with no reprieve and representatives on both sides of the slavery question had their say. One representative opposed to slavery, previously not heard from, was William Henry Seward of New York. He attacked the South for threatening disunion and wishing to change the form of government from a national democracy back to a federal alliance as it had been under the old Articles of Confederation. Thereafter, he reminded them that the Union did not exist by voluntary consent; it existed and would be maintained by force. He accused northern businessmen having capital invested in the sugar fields, cotton fields, and rice fields of the world of holding back the tide of emancipation and reminded them of the hypocrisy and cowardice inherent in the Constitution which caused slaves to be designated as *persons.* In his mind there was a "higher law" which governed the territory bestowed upon the leaders of America by the Creator of the Universe. And this law demanded that slavery be abolished and the Union preserved.

Debate over the terms of California's admission lasted for three months. During this period not a single law of national signifance was passed. Finally, a bill put together by Clay in the last of his great compromises was agreed to by the Senate. When it reached the House they were overjoyed with its contents and voted to accept it. The measure, referred to as the Omnibus Bill, admitted California as a free state on September 9, 1850, organized the territory of New Mexico and the Utah territory, and established the boundary of Texas. The bill also abolished the slave-trade in the District of Columbia and enacted a fugitive slave law.[9] President Millard Fillmore who had come into office upon the untimely death of Zachary Taylor on July 9 signed the measure into law.

The adoption of the Compromise of 1850 momentarily established a new era of good feelings. Extremism on both sides of the slavery issue was seen to diminish in Congress. A nation that began on the Atlantic had endured agonizing growing pains and now the air she breathed in on her eastern shore, she exhaled on the sunny Pacific. America had indeed reached her "manifest destiny." A vast expanse between the two great oceans had congealed into a mighty nation under a single chief—the President of the United States. Those men from Europe had conquered the land and the issue that had caused much consternation among them had subsided. Politically, the Democrats were the main benefactors for the other two parties had lost votes. In the Congressional elections of 1850, the Whig strength in the House fell from 104 to 88 and the Free Soilers lost 9 of the 14 seats they had previously held. The Democrats picked up 29 seats to increase their total to 140; consequently they were able to elect the Speaker of the House.

This new era of good feelings would carry over into the presidential election of 1852. Both major parties in their national conventions would nominate candidates who were "sound on the goose."[10] On the forty-ninth ballot, the Democratic party in their June convention held in Baltimore would nominate Franklin Pierce of New Hampshire, a dark horse candidate, to run for the presidency. The Whig Party Convention, of no shorter duration (in spite of the fact that only a simple majority was required for nomination) due to the uncompromising candidacies of Fillmore and Webster, nominated General Winfield Scott, an aging Mexican War hero, on the fifty-third ballot. Paradoxically, Webster and Fillmore, both of whom shared similar pro-Compromise views, could not come to terms with each other. Scott, the candidate who admitted possessing no views of his own on the matter, received the nomination with the backing of the Seward faction—"Conscience Whigs." Both major party conventions endorsed the Compromise. The Free Soilers who attacked the Compromise nominated John P. Hale of New Hampshire for the Presidency.

The presidential election of 1852 was won by Franklin Pierce. When the results were in it was obvious that popular support for the Compromise was widespread. Pierce, the Democratic party candidate, carried all but four states. The Free Soil party vote total dropped some 100,000 compared with 1848. As far as most politicians were concerned, the slavery question was dead and buried. The issue that had threatened the Union was laid to rest. Franklin Pierce, in his Inaugural Address of March 4, 1853, appeared to confirm the rights of slave holders to their property by stating his belief that the Constitution recognized slavery. And, in light of this recognition, it was therefore necessary to make available to those states in which the institution existed "efficient remedies to enforce the constitutional provision."

The Democratic party, the party of the slaveholders, was in power. They controlled the national government in Washington and their man, Pierce of New Hampshire, sat in the White House. True, the people of the nation had spoken. But what had they said? Did the popular mandate the Democratic party had received mean that the people were proslavery, as interpreted by the President? Or, did it mean that they were opposed to war—the ultimate conflict that daily became inevitable?

A mighty nation stretching from ocean to ocean had been forged from granite. But beyond the horizon of that nation there hovered close by ominous and foreboding thunderclouds. And one day a storm would appear and lightning would strike that rock and cause a cleavage that only the wisdom of time could mend. And when that storm would appear there would be no more debates, no more gentlemen's agreements, no more compromises. There would be war. For, if reasonable men could not agree upon the status of the black man it would be necessary to take up the sword, to "speak the fraternal language," to defend one's honor.

4

ON THE BROTHER'S BACK

Supposedly reaffirmed by the election of 1852, the Compromise of
1850 brought to an end one of the most stirring epochs of American political history. The question of the black man's status had become the
stage on which the major American drama was being acted out. Momentarily, the show was canceled, for the old actors had passed from the scene
and their replacements had not yet arrived. On both sides of the slavery
question, the leadership ranks had been depleted. Death claimed Andrew
Jackson in 1845, John Quincy Adams in 1848, and Calhoun in 1850.
Henry Clay and Daniel Webster, two men who on several occasions had
held the Union together through their abilities to effect compromise,
passed away in 1852 and were laid to rest in Ashland, Kentucky und
Marshfield, Massachusetts, respectively. Martin Van Buren, "The Little
Magician," founder of the Albany Regency and eighth President of the
United States, was in retirement and Thomas Benton of Missouri had lost
his Senate seat to Atchison for opposing the Compromise of 1850.

The new players who were soon to occupy center stage would differ
drastically from the men they replaced. To those on both sides of the
slavery question the term "compromise" would be anathema. The back
door alliance between the Lords of the Lash and the Lords of the Loom[1]
would have to be broken. President Pierce's wish for continued "repose"
as expressed in his message to the opening session of Congress on December 6, 1853, would soon be dashed. The Senate floor would once more
become the battleground on which the most significant battle in the political history of a nation would be fought. Leading the charge on behalf

of the pro-slavery forces would be Archibald Dixon of Kentucky, successor to Henry Clay; Stephen A. Douglas of Illinois, a northern Democrat; and Jefferson Davis of Mississippi, son-in-law of former President Zachary Taylor. They would soon be met at mid-stripe by cadremen of opposite persuasion led by William Henry Seward, Whig Senator from New York, and Salmon P. Chase, Democrat—Free Soiler (recently founder along with Charles P. Sumner of Massachusetts of the Free Democratic party)[2] from Ohio.

Late in December of 1853 the committee on territories headed by Senator Douglas of Illinois issued a report favorable to the organization of the Nebraska Territory on a squatter sovereignty basis. Included among the provisions of the measure were several propositions reaffirming the Fugitive Slave Law of 1850. The aim of the committee was to leave the territory open to slavery in spite of the obvious fact that it lay north of 36° 30′ north latitude. However, they refrained from stating their purpose in order to avoid unwarranted debate on the subject. Considering solely what they judged the mood of the country to be, the Democrat-controlled committee was prepared to take full advantage of the mandate presented to their party by the election of 1852.

As reported out of committee, the measure itself represented somewhat of a compromise since it soft-pedaled the issue of slavery in the Nebraska Territory—a violation of the Missouri Compromise of 1820. But abruptly and without warning an arrow had pierced the Achilles' heel of a nation and compromise was no longer possible. On January 16, 1854, Archibald Dixon of Kentucky gave notice of an amendment to the committee report, unequivocally repealing the Missouri Compromise. Debate on the measure was begun on January 30 when Douglas rose to its defense by arguing that Congress itself had already repealed the Missouri Compromise by defeating in 1848, after the acquisition of Mexico, a bill that would have extended the Compromise line all the way to the Pacific Ocean. He stated that it was the defeat of this measure that had necessitated the Compromise of 1850 which, on the basis of the California question, had left the whole issue of slavery to be settled by the people within the territory. This principle, he asserted, was to be applied to the whole country—both north and south of 36° 30′. Evidently concerned about the eroding effect of the slavery issue on the northern wing of the Democratic party and in an oblique slap at Senator Chase of Ohio, one of the founders of the Free Democrat party, and at the abolitionist movement in general, he scorned them for falsifying the law and the facts before the public as to the real meaning of the Compromise of 1850.

Realizing the motives of Mr. Douglas, Senator Chase took to the floor of the Senate on February 3 to defend his person and position against the charges placed against him. In his mind, it was not he who should be held responsible for the renewal of strife and controversy over the question of slavery. It was his accusers who had recently brought the issue of territorial slavery before the Senate. Had they forgotten that the "two old political parties" had agreed that the slavery issue had been settled "forever" by the Compromise of 1850? Had they failed to recall that the electorate had acquiesced in their agreement? Well then, what was the source of their present irritation that required congressional repeal of the Missouri Compromise by legal enactment, as called for by Senator Dixon or by supersedure as envisaged by Douglas? The answer—water. The South knew that east of the 98th meridian where the dry country began that the annual rainfall was above twenty inches and slave labor could prosper. A large portion of the proposed Nebraska territory lay east of that meridian and the South sought an unencumbered right to introduce slavery into the region. They demanded that the Federal Government protect the rights of slaveholders in the territory irrespective of the wishes of the inhabitants. For this reason, the Missouri Compromise had to be repealed by law. The South through their control of the Democratic party held the trump cards and, make no mistake, they would not fail to play them at the right moment.

Intermediary appeals from all quarters on behalf of the Missouri Compromise fell on deaf ears. Sam Houston, a man who by no stretch of the imagination could be labeled a northern sympathizer, inveighed against repeal of the Compromise. In his mind the latter document remained the final word on the question of slavery. It was best to let sleeping dogs lie. For to bring the mooted issue before the Congress at this time would place heavy strain upon the sinews of that body. He warned the South that on a sectional vote it was in the minority and that to repeal the compact would be to establish a dangerous precedence, one that might backfire on them in days ahead. Lewis Cass, author of the "squatter sovereignty" principle, regretted that the Pandora's Box of disputed constitutional points had again been reopened by the attempts to repeal the Missouri Compromise. He chided the South's paranoia by explaining that the prohibition of slavery by territorial legislation did nothing to exclude the South more than the North. In fact, slaveholders and non-slaveholders were equally entitled to go into such regions, and Congress, as charged by the southerners, should not be held responsible for legislation emanating from the territorial governments.

The South, eager to spread slavery—the source of its economic and political strength— into every region of the country, would hear none of this. It was prepared to rescind the Missouri Compromise. The North, eager for battle but politically outmaneuvered and led by William Henry Seward of New York, would sound the horn of retreat and lay plans for a future day.

On March 3, 1854, aware of recent events at Ripon, Mr. Seward would rise to address the Senate and make a halfhearted attempt to have the issue brought before the public in a national referendum. Realizing that the political battle to curtail the spread of slavery had been lost, he would state: "The sun has set for the last time upon the guaranteed and certain liberties of all the unsettled and unorganized portions of the American Continent that lie within the jurisdiction of the United States."

His purpose for speaking was not to rescind the measure currently before the Senate, nor even to delay its passage. Rather, he spoke in order to lend perspective to the actions about to be taken and to determine what effect they would have upon future relations between the two sections of the country and, indeed, upon the Union itself. Acknowledging that in the Senate those who viewed the debate over the current bill as a struggle between freedom and slavery were greatly outnumbered, he nevertheless cautioned that throughout the country the situation differed immensely. The people of the nation had been brought to the point where they viewed any gain for slavery as a loss for freedom. The political battle in Congress was fast becoming an ideological contest between the two antipodal forces of freedom and slavery. Not since the beginning days of the nation had the "rights-of-man" doctrine been brought into such sharp focus. And never had there been such organized opinion among the people, regardless of their point of view. In the southern states, the population was "passive, quiet, and content" with prospects for expansion of their way of life that an abrogation of the Missouri Compromise represented. They understood the importance of slavery to their political and economic systems. The northern temperament was quite the opposite. Egged on and aroused by the abolitionists, the northerners were "excited and alarmed with fearful forebodings and apprehensions" reinforced by their recognition of slavery as a direct threat to the system of free labor.

William Henry Seward, the Senator from New York, had not sought shelter when the clouds began to appear. When the thunder came he would remain near the "eye of the storm." From that vantage point, in response to his acute political instinct for an issue, he began laying the foundation for a new political party. The philosophical tenets of that party would have to weld people together emotionally around an issue that would take full advantage of the growing division in the country. To him, there was only one issue that could do this—slavery. If properly

presented to the public there would be no room left for compromise.
You would be for it or you would oppose it. As a moral question there
could no longer be inter-sectional accommodation. Morality is absolute,
not relative. Because slaveholders viewed the black man as inferior, they
would find African slavery neither erroneous, unjust, nor "inconsistent
with the advancing cause of human nature." On the other hand, the Senator from New York would declare slavery, because of its oppressive nature, "absolutely inconsistent with the principles of the American Constitution and government."

In the 1840's and 1850's the country received, mainly from Europe,
4.3 million immigrants. For obvious economic and political reasons
these newcomers were viewed apprehensively by the slaveholders. The
California Constitutional Convention and statehood referendum, effected largely by an immigrant population, had clearly demonstrated that
this group of people was opposed to the spread of slavery. The South
recognized this and attempted to prevent from recurring in the Nebraska
Territory what had taken place in California when all of the free inhabitants were allowed to vote. The Clayton Amendment sponsored by the
Senator from Delaware represented a halfhearted attempt at denying the
immigrant the ballot. Seward, recognizing the immigrants as a potential
anti-slavery constituency, opposed the Clayton Amendment and espoused
the cause of enfranchisement for all free inhabitants of the territory. But
the South, anxious to obtain speedy congressional passage of the measure
rescinding the Missouri Compromise, was willing to forego this safeguard.
Even this was a minor consideration considering the large stakes involved
in the Nebraska issue. On this important issue the South would not budge.
Its leadership was sound, its cause was sound, and it had the votes. If the
country were to be divided as a result of the vote, so be it. Who could
suffer? Certainly not the South. It was prepared to gain politically and
economically from the opening of vast new regions to the institution of
slavery.

Realizing that the time for the crucial vote was rapidly drawing nigh,
Seward began concluding his speech. In his closing remarks he carefully
delineated the sectional relationships between the states of the Union as
well as that which existed between the political parties over the question
of the black man's status. To lend a historical perspective to the occasion
he recounted how the founders had framed the Constitution with full
knowledge of the fact that there existed a natural antagonism between
those who espoused freedom and those preferring slavery. Indeed, they
had not been immune to it despite their having used it as a basis for the
Revolution. They had preferred to let it work itself out in a natural sort

of way. But the economic and political interests involved overshadowed all other considerations, and from the beginning the systems of slave-labor and free labor had remained irreconcilably antagonistic. They had always been at war with each other but the assuaging balm of compromise had repeatedly intervened to avert outright conflagration.

Much had been accomplished since the founding of the nation. The country now stretched from ocean to ocean—an expanse of some 2,800 miles. The process of expansion had been constantly marred by increased antagonism between the two sections of the country over the unending question of the black man's status. This antagonism would have to end. And it would end either in the separation of the antagonistic parties or in the complete domination of one party over the other. As to the former course, it was very unlikely that it could be achieved by voluntary secession. For as expressed by Seward, "Commercial interests bind the slave-states and free-states together in links of gold riveted with iron" that neither passion nor ambition can break. "Political ties bind the Union together" into an empire that the world had never before witnessed. Make no mistake, the Union would endure. Its form, though unpredictable, depended upon whether slavery or freedom would ultimately predominate. In the end, the seat of power would still be the Federal Legislature and from there the strong would rule over an undivided nation.

The passage of the measure before the Senate would put an end to compromises. To rescind a congressional agreement that at the time of its passage was thought to be the final word on the question of slavery would not be acquiesced to by the free states. Who was to say when another purely sectional interest would determine the next compromise to be broken? No. The nation could not be run by whimsey or dubious congressional compact. The affairs of state required a sounder basis for operation. The shifting sands of compromise were no longer adequate. Indeed, the day had arrived when questions of freedom or slavery coming before the legislature should be decided upon their merits "by a fair exercise of legislative power, and not by bargaining of equivocal prudence, if not of doubful morality."

The bill emanating from the Douglas committee organizing the territories of Kansas and Nebraska from the originally contemplated Nebraska Territory was voted on in the Senate after four months of bitter debate. According to one section of the bill, the Missouri Compromise of 1820 was declared inoperative and void on grounds that it was "inconsistent with the principle of non-intervention by Congress with slavery in the States and Territories as recognized by the Compromise measure of 1850." As envisaged by Senator Douglas of Illinois, Chairman of the Committee on Territories, based on the principle of "squatter sovereignty," "its true intent and meaning was not to legislate slavery into the territory or state and not to exclude it therefrom, but to leave the people perfectly free to regulate their domestic institution in their own way." The measure passed the Senate on March 3, 1854, by a vote of 37 to 14. John Bell of Tennessee was the only southern Whig voting against its passage. On May 22, 1854, the bill was adopted by the House by a vote of 113 to 100. No Conscience Whigs voted for the measure and only seven southerners voted against it. Of a possible 145 Democratic votes, 44 came from the North with 57 being cast by the southern wing of the party. The Cotton Whigs of the South cast twelve votes in favor of the bill.

Another congressional battle had ended. The South had won and 350,000 slaveholders through the aegis of the Democratic party had worked their will on the 30 million people of the United States. The undisputed power of the slavocracy was poised to spread its tentacles into the far west—if not Cuba and Central America. Stephen A. Douglas, the little giant, Senator from Illinois, and railroad lobbyist, was victorious. He had beaten back all opposition.[3] Each of the authors of "The Appeal" had in their own way apologized. Douglas, unlike Seward who ascribed to a "higher law," viewed events first and foremost as purely political and scoffed at his fallen adversary for attempting to "crawl behind that free nigger dodge." To this Seward had but one reply, "Douglas, no man who spells Negro with two g's will ever be elected President of the United States." Time has held this law inviolate.

Repeal of the Missouri Compromise sounded the death knell for the Whig Party. Its North—South alliance was irreparably shattered since the Conscience Whigs of the North could find no room for compromise over the question of slavery with the Cotton Whigs of the South. Attempts at reorganization under the name of the American Party were moderately successful. Having as its creed open hostility to the Catholic Church and the proscription of foreigners (mainly the Irish who had emigrated due to the famine of 1845—46), it appealed to the Whig constituency who considered immigration a threat to their way of life. Conservatives in the North and South alike viewed agitation over the question as less disquieting than over the question of slavery. The working class of the North feared competition from alien labor and the Protestant Church was inordinately fearful of Roman Catholicism. These groups proved to be the natural constituency of the American party, nicknamed the "Know-Nothing-party" because its members met in secret lodges and when questioned about the organization gave the pat answer, "I know nothing." The Order's influence extended westward into Texas but in these areas it met with little success. In the East, due mainly to the disintegration of the Whig party, it was more successful. It was able to carry both Massachusetts and Delaware in 1854. However, oppositon to foreign immigration and ecclesiastical doctrine proved wanting as a basis for building a durable party. In spite of several short-lived successes, it soon vanished as rapidly as it had appeared. There was only one issue upon which a new organization to replace the old Whig party could be built. That issue was slavery—the status of the black man in society. And it was on the brother's back that the Republican party would come into being.

The Republican party sprang into existence in 1854. The actual site of its founding remains somewhat of a mystery, but Ripon, in Fond du Lac County, Wisconsin, has been accorded that distinction. It was here that on February 28, 1854, Alvan E. Bovay, a New Yorker by birth, called a public meeting "to consider the now alarming situation."[4] Bovay, a Whig, was joined in this venture by a Mr. Baker (Free Soiler) and a Mr. Bowen (Democrat). The meeting adopted a resolution stating that if the Kansas–Nebraska Territory Bill then pending in the Senate that opened that vast region to slavery were passed, the old Whig party organization in Ripon should be dissolved and a new party formed. The new party to be called "Republican," was to be formed on the sole issue of opposition to slavery extension. This was Bovay's belated response to Calhoun, who had realized in 1850 just prior to the adoption of the Compromise, that the South was stronger politically and morally than they ever would be. And therefore, regarding the issue of slavery, the time for adjustments had passed. It was the duty of the South to seize the moment and "force the issue on the North."

After the bill had passed the Senate on March 3, 1854, a second meeting was held in a schoolhouse on March 20. This meeting over which Bovay presided was attended by representatives from all political parties who voted to dissolve the town committees of the Whig and Free Soil parties. A committee of five, consisting of three Whigs, one Free Soiler, and one Democrat, was formed. It was the task of this committee to begin forming the new party.

The spirit that gave birth to the organization was, in 1854, to be found throughout the free states of the North. Bovay should be rocognized as the first person to organize the party in a practical and resolute manner. He was also the first to suggest its name. In speaking of the March twentieth meeting, he said, "We went into the meeting Whigs, Free Soilers, and Democrats. We came out of it Republicans, and we were the first Republicans in the Union." At first, his personal friend, Horace Greeley, Editor of the *Daily Tribune* and himself a prosperous Whig from the East, was not prepared to accept the name "Republican." Nor, like many other prominent members of the eastern Whig establishment, was he overly anxious to be identified with the new party. Nevertheless, Bovay insisted that it was "the only name that will serve all purposes, present and future, the only one that will live and last." It was only after the Kansas–Nebraska Bill had passed, some three months after his original correspondence with Bovay concerning the new party, that Greeley agreed to the name "Republican." In the *Daily Tribune* of March 16, 1854, he called for a union of the Whig party and the Free Democratic party on the basis of their common opposition "to the extension of Slave Territory and Slave Power." In this editorial he suggested that the name "Republican" would be appropriate for the new party since it "would more fitly designate those who had united to restore our union to its true mission."

Bovay's idea spread like wildfire and within the space of a few months, as if by spontaneous combustion, state political conventions had met and adopted the Republican banner. On May 23, 1854, the day after the passage of the Kansas–Nebraska Bill in the House and three months after Bovay's original meeting, thirty members of that body were called together by Israel Washburn of Maine. The group which met in the Willard Hotel, in quarters occupied by Thomas D. Eliot and Edward Dickinson of Massachusetts, was composed of both Whig and Democratic representatives. Outraged by the passage of the Kansas–Nebraska Bill, the meeting was called for the purpose of forming a new party whose sole purpose would be to restrict the ever-increasing power of the slavocracy. Those present at the meeting adopted the name "Republican" for the new party and pledged to battle the extension of slavery into the territories.

A convention of the Free Democrats of Michigan held on February 22 had adopted a resolution declaring sectional slavery and freedom, national. In nominating their own slate of candidates, which included both Democrats and Whigs, the convention expressed the hope that the day would soon come when "all the friends of freedom would be able to stand upon a common platform against the party and platform of the slave propagandists." To accomplish this would be a formidable task indeed especially since the Whigs, who were in the majority, were not anxious to give up their name, and the Free Democrats and Free Soilers combined were not powerful enough to work their will on the gathering. One of the first to recognize this political fact of life was Joseph Warren, editor of the Detroit *Tribune,* who used the influence of his paper to produce a climate conducive to the withdrawal of the Free Democratic slate. A mass meeting held in Kalamazoo provided the setting for the withdrawal of the ticket nominated on February 22 and issued a call for a gathering of all opponents of slavery extension. This call, signed by thousands of citizens from every nook and cranny in the state, set July 6, 1854 as the date for the next meeting which was to be held in Jackson.

The meeting in convention took place in Jackson according to prior arrangements but because of the enormous gathering of people sharing every shade of anti-slavery feeling, the town's largest meeting hall could not accommodate it. Consequently, it had to be moved outdoors to a tract of land located between the village and the county race course called "Morgans Forty." Despite the great difference of opinion over the question of slavery held by the participants, which by itself would have been enough to disrupt even the most carefully conceived agenda, the incipient discord was minimal. Thanks to experienced, shrewd, and sagacious political managers who understood the importance of the undertaking, buttressed by the overwhelming fervor for fusion among the participants, earnest effort was not wantonly dissipated but channeled into constructive and creative endeavor. Levi Baxter, a former Whig and Free Soil State Senator, was agreed to as Chairman pro tempore. With the filling of the Chair, the gathering, after listening to a number of brief speeches, went on to elect officers of the first Republican State Convention ever held. David S. Walbridge, of Kalamazoo, a prominent Whig member of the State Legislature, was elected President.

With the election of permanent officers, the next item of business, the formation of the resolution committee, was taken up by the body. After separating into smaller groups representing four congressional districts, a committee on resolutions was formed under the chairmanship of Jacob M. Howard. It was the duty of this group to write the party platform. The platform which was adopted unanimously contained among its many resolutions one stating that those gathering in Jackson on that date "will cooperate and be known as *Republicans*" and another acknowledging slavery to be "a violation of the rights of man as man: that the law of nature, which is the law of liberty, gives no man rights superior to those of another; that God and nature have secured to each individual an inalienable right of equality."

In concluding the business of the convention the body nominated a slate of candidates for statewide office. Kinsley S. Bingham was nominated to run as the state's first Republican gubernatorial candidate. Because Jackson, Michigan, was the first place to hold a Republican convention, it, in the minds of many people, shares with Ripon the honor of being the birthplace of the party.

The influence of the movement spread and the party continued to grow. Back east in New York State, Asher N. Cole, a newspaper editor in Allegany County, called a meeting late in July 1854 which resulted in the formation of the Republican party in that state. In Wisconsin and Vermont on July 13, sixty-seven years to the day since the nation's first anti-slavery legislation was adopted, state conventions met and adopted the name "Republican." Within a two-month period following these meetings, state Republican conventions would be held in Maine (August 7), New York (August 16), and Massachusetts (September 7). Similar gatherings occurred in many other communities throughout the North. The new political party, fast gaining momentum throughout the North, was referred to in the South as the Abolitionist Party in spite of its limited objectives which merely called for restricting slavery's extension—with the exception of the District of Columbia where it sought abolition.[5]

A syncretic event unparalleled in the history of partisan politics had taken place with the formation of the Republican party. The combination of Whig wealth and influence, Democrat solidarity and experience, and Free Soil vigor would prove politically synergistic beyond all expectations in the forthcoming congressional elections in 1854. Although the Democrats would return in control of the Senate in the thirty-fourth Congress by a margin of 38 to 22 (5 Know-Nothings), the Republicans would take control of the House by a 108 to 83 advantage. The 43 Know-Nothings would hold the balance of power.

In a manner of speaking, the Republican party was not founded; instead, like Topsy in *Uncle Tom's Cabin,* it just grew. Basically, the phenomenal success witnessed in the 1854 elections was the by-product of years of evolutionary change within northern political leadership over the question of the black man's status. Accompanying this was a simultaneous increase, due to the activity of the abolitionists, in awareness in the body politic. The death of the Whig party with the passage of the Kansas—Nebraska Act left the northern political leaders party-less and issue-less. It would be just a matter of time before their electorate would come unglued. Once this happened it would be extremely difficult to bring them back together. Perhaps Bovay recognized this and in reading the Presidential election results of 1852 saw the possibility of forming a new national party oriented around the issue of slavery.[6] At least it was worth a try and had it not been successful the interlocking histories of the two-party system of America and, indeed, of the world would today be written in another fashion. Slavery, the legal status of the black man in America, did prove to be the issue around which a new party could be formed and an abandoned Whig electorate reconstituted.

The thirty-fourth Congress convened on December 3, 1855, the first order of House business being to elect a Speaker. Quickly the lines were drawn taut along sectional lines. On January 23, after 121 ballots, the southern-backed Democratic candidate, William A. Richardson of Illinois, former House leader on the Kansas–Nebraska Bill, was unable to obtain a majority vote. He withdrew and was replaced by William Aiken of South Carolina who, after nine additional ballots, also could not be elected. In order to break the stalemate the House agreed, on a motion offered by John Hickman of Pennsylvania, to the election of the Speaker by a plurality vote. Consequently, on the 133rd ballot, taken on February 2, Nathaniel P. Banks, Republican of Massachusetts, and the anti-Nebraska favorite, was elected Speaker of the House. He was chosen on a purely sectional vote of 103 to 100 for Representative Aiken, the slavery candidate, with ten other votes being scattered among three candidates. Never before had the Speaker of the House been elected without support from both sections, and with this historic event a new technique for dealing with slavery expansion was beginning to evolve which would lend stability and direction to the Republican party. On the floor of the House, the harsh abuse and insults mutually heaped upon colleagues of opposing views immediately following the election ominously portended the course of events that were soon to take place in Kansas over the question of slavery.

The first step in organizing the Kansas Territory was the establishment of a territorial government. To accomplish this, President Pierce appointed Andrew H. Reeder of Pennsylvania as Governor and Daniel Woodson of Arkansas, Secretary of the Territory. As expected, the appointment of Reeder was not well received by the South, but Pierce offered quick assurance that Reeder was strictly a national man and not an agent of the North. In addition to Reeder and Woodson, several other judicial officers, all Democrats, were sent to the territory. Each of the judges was a strong supporter of the Administration and of the squatter sovereignty principle. As a matter of fact, one of the officials had carried slaves with him into the territory.

One of the first duties of the overseers was to hold an election for territorial delegates to Congress. This took place in November of 1854. John W. Whitfield, the pro-slavery (Missouri) candidate, received a total of 2,871 votes of which only 1,114 were considered legal, the rest being cast fraudulently by Missouri residents who had crossed the border into Kansas for the sole purpose of voting to elect a pro-slavery candidate. The next election ordered by Governor Reeder was for naming the Territorial Legislature and was to be held on March 30, 1855. Based on a census taken by Governor Reeder early in 1855, the territory had a population of 8,501. Of this number, there were 242 slaves and 2,095 eligible voters. This fact did nothing to deter the Missourians from their stated objective of controlling the election. The stakes were too high. Realizing the relative ease and impunity with which they had effected the outcome of the previous election, all border Missouri turned out for this election. In a concerted move to offset the aims of the Emigrant Aid Society,[7] armed Missourians were sent from Andrew County in the north, Jasper County in the South, and as far eastward as Boone and Cole counties into nearly every election district. The surplus of squatters detached to Lawrence were soon transferred to two other election districts which they carried handily. When the results were in, pro-slavery candidates had been elected in every legislative district save one. In this remote inland district two anti-slavery representatives—one for each house—had been chosen. As in the previous election the vast majority of the votes were fraudulently cast. Of the total 6,278 votes cast, 4,968 were illegal. The pro-slavery candidates garnered 5,427 votes compared with a paltry 791 for the opposition. And so it was that Kansas' first territorial government was chosen by the people of Missouri.

The Missourians, jubilant with victory, made no attempt to camouflage their true feelings. *The Squatter Sovereign,* the official organ of the Missourians located in Atchison, declared, in reference to the Emigrant Aid Society, that "we will continue to lynch and hang, tar and feather, and drown every white-livered abolitionist who dares to pollute our soil." In scoffing at Governor Reeder, the Weston *Reporter* boldly claimed that "two thousand squatters have passed over into the promised land" to take part in the election. When it was learned that the Governor had refused certificates of election to thirteen members of the House, the Missouri *Brunswicker* labeled him an "infernal scoundrel" and warned that he would "have to be hemped yet."

Realizing that a travesty of justice had taken place, Governor Reeder took immediate steps to partially rectify the situation. He issued a proclamation calling for new elections to be held in six districts. Most of these districts were carried by Free Soilers who, in turn, received election certificates from the Governor. In the twelfth election district, Leavenworth, where armed Missourians returned to vote, a pro-slavery slate was chosen.

On July 2, 1855, the first territorial legislature of Kansas was called by a proclamation of the Governor to meet in Pawnee located on the Kansas River approximately one hundred miles from the Missouri border. The meeting was controlled by the pro-slavery faction and on the third day every delegate elected in the second election with the exception of those from the twelfth district, were ousted. They were disallowed recognition as bona fide delegates in spite of their being duly certified by the territorial governor.

In further usurpation of the authority vested solely in the governor of the Territory, the assemblage adjourned the Pawnee meeting and set Shawnee Mission, directly over the Missouri border, as the site of the meeting. General Stringfellow from Missouri was elected presiding officer. In his address to the gathering he entreated them "to mark every scoundrel among you who is the least tainted with abolitionism or Free Soilism and exterminate him." In this setting the Legislature enacted franchise and sedition laws by which the territory would be governed. According to these ordinances, actual residence was not to be considered a prerequisite to voter eligibility. And in prohibitive legislation aimed directly at their anti-slavery opponents, they declared it a felony punishable by imprisonment for not less than two years at hard labor, for any free person to publicly express or maintain opposition to the rights of others to possess slaves. It was likewise a felony to introduce any written material into the territory critical of the institution of slavery and persons failing to admit to the right and righteousness of slavery were disqualified to sit as jurors. The Legislative assembly continuously passed laws from July 16 to August 31, 1855, which were thereupon vetoed by the Governor who, as a result of his activities, which included his declining to recognize the Legislature as a legitimate assembly, was placed on a direct collision course with President Pierce. On August 15, 1855, Governor Reeder was removed from office and replaced in that position by Wilson Shannon of Ohio. The new Territorial Governor immediately declared that he "was for slavery in Kansas" and that he recognized the pro-slavery assembly as the legitimate Territorial Legislature.

The appointment of Shannon, intended as a ploy to frustrate the anti-slavery element in Kansas, produced, in fact, an opposite effect. The ranks of the settlers from the East, swollen by the large number of European emigrants, remained steadfastly opposed and refused to submit to either the pro-slavery laws or law-makers. At the time that Governor Reeder was being officially removed from office, a large meeting was held in Lawrence, Kansas, in which "many voters" took part. The participants were called upon, irrespective of their party affiliations, to consult with one another regarding the political and social condition in the Territory. On September 5, they held another meeting at Big Springs which was to be followed by a third meeting, previously agreed to in Lawrence, in Topeka on the nineteenth of the month. The purpose of the Lawrence meeting had been "to take into consideration the propriety of calling a territorial convention, preliminary to the formation of a state government, and other subjects of public interest." On the basis of the turnout, the anti-slavery assemblage called for the election of three bona fide Kansas delegates from each election district as required by Governor Reeder's proclamation of March 10, 1855. Once chosen, these delegates were to assemble in Topeka on September 19, 1855, "to consider and determine upon all subjects of public interest, and particularly upon that having reference to the speedy formation of a state constitution, with an intention of an immediate application to be admitted as a state into the union of the United States of America."

The Topeka delegates' convention took place on September 19, 1855. In attendance were delegates from across the state who resolved that an election should be held on the second Tuesday in October, the purpose being to elect members to a constitution convention who would adopt a bill of rights and take the necessary steps for organizing a state government, preparatory to admission into the Union. In other business, the convention nominated Governor Reeder for delegate to Congress from the Kansas Territory. On October 23, delegates elected by the citizens of the territory met in Topeka to frame a constitution which was in turn accepted by the people on December 15. The constitution called for admission to the Union as a free state.

Both elements had chosen their delegates; Whitfield was the choice of the pro-slavery faction, and the anti-slavery proponents had selected Reeder. This selection of rival congressional delegates from the same territory epitomized the untoward political manifestations of the squatter sovereignty principle that everywhere were being repeated. Between November 1, 1855, and December 1, 1856, over two hundred lives and two million dollars in property would be consumed in the fiery furnace of Kansas. Vast multitudes of emigrants from the East and South began pouring into the Territory. Thoroughly aroused by the atrocities at the ballot box,[8] settlers, many of whom had been neutral up to this point, began supplying anti-slavery emigrants with rifles and ammunition. In the opposing camp, the Missourians were being joined by large bands of southerners who wished to see Kansas under control of the slavocracy. The Territory was now in a state of anarchy. A civil war was taking place in nearly every community. The town of Lawrence, headquarters for the Emigrant Aid Society, was held in siege for two weeks by 2,000 Missourians armed with artillery. Late in November of 1855, they assailed the town intending to destroy it and slaughter its inhabitants. Printing presses in Lawrence, Leavenworth, and Osawatomie were destroyed and a hotel in Lawrence which served as a temporary refuge for northern emigrants was sacked, robbed, and burned to the ground. In the Battle of Black Jack, noted because of one of its participants, twenty-eight free-staters led by John Brown of Osawatomie fought and defeated fifty-six Missourians led by Captain H. Clay Pate of Virginia.

Reacting to the events in Kansas, the thirty-fourth Congress, under the leadership of Speaker Banks, took steps to more fully apprise itself of the political conditions extant in the territory. On a vote of 101 to 93, the House resolved on March 19, 1856, to send a special committee to the Territory whose task would be to determine the conditions then prevalent. After several weeks of on-the-spot investigation, which included taking testimony, the committee, made up of William A. Howard of Michigan, John Sherman of Ohio, and Mordecai Oliver of Missouri, returned with a very lengthy report. The report showed that the free-state elections were not held in pursuance of any valid law and that no fair election could be held in the Territory without the presence of United States troops at every polling place. Thus, delegate Whitfield, representing the pro-slavery faction, was allowed to hold his seat. Subsequently, a bill admitting Kansas as a free state was passed in the House on July 3, 1856, by a vote of 99 to 97. However, the pro-slavery Senate failed to concur.

Considered against the backdrop of events in Kansas and being the time of a national election, 1856 was an extremely important year in the history of American politics and the evolution of the party system. On January 17 of that year, a call, sent out from Washington D.C. over the signatures of A.P. Stone of Ohio, J.Z. Goodrich of Massachusetts, David Wilmot of Pennsylvania, Laurence Brainerd of Vermont, and William A. White of Wisconsin, summoned the Republicans of the United States to a meeting in Pittsburgh for the purpose of "perfecting" a national organization. The letter sent out read as follows:

To the Republicans of the United States:
    In accordance with what appears to be the general desire of the Republican Party, and at the suggestion of a large portion of the Republican press the undersigned, chairmen of the State Republican Committee of Maine, Vermont, Massachusetts, New York, Pennsylvania, Ohio, Michigan, Indiana and Wisconsin, hereby invite the Republicans on the 22nd of February, 1856 for the purpose of perfecting the National Organization, and for providing for a National Delegate Convention of the Republican Party, at some subsequent day, to nominate candidates for the Presidency and Vice-Presidency to be supported at the election in November 1856.[9]

The convention, held as planned on February 22, attracted, in addition to delegates from all of the free states, representatives from Maryland, Virginia, South Carolina, Kentucky, and Missouri. John A. King served as president pro tempore and Francis P. Blair, Sr. was elected permanent president. Speeches were made by several prominent opponents of slavery, including Horace Greeley, who sent a report of the meeting to the New York *Tribune.* The convention adopted resolutions demanding the repeal of the Kansas–Nebraska Act, supporting the activities of the free-state men in Kansas, and urging the Republican Organization to "overthrow the present National Administration" so deeply aligned with the slavocracy. The meeting was adjourned sine die on February 23. That same evening a mass meeting was held and addressed by Horace Greeley. All of the speeches delivered, like that of Greeley, were in favor of rendering every possible assistance to the people of Kansas in their struggle.

Things were happening fast; it was time to involve the electorate. Therefore, several weeks after the convention, the executive committee, appointed by that body, met in Washington on March 27 and issued a call *To the people of the United States,* "without regard to past political differences or divisions . . . who are opposed to the spread of slavery into the territories," to meet in a national convention on June 17, 1856. The convention to be held in Philadelphia would recognize the delegates from each state congressional district within a state and six delegates-at-large. The purpose of the convention would be to nominate candidates to be supported in November for the offices of President and Vice-President of the United States.

Notwithstanding the prospects for the formation of a new party, there were in the Spring of 1856 three active major political parties north of the Mason-Dixon line—the Democrats, the Whigs, and the Know-Nothings. Each group held a National Convention. The Democrats met in Cincinnati, the Whigs in Baltimore, and the Know-Nothings in Philadelphia.

The Democratic National Convention met in June. Four candidates sought the presidential nomination of the Convention—President Pierce, James Buchanan, Lewis Cass, and Stephen A. Douglas. The two-thirds rule being maintained, Cass was eliminated from the outset. When the balloting began, the contest between President Pierce and Buchanan was about equal, with Buchanan having a slight edge. Neither candidate could muster enough votes to obtain the nomination. After several rounds of balloting, as slippage appeared in Pierce's support the South began to desert him in favor of Douglas, their ally from the days of the Kansas–Nebraska battle. In the eye of the southern leadership, if their favorite, Pierce, could not be nominated, Douglas would automatically become the heir-apparent. But the northern Democrats would have none of this. Their support for Buchanan remained unflagging. Buchanan's day had come. Several times since 1844, he had been a presidential aspirant. Vying in the past for the honor against Cass, Polk, and Pierce, he had never been able to sustain his candidacy. But things were different this time. Not only had he maintained the lead from the outset, he had also gradually increased it as many of Pierce's delegates went over to Douglas. Based upon his role in the formulation of the Ostend Manifesto,[10] the South considered him a dough face, which meant a northerner with southern principles, and was, on that account, not opposed to his nomination. After sixteen ballots, Pierce withdrew from the race and Buchanan was nominated for the Presidency on the Democratic ticket. John C. Breckinridge of Kentucky was placed on the ticket as the Vice-Presidential candidate.

The Know Nothing Convention, split over the question of slavery, adopted a platform condemning the repeal of the Missouri Compromise but reaffirming the right of territorial inhabitants "to regulate their domestic and social affairs in their own mode, subject only to the Constitution." This platform, offensive to delegates from New England, Ohio, Pennsylvania, Illinois, and Iowa who subsequently went over to the Republican party, was adopted at the Convention. The nomination of Millard Fillmore for the Presidency at this Convention was later ratified by the Whigs who likewise had lost their anti-slavery faction to the Republican party. To the Whigs, both the Democratic and the Republican parties were sectional parties wishing, like spoiled children, to have their way in Kansas. Opting in favor of what they considered was the middle ground, they adopted a platform calling for peace in Kansas and a cessation of hostilities between Union members.

The Republican Nominating Convention, as earlier agreed to, met in Philadelphia on June 17, 1856. Robert Emmet of New York was elected Chairman pro tempore. In attendance were 565 delegates representing every free state plus Delaware, Kentucky, and Maryland. Based upon the fact that no uniform rules had been adopted regarding delegate selection and voting, several seats were contested. However, these minor contentions were easily set aside and a permanent Chairman (Henry S. Lane, Indiana) was elected. The largest bloc of votes would be held by New York, Pennsylvania, and Ohio who would each cast 96, 81, and 69 votes, respectively, in the Presidential and Vice-Presidential balloting.

The make-up of the Convention, a conglomerate of delegates meeting for the first time under a unitary party banner, represented every shade of anti-slavery opinion. There were Abolitionists, Free Soilers (Democrats who had supported the Wilmot Proviso), and Whigs like William Seward, Thurlow Weed, and Horace Greeley, who had broken away from the temporary Know-Nothing party fusion late in 1855. On the first day of the three-day Convention, stirring speeches were made by the temporary and permanent chairmen. They were followed by several more speeches of like caliber and intensity denouncing slavery and exalting the Republican Call. On ascending to the podium, the temporary Chairman referred to squatter sovereignty, as applied to the Kansas Territory, as "a fallacy, a delusion and a snare [which enabled] quasi-squatters from Missouri . . . with their bowie-knives and revolvers to control the elections." The Democratic charge that the new party was composed of "Negro worshippers and Black Republicans," he rebuked by labeling his opponents "traitors and buffoons" lacking sufficient imagination to create a more substantive issue.

In the afternoon session of the second day Chairman Lane addressed the Convention. Referring to the delegates there assembled as "Friends of Freedom and Freemen," he questioned the wisdom of the laws passed by the Kansas Legislature which made it a felony to introduce any written literature into the Territory opprobrious of slavery. For it followed, based on that standard, that neither the Constitution nor the Bible could be read in the Territory, as both were anti-slavery documents. The historic promise of the Democratic party to abide by the Missouri Compromise of 1820, broken again and again—most recently in their Cincinnati Convention—bordered on sublime effrontery. "Their declarations were like Dead Sea fruit—pleasant to the eye, but that turned to ashes on the lips."

Following the chairman's speech, Caleb Smith of Indiana, speaking in behalf of the northern men in Kansas, recognized the Republican party as the only party capable of bringing to fruition the dreams of the Founders. The notion that the new party was simply an organization sectional in scope, he dismissed outright. "There never was a party since the days of Washington so national in its aim as this, for its object was to preserve and extend freedom and was not freedom national?" In his manner of thinking, the only party that could insure freedom was the Republican party. To him, the Republicans were "a party not organized to advance the interests of any man or set of men, but to maintain the principles of Freedom." The audience received each speaker enthusiastically, frequently interrupting to show signs of approval.

When it came time to choose the Presidential candidate, the name most prominent in the minds of a large majority of delegates was William H. Seward. He declined the nomination feeling that his time had not yet come. Salmon P. Chase, then Governor of Ohio, was equally reticent and likewise declined the nomination. Like Seward, he was a favorite among the delegates, but opposed to spearheading what he considered a forlorn hope. Judge John McLean, an eminent jurist serving in the Supreme Court of the United States, was put forth as the Presidential candidate by the Whig element at the convention on the notion that he was the only candidate capable of carrying the state of Pennsylvania. His support came mainly from Maine, New Hampshire, New Jersey, Pennsylvania, Delaware, Ohio, Indiana, and Illinois. On the informal ballot he received 196 votes.

The younger men of the party, eager to accept the challenge of the South and unwilling to compromise, felt that the young party should look to the future and not to the past. For their purposes, McLean at seventy-one years, was too old. Their bill of particulars, politically speaking, required a younger, more energetic, and more attractive candidate. John Charles Fremont, "Pathfinder of the Rockies" and son-in-law of Senator Thomas Benton, was their man. Ordinarily, such factional differences of opinion between convention delegates would be more than enough to delay deliberations. But the purpose for which the Convention had assembled was too important. Differences had to be submerged. The nomination that had to be made was one which would bring together all the friends of freedom in a concerted effort to overthrow the national slavocracy and preserve the Union. Fremont received 359 votes for President on the informal ballot. On the formal ballot, taken immediately thereafter, Fremont received 520 votes, McLean 37, and Seward 1. This nomination was then made unanimous by the Convention.

On the third and final day of the Convention, William L. Dayton of New Jersey was unanimously elected the Vice-Presidential candidate. On the formal ballot he received every single vote. On the informal ballot he received 253 votes to be followed next by Abraham Lincoln of Illinois who received 110. Nathaniel Banks, first Republican Speaker of the House, polled 46, David Wilmot and Charles Sumner received 43 and 35, respectively.

The work of the Republican Nominating Convention had come to an end. Those assembled there had been summoned to unite in a common cause to defeat the spread of slavery. Speaker after speaker had denounced the odious institution and harangued the Democratic party for its role in support of the slavocracy. The platform committee, headed by David Wilmot, had reported out a series of resolutions patently opposed to the spread of slavery and strident in their denunciation of the Ostend Manifesto. As accepted by the Convention, not only did the platform "deny authority of Congress or of a Territorial Legislature, of any individual or association of individuals, to give legal existence to slavery in any Territory of the United States" but it further resolved "that the Constitution

ON THE BROTHER'S BACK

confers upon Congress sovereign power over the Territories of the United States for their government, and in the exercise of this power the right and duty of Congress to prohibit in Territories those twin relics of barbarism—polygamy and slavery." In reference to Democrat nominee Buchanan, one of the formulators of a foreign policy document which if enacted would permit the spread of slavery into Central America, the platform declared that "the highwayman's plea that might makes right, embodied in the Ostend circular, was in every respect unworthy of American diplomacy, and would bring shame and dishonor upon any government of people that gave it their sanction."

A new party had been born. If geography delimited its appeal, its aim would remain, nonetheless, universal. By any stretch of the imagination, the platform adopted that summer of 1856 was exceedingly bold. Could such a set of principles catch hold, even in the North, where a once solid Whig constituency was undergoing a process of interminable fragmentation? Was it possible to form a national party whose sole *raison d'être* was its opposition to the spread of slavery? When the first National Republican Convention adjourned on June 19, no one there was in a position to supply the answers—only the electorate could do that. And how they would react, time alone would tell. A widespread and sizeable vote would indicate that the time had come to move against the slave system of labor. A small vote, purely sectional in character, would relegate the new organization to the fate of the previous third party movements. Everything was in the hands of the people. On the basis of how they voted would be decided whether or not the Republican party would be able to sustain itself as an effective national party.

5

" ...AS AMERICAN AS CHERRY PIE "

That vast array of colligative events surrounding the campaign of 1856 would make all that had gone before seem like child's play and prove ultimately to have a causal effect upon the future of the nation, second to none in its history. On the eve of the Republican Convention, while incipient civil war bloomed in Kansas, the scene of the battle momentarily shifted to the halls of Congress. As in Kansas where the struggle for land pitted man against man in deadly strife, so it was on the Senate floor where the rhetorical clash over principle became at times physical. On May 22, 1856, the sanctity of the Senate was invaded when Charles Sumner, Senator from Massachusetts, was brutally assaulted by Preston S. Brooks, Representative from South Carolina. On the 19th and 20th of May, Sumner, borrowing from the classics, attacked the South in general and southern senatorial leadership personally for their designs in Kansas on behalf of slavery.[1] The assault upon the Senator came about as the result of a philippic delivered by him against the South.

In a stinging denunciation of the slavocracy, Sumner delivered a peroration against slavery which he divided into three parts: 1) *"The Crime Against Kansas;"* 2) *"The Apologies for The Crime;"* and 3) *"The True Remedy."* He referred to Senator Butler of South Carolina and Senator Douglas of Illinois as the Don Quixote and Sancho Panza of the pro-slavery forces sallying forth together in the same lurid adventure. They had risen to their positions of eminence on the Senate floor through their "championship of human wrongs." The Senator from South Carolina, beguiled by the books on chivalry he had read, now began to view himself in that light. His mistress, the "harlot slavery, to whom he has made his vows, though ugly to others, is always lovely to him. . . . Let her be impeached in character, or in any proposition made to shut her from the extension of her wantonness, and no extravagance of manner or hardihood of assertion is then too great for this Senator. The frenzy of Don Quixote in behalf of his wench, Dulcinea del Toboso,[2] is all surpassed." In the same vein Sumner went on to label Senator Douglas from Illinois, the "squire of Slavery, its very Sancho Panza, ready to do all its humiliating offices." Douglas was viewed as an agent of the South who, by judicious use of influence in the Democratic party, was attempting to subdue the North. The logical conclusion to the squatter sovereignty principle which he championed would be the spread of slavery throughout every state of the Union. Popular sovereignty was nothing more than a cover for "Popular Slavery." Quite naturally, the North inveighed against that doctrine.

One of their most able orators was now holding forth on the floor of the Senate. Part one of Sumner's speech "The Crime Against Kansas," dealt in detail with the evolution of current events in the Territory beginning with the Missouri Compromise of 1820. The "consummate transgression" taking place in Kansas he likened to the Crime of Crimes which surpassed even the old *crimen majestatis.*[3] It was a *crime against* nature and contained "all other crimes as the greater contains the less."

Moving to the second part of his discourse called "The Apologies," he divided the latter into four sub-sections called "The Apology Tyrannical," "The Apology Imbecile," "The Apology Absurd," and "The Apology Infamous." It was his purpose in writing this section to show that in Kansas as in ancient times "the great Crimes of history have never been without apologies. . . . But the Apologies for the Crime are worse than efforts at denial. In cruelty and heartlessness they identify their authors with the great transgression." The final portion of his speech was delivered on June 20, 1856. It was called "The True Remedy" and began with the simple axiom that "the Remedy should be coextensive with original Wrong." Since by passage of the Kansas–Nebraska Bill not only were these two territories opened to slavery but the possibility of its extension into Minnesota, Washington, and Oregon became manifestly real. This is what worried Sumner and it can best be appreciated in his own words in reference to events in Kansas. In order to prevent its further extension, Sumner wanted the original prohibition against slavery, dating back to 1787, invoked. This was "the Alpha and Omega of our aim in this immediate controversy."

Like the "Apologies," his final section contained four sub-sections,

"The Remedy of Tyranny," "The Remedy of Folly," "The Remedy of Injustice and Civil War," and "The Remedy of Justice and Peace." Not unlike a sick person in search of the best cure that medical science had to offer, the nation would have to prescribe for its health and safety a Remedy favorable to its best long-range interests. This was the job of the Congress.

Under the sub-section entitled "The Remedy of Tyranny," the pronouncements of King George III in response to the complaints of the Province of Massachusetts Bay were compared to the activities of President Pierce in the current conflagration. In a speech delivered at the opening of Parliament on November 30, 1774, in reference to colonial opposition (Boston Tea Party, December 16, 1773) to the Tea Act of 1773, King George complained of a "daring spirit of resistance and disobedience to the law. . . . Which has broke forth in fresh violences of a very criminal nature." This was equivalent, in Sumner's thought, to President Pierce's declaration in a special message submitted to Congress on January 24, 1856, that those persons in Kansas opposed to the spread of slavery into the Territory had no right to form a constitution. That right was conferred upon the people of the Territory and not upon a "mere party" among them. In fact, this latter group of individuals was involved in acts of a "revolutionary character" which if carried to the point of organized resistance would become "treasonable insurrection." Should this happen the power of the Executive would immediately be summoned forth to quell the uprising. Whereas the King proclaimed to have taken the necessary precautions "for carrying into execution the laws" of the British Empire, President Pierce promised to "exert the whole power of the Federal Executive" to support the institution of slavery in Kansas. The parallel was complete. To the Senator from the Bay State of Massachusetts, President Pierce's prescription for solving the most crucial problem facing the nation was indeed the remedy of a tyrant.

Sumner next launched a direct verbal assault upon Senator Butler of South Carolina, the man whom earlier he had called the Don Quixote of the pro-slavery forces. Under the sub-section entitled "The Remedy of Folly," the South Carolinian was chided for his suggestion that the antislavery forces in Kansas be deprived of their Constitutional privilege, "to keep and bear arms." Surely this suggestion could also be placed in the category of the tyrant's remedy but as defined by Sumner "its Folly is so surpassing as to eclipse even its Tyranny." For if you took the rifle away from the pioneer how could he protect himself against the red man and the beasts of the forest? The weapon was needed in self-defense and the venerable Senator from South Carolina was foolhardy to believe that

. . . AS AMERICAN AS CHERRY PIE"

his allies and constituents, the fanatics of slavery, would find respite by trampling on one of the plainest provisions of constitutional liberty.

"The Remedy of Injustice and Civil War," also an offshoot of "The Remedy of Tyranny," as labeled by Sumner, originated in the Committee on Territories headed by Senator Douglas of Illinois. According to Douglas' bill, the territory of Kansas would be authorized to hold a State Constitutional Convention and form a State Government preparatory to admission into the Union contingent upon a census to be taken by the Governor under legislative authority. As in the previous instances Sumner viewed the suggestion with disgust. He was not about to accept the main contingencies of the bill, for to do so would be to recognize the legitimacy of the legislative and gubernatorial authority resident in the Territory. If Congress acquiesced and passed this bill it would become a member in the conspiracy to legislate Kansas into slavery. But there was every indication that the people of the Territory would not willingly accept that injustice and the result would be civil war. And when civil war would come there would arise a William Tell[4] who, in refusing to salute the tyrant's cap, would arouse the passions of the people to overthrow the Territorial Government. The Remedy of Injustice and Civil War would not put an end to the conflicts in Kansas—on the contrary, it would only serve to inflame the already caustic conditions prevalent.

The final remedy offered was proposed by William Seward of New York. It was embodied in a bill offered by the New York Senator for the immediate admission of Kansas as a free state. Referred to by Sumner as "The Remedy of Justice and Peace," it was supported by a petition of the anti-slavery forces in the Territory and, as might be expected, it was in opposition to the Douglas bill. To Sumner it was the only possible way to avoid further conflict. He pleaded for his colleagues in the Senate to recognize this simple fact. Should they fail to recognize it, and fall prey to the propositions of Tyranny and Folly, the result would be injustice and civil war. To avoid such a conflagration he counseled his compeers to seek the True Remedy of Justice and Peace.

The oration, which later became known as "The Crimes Against Kansas" speech, was delivered before standing-room-only audiences. In the lobbies, House members and politicians from all over the country had assembled to hear the well-known orator deliver one of America's most famous philippics against the slavocracy. With the exception of two, all of the Senators were in their seats. The ladies' gallery overflowed with the fashionable of the City. No one to whom the speech was addressed "failed to feel the shock of Sumner's lance." Stephen A. Douglas who had been labeled Sancho Panza by Sumner "listened with ill concealed hate and a rage that he was scarcely able to *repress*." Both he and Senator Cass of Michigan were quite severe in their denunciation of him. His friends and anti-slavery ally, Benjamin F. Wade, Senator from Ohio, questioned whether he had gone beyond the normal limits of propriety. Why had he not once been called to order during the delivery of the entire speech? Senator Andrew P. Butler of South Carolina, who had absented himself from the floor during the speech due to illness, was shortly to be avenged by Representative Preston Brook of his home state. The debate over the question of the black man's status would soon bring the opposing parties to blows on the floor of the United States Senate.

During the course of his speech, Butler had been scathingly referred to by Sumner as one who "touches nothing which he does not disfigure with error, sometimes of principle, sometimes of fact." His home state of South Carolina was arraigned for its prominent role in support of slavery. "Has he read the history of the State which he represents?" Sumner asked. "He cannot surely have forgotten its shameful imbecility from slavery, continued throughout the Revolution, followed by its more shameful imbecility from slavery, since."

This two-pronged attack upon the Palmetto State and one of its favorite sons would not go unanswered. On May 22 Sumner, who remained at his desk writing letters after the Senate had adjourned, was approached by Representative Preston Brooks from South Carolina. Brooks said, "I have read your speech twice over carefully. It is libel on South Carolina and Mr. Butler who is a relative of mine." With these utterances, the South Carolinian raised his heavy gutta-percha cane and laid siege to Sumner's head. Sumner, unable to defend himself, was continually beaten by Brooks. James W. Simonton, the New York Associated Press agent, attempted to intervene but was stopped by Laurence M. Keith, Brooks's colleague from South Carolina who rushed in saying, "Let them alone, G - d d- - n you."[5] The assault continued until Sumner reeled bleeding to the floor. It is said that only the thick mass of hair covering his scalp saved him from a fatal fracture of the skull. Sumner would spend nearly four years in recovering from the assault but his normal strength and vigor would never return. He would return to the Senate in December of 1859, having been reelected by the Massachusetts Legislature by an almost unanimous vote in the Senate and 333 out of 345 votes in the House.

On the day following the assault, congressmen from both houses armed themselves before taking their seats. In the Senate, Henry A. Wilson of Massachusetts moved the appointment of a committee to investigate the matter. After being amended by Mason of Virginia, the motion carried and a committee containing no Republicans was formed. However, having decided that the South was unable to act in the matter, a committee was appointed by the House to consider the situation. The House committee sought expulsion of Brooks as just punishment for his undisciplined act. On a resolution to the effect brought before the entire House, the vote was 121 to 95 in favor of expulsion. Had a simple majority been required for expulsion, Brooks would have been dismissed by his colleagues. Since a two-thirds vote was required in this type of action, the motion to expel failed. A resolution to censure Brooks and Edmundson as accomplices failed in the case of the latter but carried in that of Brooks. Thereupon Brooks resigned his seat, only to be reelected by his district with all but six opposing votes.

In the North, Brooks was universally denounced and condemned for his actions. In the South he was made a hero. The effectiveness of indignation meetings held in hundreds of cities and towns above the Mason–Dixon Line was all but canceled by the vast outpouring of concurring sentiment in the South. Emblematic of their endorsement of his tactics, Brooks received canes and whips bearing such inscriptions as "Use knockdown arguments" and "Hit him again." Southern admiration for Congressman Brooks approached idolatry. When, in the Senate, his attack upon Sumner was referred to as "brutal, murderous and cowardly" by Senator Wilson, he responded by calling the latter a liar and challenging him to a duel.[6] Wilson declined the challenge, but like many other Senators, armed himself in case he should be accosted. Over in the House, Anson Burlingame of Massachusetts, a deadly shot with the rifle, denounced the assault and accepted Brooks's challenge. The duel, to take place at the Clifton House in Canada, never materialized as Brooks objected to the meeting place. Later, he was tried by the courts of the District of Columbia and fined three hundred dollars. He was to die shortly thereafter in January of 1857. Numbered among his many defenders were Jefferson Davis and James Buchanan, the latter soon to be the Democratic standard-bearer in the national election of 1856.

The caning of Sumner had an incendiary effect upon the politics of the nation, unparalleled in congressional history. The South applauded; the North reacted. The nation was unmistakably divided. Events in Kansas continued to flare up before the public. The campaign of 1856 would be the vilest of any yet seen in American history. Brooks's attack upon Sumner rounded out the Republican organization's campaign appeal and served as an incentive to action. At each indignation meeting held throughout the North the assault was denounced and interpreted to the audience as an attack upon northern manhood. "What are you going to do about it?" was the headline cry of the Republican papers. Massachusetts, Rhode Island, Connecticut, and Maine sent resolutions to Congress deploring the attack. In the newspapers and at each public gathering, health bulletins regarding Sumner's physical and mental status were issued. Symbolically, his Senate seat was left vacant as silent testimony to his martyrdom. This attack upon Sumner when coupled with northern rage over events in Kansas confirmed in the minds of those above the Mason–Dixon Line the abolitionist thesis that the South and the Democratic party were involved in a conspiracy to spread slavery. This alone was a victory for the fledgling organization, since few northerners had ever gone so far as to accept the abolitionist viewpoint that slavery ought to be abolished. Northern sentiment was now ready to agree that the expansion of slavery ought to be stopped. In this belief they automatically became ideological Republicans.

"Free-Soil, Free Speech, Free Men, Fremont" was the battle cry of the Republican army. The Republican campaign of 1856 was a young man's campaign and they were the ones who were the makers of the party. Many of the leaders who would come to the front in later years were still cautious as to their involvement in the new organization. Although Chase endorsed the platform, his support of Fremont was mostly perfunctory. Sumner was disabled. Seward, in spite of his "irrepressible conflict" proclamation, lacked confidence in the ability of the candidate to govern the country if elected. For the most part, the men who did the work were dynamos of energy, little known in establishment politics but, nevertheless, destined to affect the future of the country. There was Anson Burlingame, friend of Sumner, first elected to the House during the thirty-fourth session of Congress; Nathaniel Banks, first Speaker of the House to be elected by Republicans; John Sherman of Ohio, who, like Banks, was serving his second term in Congress; Eli Thayer, prime mover in the organization of the Emigrant Aid Society. There was also Roscoe Conklin, John A. Bingham, and Thaddeus Stevens. In terms of public exposure, there was a still younger group consisting of such men as Austin Blair, James G. Blaine, Schuyler Colfax, Andrew G. Curtin, and Oliver P. Morton. These political parvenus, followers of Dayton and Fremont, went into the campaign filled with moral enthusiasm. They attempted to define the issues in moral and philosophical terms. Their approach appealed to the ministers of practically all the Protestant churches. In the universities, their pitch was particularly attractive to the liberal faculties and literary men of the day.

Elsewhere, the campaign followed a basic pattern built upon a denunciation of the South, coupled with an exploitation of "Bleeding Kansas" and the attack upon Sumner. The South was pictured as attempting to undermine free labor by surreptitiously, under the guise of squatter sovereignty, expanding slave labor and thus diverting lands from the use of the former. In essence, this had been the purpose of the recently enacted Kansas–Nebraska Act. Clearly, the more canny of the Republican strategists wanted the debate limited to the state of affairs in Kansas and the martyrdom of Sumner. At this juncture, their wish was not to "trouble the waters" over the question of slavery. They did not want to be identified with the broader topic of the black man's status and, in this respect, the general thrust of the campaign can best be appreciated through material released by the Republican National Committee. This group issued campaign documents on such subjects as *The Border Ruffian Code in Kansas, The Poor Whites of the South,* and *The Vacant Chair of Sumner.* Notwithstanding the historical reality of the African's travail in North America and the fact that the Republican party owed its genesis and existence to two major factors associated with this journey—the unending debate over the status of the black man and the evolution of slavery as a political issue—everything that could be expected was done by the new organization to divorce the Republican cause from the anti-slavery cause in the campaign of 1856.

The Democrats saw things differently. Realizing that every vote cast for Fillmore was a vote taken away from Fremont, they cleverly exploited the fear of the Whig element that Fremont's election would speed disaster for the Union. Buchanan's supporters denounced the Republicans as a purely sectional party. Howell Cobb, a House member from Georgia, declared that if Fremont were elected he would immediately return home and take the stump for secession. The Democrats labeled the Republican standard-bearer a freak from Barnum's menagerie. Every attempt made by the Republicans to play up the Conqueror of the Rockies was met and successfully counteracted by the Democrats. Republican opponents, north and south of the Mason–Dixon Line, described Fremont as vain, shallow, and pretentious and called him a "woolly horse," "mule eating," "free-love," "nigger embracing" black Republican who dined on "black, mutton sheep" and had "nigger hash" for dessert. These were the views held by many in the Democratic party regarding the first Republican Presidential candidate.

Maryland, Ohio, Pennsylvania, and Indiana were then "October States"[7] In order to elect Fremont, the latter two would have to be carried by the Republican party. The Democratic leaders, familiar with political facts of life, were taking no chances on losing these two important states. Since money and patronage were important factors in the success of any

81

campaign, they made every effort to increase their campaign chest. The Pennsylvania Democrats assessed every state job holder three days' pay and the Pierce Administration, making use of their federal patronage, put on additional workers at the navy yard in Philadelphia. In Pennsylvania alone the Democrats had an election fund of 70,000 dollars. The Republicans began their fund-raising efforts late in August and it was not until September that funds began coming in. By October 8, 15,000 dollars had been alloted by the National Committee for use in Pennsylvania. This was no match for the combined Democratic war chest and federal patronage. When the results were in, the Democrats won Pennsylvania by only 3,000 votes. They had won fourteen congressional seats compared with four carried by the Republicans. The Republican ticket received a similar setback later that month in Indiana where the Democrats, in addition to winning the governorship, carried six congressional districts compared to the Republicans' five. Ohio was carried by the Republicans.

As acknowledged by the political pros, the October results were an accurate prediction of what was to happen in November. Thirty-one states took part in the national election of that month. Buchanan carried nineteen, including Pennsylvania, Indiana, New Jersey, Illinois, and California, plus all of the slave states except Maryland where Fillmore prevailed. Fremont carried eleven states—Connecticut, Iowa, Maine, Michigan, Massachusetts, Ohio, New York, New Hampshire, Vermont, Rhode Island and Wisconsin. Buchanan received 1.8 million popular votes contrasted to 1.3 million for Fremont and 874,534 for Fillmore. In the electoral college, Buchanan ended up with 174 votes while Fremont obtained 114. Fillmore received eight votes of the Maryland electors. Buchanan tallied 1.2 million votes in the free states and 611,879 in the slave states. Fillmore's total was more evenly distributed and he received 394,642 and 479,892 votes above and below the Mason–Dixon Line respectively. Fremont's popularity was unquestionably in the North. Outside that area he collected only 1,194 votes (Delaware, 308; Maryland, 281; Virginia, 291; Kentucky, 314). Not a single vote was cast in his behalf in Alabama, Arkansas, Florida, Georgia, Louisiana, Mississippi, Missouri, North Carolina, Tennessee, and Texas. On a county-wide basis, the Republican candidate won 362 to the Democrat's 1,067. In New England where the former made his best showing, he captured 63 out of 67 counties. Obviously, the Republican party was entirely sectional.

The results of the election of 1856 were a sobering blow to the Democratic party. True, they had won the Presidency, but only by a plurality. On a percentage basis, Buchanan polled 45 per cent of the popular vote while Fremont and Fillmore polled 33 and 22 per cent respectively. This

". . . AS AMERICAN AS CHERRY PIE"

meant that the Democrats were a minority party having come to control of the National Administration on the basis of several political factors not under their direct control. In this vein, the two items that emerge as having contributed significantly to Buchanan's election are the exploitation of the fear by southern leaders that if Fremont were elected the South would secede, and the inability of the Republican party leaders to entice the more conservative Whig element to vote for their candidate. Following the October election, if the Republican leadership had succeeded in being able to bring about a fusion ticket between their party and the American party, perhaps the outcome of the election would have been quite different. But in Pennsylvania and elsewhere the mutual antagonism between the followers of Fremont and Dayton was too great to overcome.

In spite of the outcome of the election, the Republicans, barely in existence for two years, had something to crow about. Their showing in their first Presidential election was nothing short of spectacular. Overnight they had become the nation's second major party, not just another also-ran third party that "struts and frets its hour upon the stage and then is heard no more." The results of the election caused Thaddeus Stevens to describe the campaign as the "victorious defeat" and ex-Barnburner Preston King of New York predicted, in private, that the Democrats had won their last election. The full impact of the Republican party's triumph would only become apparent when the northern state legislatures met to choose United States senators. The new organization picked up five Senate seats and in so doing were able to unseat several Democratic wheel horses. Most conspicuous in his absence from the thirty-fifth Senate was the Democratic Presidential candidate of 1848 and the author of the squatter sovereignty principle, Lewis Cass, of Michigan. He was replaced by Zack Chandler and went on to become Secretary of State in the Buchanan Administration. In New York the Democrats foamed at the mouth when the Legislature elected renegade Preston King, a Republican, to the Senate. Despite having lost the election to Buchanan in Pennsylvania, the Republicans were able to place Simon Cameron in the Senate. This came as a direct slap in the face to the newly elected President who had hoped to see J.W. Forney, his statewide campaign manager, in that seat.

When all of the factors associated with the formation of any new political party are considered, it becomes obvious that the Republican party fared quite well in the election of 1856. Its success in its first national outing was due to its appeal based upon its opposition to the extension of slavery. This opposition derived from its interpretation of the squatter sovereignty principle as expostulated by Senator Douglas of Illinois. To the South and the Democratic party, squatters' sovereignty was construed as meaning that slavery was to be protected by Congress in the territories until state governments were formed and admission to the Union secured. From this perspective, Democratic doctrine argued that territorial legislatures could pass laws to protect slavery, but not to exclude it, the main point being that slavery was the natural condition of the territories. The Republicans saw things differently. They argued that freedom, not slavery, was the natural condition of the territories and that Congress was empowered and duty-bound to exclude slavery from those areas. This Republican viewpoint was clearly enunciated in its Philadelphia platform. The Republican party was aided in the campaign of 1856 by its willingness to deal with the question of slavery as a real issue—albeit in limited terms—and not as a mere abstraction. This tactic earned for the party the allegiance of the masses north of the Mason—Dixon Line and enabled it to replace the Whigs and the Americans as the nation's second major party. The fact that the Republicans were sectional in character and lacked the support of the powerful northern commercial classes, who voted for Fillmore purportedly to avoid disunion, proved a hindrance in their initial assault on the White House. However, the young party, less than three years old, was a vital party and it would live to see a better day. The main task that lay before it in the days ahead was threefold. First, it had to bring into the fold the northern commercial interest. Second, it had to avoid the deleterious effects produced by a third party effort appealing to its general constituency. Third, it had to produce a candidate for the 1860 election who was basically political in orientation and capable of dealing with the question of slavery in the most intricate of its political detail. Should the Republican party rise to the occasion and successfully meet these essential pre-conditions, there would be nothing to prevent its capturing the White House four years hence.

James A. Buchanan, the fifteenth President of the United States, took office on March 4, 1857. In his inaugural address he alluded to the pending Supreme Court action that would "speedily and finally settle" the question of slavery in the territories. Actually what Buchanan was referring to was the Dred Scott Decision[8] which would declare, when rendered, that a slave was not a citizen and neither Congress nor a territorial legislature had the power to exclude slavery from the territories. However, the Court decree did not stop at this point. It went a step further and declared in its precedent-setting opinion that the Missouri Compromise was unconstitutional. For the first time in over fifty years the Court had overridden the Congress.

". . . AS AMERICAN AS CHERRY PIE"

The decision pronounced by Judge Roger B. Taney remanded Scott back to slavery and forbade the reenactment of the Missouri Compromise. Taney, who had been appointed Chief Justice[9] of the Court twenty years earlier by Andrew Jackson, was a pro-slavery partisan. He was supported in all his conclusions by three of the Associate Judges—Wane of Georgia, David of Virginia, and Campbell of Alabama. Judge Catron of Tennessee supported Taney in his conclusion that Scott's two-year residency in Illinois gave him no right to freedom, in other words, Scott should be remanded to slavery. He would not go so far as to say that Congress had no right to govern the territories. To this he appended the right of slaveholders to their property in all territories of the United States. In essence the five southern judges agreed wholeheartedly with Chief Justice Taney. The two northern Democratic Justices, Nelson of New York and Grier of Pennsylvania, disagreed with Taney's conclusion but voted with their southern colleagues. The dissenting opinions came from Justice Curtis of Massachusetts, the only Whig member, and Justice McClean of Ohio, the only Republican on the bench. The dissent of Justice Curtis, recognized by Fillmore and almost the entire legal association as "unanswerable," was related to "that part of the opinion of the majority of the court in which it is held that a person of African descent cannot be a citizen of the United States." To Curtis the thought of denying citizenship based on color was ludicrous. Had America forgotten that at the time of the ratification of the Articles of Confederation that all free natural-born inhabitants of Massachusetts, New Hampshire, New Jersey, New York, and North Carolina possessed the electoral franchise? Had it been overlooked by the Democratic Justices that among the citizens of these states were many of African descent? Did these seven Justices realize that they were decreeing a whole race of men into slavery and providing that odious institution with a political subterfuge for its extension into all the territories? Obviously they did, for Taney's opinion carried seven to two. What had been authorized by implication in the Constitution had been made manifestly real by the Supreme Court of the United States.

The Court decision produced unexpected results and had an immediate effect upon national power. Buchanan had made a smart political move but also a dangerous one. Would a Supreme Court decision put to rest the question of slavery in the territories as he had anticipated? Obviously not, for by now the highest tribunal in the land had become recognized as a mere instrument in the hands of the slavocracy-controlled Democratic party. Buchanan himself was recognized as having been a party to rigged dealings of the Court when he indiscreetly predicted the Court's decision in his inaugural address on March 4, just two days prior to its public pronouncement. The most immediate effect of the decision was to give renewed life to the question of slavery in the territories. Public opinion became polarized and the conflicting opinions of the Court were seen by the people north and south of the Mason–Dixon Line according to the views of either Taney or Curtis. Overnight the abolitionists' propaganda mills were set in motion churning out anti-slavery literature. Horace Greeley wrote in the March 7 New York *Tribune* that the majority opinion warranted no more respect than that of a majority "congregated in a Washington bar." From the pulpits, abolitionist ministers preached that the Dred Scott Decision was ample proof of the conspiracy to spread slavery throughout the entire hemisphere. The northern mood, angered by the decree, began cries of secession and in Wisconsin the legislature of the state actually passed a resolution supporting nullification in principle. While Garrison called for "No union with slaveholders," Wendell Phillips, a fellow abolitionist, declared the Union to be a curse of God that must be done away with. All in all, the Dred Scott Decision, while not proving of any value to the South, engendered fierce hostility in the North. Politically speaking, the decision was a boon to the Republican party giving it added strength and vigor during its initial period of growth.

Slavery was now irrevocably fastened upon the territories by the Supreme Court of the United States. The next logical step to be taken by the Buchanan Administration would be to secure a pro-slavery constitution in Kansas. Efforts in this direction had failed in the past and had led to the resignation of three territorial Governors. The third, John W. Geary of Pennsylvania, resigned March 4, 1857, the day Buchanan took office. In an attempt to bring both peace and slavery to the territory, the Administration appointed Robert J. Walker to the office of Governor. Walker, born in Pennsylvania, had been a Senator from Mississippi for ten years and Secretary of Treasury under President Polk. He was a man of no mean political ability, having secured the Democratic nomination for Polk over Van Buren at their party's convention in 1844. Therefore, if any one individual could carry out the President's wishes, certainly Walker was that man. For by now the situation had become complicated and the allegiance of the northern Democrats began to waver.

Walker arrived in Kansas on May 25, 1857, his primary object being not to make Kansas a slave state, which he deemed an impossibility, but rather to settle the territory with people of a southern outlook who could be counted upon to support the Democratic party in their allegiance with the southern plantation class. He rationalized that if he could bring peace to Kansas and at the same time increase the pro-slavery-oriented population, eventually he would be able through the judicious use of Federal patronage to bring about *de facto* slavery in the territory. If this could be pulled off everybody would have gained something. The anti-slavery elements would rejoice because Kansas had entered the Union as a free state. The pro-slavery faction would revel in being able to enjoy the fruits of slavery, albeit *de facto*, based on support of the National Administration and the Supreme Court. The Buchanan Administration would profit by having "Bleeding Kansas" removed as a political issue, the major advantage being that a party split could be avoided. In fact, the only ones to suffer should Walker succeed would be the Republican party.

Walker was to come closer then any other territorial Governor in bringing peace to Kansas. Being able to gain the trust of the free-staters in the territory, he was able to persuade them to participate in an election, held in October of 1857, for the territorial legislature. As a result of this election, a free-state legislature and delegate to Congress were chosen. The pro-slavery forces in Kansas did not trust Walker so they held their own constitutional convention on September 5 of that year at Lecompton and adopted the Lecompton Constitution. One article of this constitution declared slave property inviolable. The people were not allowed to vote upon the whole constitution as they had been promised by Governor Walker. Instead, they were only allowed to vote upon the aritcle covering slavery. They could either accept or reject slavery—not the entire constitution. Furthermore, in the event they rejected slavery the constitution provided that there could be no interference with the institution before 1865, nor could there be any amendments to the constitution prior to that date. In essence the Lecompton document was a compromise offered by the pro-slavery forces that would allow them to maintain control of the territorial legislature while ostensibly appearing to abolish slavery. They hoped to have their cake and eat it too. On December 21, only that portion sanctioning slavery was submitted to the voters. The Free Soilers in Kansas refused to vote and being in control of the legislature held an election January 4, 1858. They submitted the entire Lecompton Constitution to the electorate. By a vote of 10,226 opposing and 138 for the constitution with slavery, the measure was defeated. Twenty-four persons cast ballots in favor of the constitution without slavery.

Once more the affairs in Kansas had come to an impasse. Robert Walker, perhaps the most able of all the territorial Governors, had failed to find the formula that would bring peace to the warring factions. The scene of the battle again shifted to Congress. President Buchanan, having received a copy of the Lecompton Constitution late in January 1858, forwarded it to Congress with his blessings. He did this against the best advice offered him. Long before even the elections in Kansas had taken place, Walker and Stephen A. Douglas, the foremost exponent of popular sovereignty, had warned the President of the injudiciousness involved in supporting the Lecompton Constitution. They advised him to use his influence rather against it and to look forward to a new beginning in Kansas. Not to oppose the document would be to court political disaster, for the northern wing of the Democratic party would not stand idly by and permit the already southern-dominated organization to slip completely from their grasp. If for no other reason than pure political survival, the northern congressional Democrats would have to oppose the constitution. If Buchanan supported it, eventually they would be forced to oppose him. Without question, this would lead to a split within the party that would have calamitous effects upon the organization, if not upon the nation itself.

Buchanan would hear none of their pleas. Instead he took the advice of his southern allies and mobilized all of his resources toward securing passage of the Lecompton Constitution. The document, accompanied by a message from the President declaring Kansas to be as much a slave state as either South Carolina or Georgia, was voted on in the Senate on March 23. There it passed by a vote of 33 to 25. In the House, the opposition was more effective and the measure had to be amended to allow for submitting the entire constitution to a popular vote. As amended by Congressman English of Indiana, it passed the House by a vote of 120 to 112. The Senate, in spite of Douglas' opposition, concurred and for all practical purposes the struggle was over.[10] Nevertheless, Kansas would not be admitted until January 29, 1861, after the South had seceded from the Union.

President Buchanan's effort to force the Lecompton Constitution through the Democratic Congress had a ruinous effect upon the Democratic party. It produced a schism in that body that has not healed to this day. Naturally, the first to feel the sting of the angry President's lash was Stephen A. Douglas. He was personally attacked by the party press for not having supported Buchanan. The South, resentful of his unwillingness to sacrifice his career in the interest of slavery, maligned him in a manner reminiscent of that heaped upon Fremont in 1856. It was more important to the South to secure Kansas for slavery than to maintain Illinois for Douglas. To Douglas, the opposite was true. Failing to carry Illinois in the forthcoming election would mean an end to his public career. The once powerful Democratic leader of the North broke with the slavocracy-controlled national organization. The foremost exponent of squatters' sovereignty who had applauded the Dred Scott Decision was no longer welcome in the party. For his actions he was heartily applauded in the North and bitterly denounced in the South. In the Senate, Douglas picked up three important votes in his fight against the Lecompton Constitution. One of those, David C. Broderick of California, was later staked out and killed in a gun duel. Also standing by Douglas in his opposition to the Lecompton Constitution were many northern Democratic members of the House.

With his state machine firmly behind him and unable to be broken by the President, Douglas was prepared to seek reelection to the Senate. So well had his actions in protest of Buchanan's Kansas policy been attended by public interests that for a time the Republican hierarchy, such as Horace Greeley, William Seward, and Schuyler Colfax were prepared to extend the hand of comradeship and help the "Little Giant" get reelected as a Democrat running on a squatter sovereignty platform. For a time a coalition between Douglas Democrats and Republicans became a distinct possibility. This attempt to widen the breach between northern and southern Democrats was looked upon with contempt by the aggressive Free Soil faction of the Republican party. To them this represented a complete surrender of principles that would lead to the destruction of the party once it abandoned its opposition to the spread of slavery. In this respect the Illinois Republicans were to have the final word. Realizing that Douglas' main purpose was to be reelected and having been more involved than the eastern wing of the party, they rebeled declaring that it was "asking too much for human nature to bear, to now surrender to Judge Douglas." Their view of the "Little Giant" was at best most uncomplimentary.

Having moved Douglas aside as the party's nominee for Senator, the Illinois Republicans met in convention at Springfield on June 8, 1858, and nominated Abraham Lincoln to run for the post. Lincoln's rise to prominence within the Republican state organization came via an extremely circuitous path beginning in 1855. In order to achieve the party leadership he had been forced to walk the political tightrope across the insidious snake pit that was Illinois party politics immediately after the founding of the Republican party. At that time the Illinois Republican organization was composed of the most radical elements from the Free Soil movement, their main spokesmen being Icabod Codding and Owen Lovejoy. Because of their platform which called for the repeal of the Fugitive Slave Law and the abolition of slavery in the District of Columbia, they did not receive the cooperation of either the Democrats who supported the squatter sovereignty principle or the Anti-Nebraska Whigs who simply wanted restoration of the Missouri Compromise. In spite of the state's being normally Democratic, the conservative Whig element preferred demise rather than fusion with Republicans. Lincoln, the Whig party nominee for Senator in 1855, was a victim of this intransigence and at the age of forty-six was faced with the possibility of having no political future, for he belonged to a party identified with issues no longer extant.

There was only one issue around which Lincoln could make a new beginning. That issue was slavery—the status of the black man in America. But how could this be accomplished in Illinois, a Democratic state whose Republican party was too far to the left to attract even those who should have been its natural allies, the Anti-Nebraska Whigs? Lincoln saw his way in a fusion of the two anti-Nebraska elements in the state. His aim would be to unite the Democratic and Whig opponents of the Kansas—Nebraska Act. He was aided in this undertaking by the unforeseen caning of Sumner. For with the attack upon Sumner coupled with events in "Bleeding Kansas" it became possible to avoid embracing the black man as a political cause.

Lincoln set about bringing together the two anti-Nebraska factions in Illinois. True it was a long shot but if it could be accomplished it would be well worth any effort expended. Besides, his very political life depended upon the success of this venture and if he were to succeed it was important that he begin to take care of business. As any successful politician knows taking care of business begins at home. Therefore, instead of running off to attend the first National Republican Convention being held at Pittsburgh on February 22, 1856, Lincoln remained at home and attended a meeting of Illinois editors held at Decatur on the same date. He did not take part in the proceedings but, being in touch with many of the delegates, he persuaded them to adopt a platform against slavery's extension and to set May 29 as the date for a fusion meeting to be held in Bloomington. In the interim, aided by the attack on Sumner, he succeeded in coaxing many anti-Nebraska-ites to attend the meeting.

At the meeting after a number of pre-arranged speeches had been delivered, the crowd began chanting "Lincoln, Lincoln! give us Lincoln!" When Lincoln ascended to the platform he gave a speech that was lauded the following day in every Illinois state paper. The effect of his speech upon the audience was such that even the reporters ceased taking notes. The time was right and Lincoln was the man to unite the foes of slavery's extension. At this meeting Lincoln, recognizing that the anti—Nebraska Democrats were in the majority, insisted that they receive the top nominations, including the governorship. In turn he and several others were chosen as delegates to the Republican National Convention in Philadelphia to be held the following month. No members of the original Illinois-Republican party were placed on the state ticket. What had seemed impossible had been accomplished. The anti-Nebraska forces had united under the Republican banner. On the issue of slavery, Lincoln had succeeded in stealing the party away from Codding and Lovejoy and moving the Republican party to a more moderate position thereby broadening its base of support throughout the state. In the process he had become its acknowledged leader and had been granted a new lease on his political life. That is how Abe Lincoln became a Republican.

Lincoln was the unanimous choice of the Illinois Republicans in 1858 for the Senate seat held by Douglas. He was endorsed for that post by the state convention on June 16. The tightrope walking act he had developed in wresting control of the party from Codding and Lovejoy would prove of particular benefit in the campaign of that year, especially in the questionable counties of central Illinois whose 37,000 Whig votes had gone to Buchanan in 1856. His "house divided" speech delivered at his acceptance of the nomination would be too radical for the people of Illinois. Speeches of this nature would supply his opponent, who freely admitted that Lincoln was "the strong man of his party—full of wit, facts, dates—and the best stump speaker . . . in the West," with too much ammunition. The historic Lincoln-Douglas debates, which "set the prairies ablaze" began on August 21 in Ottawa and took place throughout the state. The debates,[11] seven in all, lasted from August into late October and attracted large audiences at Charleston, Freeport, Jonesboro, Galesburg, Quincy, Ottawa, and Alton. During the course of the debates Lincoln was able to take advantage of Douglas' national prominence to boost himself onto the national scene. Citing Kansas as the example, Lincoln's strategy was to force Douglas to admit that his squatter sovereignty principle was not sufficient to curtail the spread of slavery. Douglas attempted to show that the "Black Republicans" favored the abolition of slavery and the equality of the black man with the white man. In this attack upon Lincoln, Douglas was extremely successful in forcing Honest Abe to declare that "I am not, nor ever have been, in favor of bringing about in any way the social and political equality of the white and black races." By the time the debates were finished, Lincoln could state only that he opposed enslavement of the black man.

Lincoln received no support from the eastern wing of the party. The New York *Tribune,* edited by Horace Greeley, favored Douglas in recognition of his stand against the Lecompton Constitution. *The New York Times* supported the "Little Giant" and his squatter sovereignty principle as a means of putting to rest forever the slavery question. But editor Henry Raymond's wish was not to be answered as throughout the North candidates for office echoed the arguments being made in Illinois. In New York where Edwin D. Morgan was seeking the Governorship and William Seward reelection to the Senate, strains of Lincoln's "house divided" speech were evident. On October 25 Seward, now running as a full-fledged Republican, gave the most important speech of that campaign. The speech given in Rochester, New York, declared that the differences between the North and the South would lead to an "irrepressible conflict" in which "the United States must and will, sooner or later, become either entirely a slave-holding nation or entirely a free-labor nation." The important question of the black man's status could not be eternally dodged.

When the results were in, the Republicans carried every northern state except Illinois. There they won the popular election by 4,000 votes, but due to the legislature apportionment, Douglas was reelected by a vote of 54 to 46. In spite of Lincoln's loss, he had gained a national reputation as a formidable debater and elsewhere his party, the Republican party, was on the march. In New York, where Morgan became the state's first Republican Governor, a Republican Legislature was elected. With the exception of four, every congressman elected was either Republican or anti-Lecompton Democrat. Pennsylvania, New Jersey, and Minnesota went to the Republicans. Maine (Morrill), Massachusetts (Banks), New Hampshire (Hale), Rhode Island (Dyer), and Connecticut (Buckingham) elected Republican Governors. The two congressional districts in Vermont came under Republican control as did the Indiana congressional delegation. In Michigan, Ohio, Wisconsin, and Iowa the Republican-dominated legislatures were increased. Minnesota, recently admitted to the Union as a free state (May 11, 1858), fell into the Republican camp. Aside from Illinois, only California among the northern states voted pro-Administration. Oregon, not yet a state, went along with California.

The extent of the Republican triumph was readily apparent when the first session of the thirty-sixth Congress convened on Monday, December 5, 1859. In that body which was to become known as the "Congress of Secession," the Republican party had taken control of the House and made substantial gains in the Senate. The House, consisting of 237 members and five territorial delegates without any voting power contained 109 Republicans, 101 Democrats, 26 Americans, and one Whig. After two months of battle, they elected William Pennington of New Jersey as Speaker. In the Senate Republican strength had climbed from 20 to 26 as against 36 Democrats. In retrospect, the newly found congressional strength of the Republican party was due, at least in part, to the resignation of Robert Walker as Territorial Governor. He, like several Governors before him, had counseled the Administration against its course in Kansas.

When Buchanan failed to take his advice he resigned and repudiated the President's territorial policies. As for Douglas, his sojourn among the ranks of the powerful within the Democratic party was shortly to be ended. Because of his opposition to the Lecompton Constitution, he had ceased to be of service to the southern-dominated Democratic party. He was stripped of his chairmanship of the powerful and important Committee on Territories and eventually forced to oppose his former southern allies on the question of federal protection of slavery in the territories. Because of these events the Democratic party was now split North and South. But more important, the nation was also politically divided North and South over the question of slavery. From the South Jefferson Davis, the favorite of the slave power, was the undisputed leader of the Democratic party. In the North, the Republican party had produced no one of comparable status to oppose the spread of slave power. The South had tossed the ball to the North. If the Republican party were to endure, it would have to produce someone of stature equal to Davis and forthrightly as committed to freedom as the latter was to slavery.

Certainly, if among the Republican politicians there had not yet arisen a leader prepared to deal bluntly with the slavery issue, one did exist among the ranks of the abolitionists. The man, John Brown of Osawatomie, Kansas, divinely commissioned "By the Authority of Almighty God," was an "abolitionist of the Bunker Hill school. He followed neither Garrison nor Seward, Gerrit Smith nor Wendell Phillips; but the Golden Rule and the Declaration of Independence." Brown, a disciple of Nat Turner, whom he believed to be an American patriot as ardently as the rest of America believed George Washington to be, "could not see that it was heroic to fight against a petty tax on tea, and war seven long years for a political principle, yet wrong to restore, by force of arms, to an outraged race, the rights with which their maker had endowed them."

The man whom Robert E. Lee referred to as "Old Osawatomie Brown" was born in Torrington, Connecticut, on May 9, 1800. He had, early in his life, sworn himself and his children to the freeing of slaves. In "Bleeding Kansas" he had distinguished himself as an able warrior not lacking in valor. Because of his exploits in the rescuing of slaves, he had gained somewhat of a national reputation. The President of the United States had offered a 250-dollar reward for his capture, whereas in Missouri there was a 3,000-dollar bounty on his head.

To successfully effect his plan of emancipating the slaves by inciting a general insurrection among them, Brown returned back East in 1858 and began a fund-raising campaign. He was aided at various times in this venture by Gerrit Smith, Frank B. Sanborn, George L. Stearns, Theodore

Parker, Dr. Samuel Howe, and some say, Thomas Wentworth Higginson, in addition to many others. In Concord, Massachusetts, he spoke to a huge gathering at the Town Hall. The eastern literati, Alcott, Emerson, and Thoreau, came to hear him and had nothing but words of praise for his bold ventures. Attempts to dissuade him by such men as Frederick Douglass and others who knew of his scheme, failed.

Brown's basic plan was simple. Take control of the armory at Harper's Ferry and confiscate the large quantity of arms and ammunition stored there. Next, free as many slaves as possible before daybreak, arm them and move into the mountains. Use the mountains as a base camp for further guerrilla sorties to free slaves. Brown reasoned that after a while panic would set in among the slaveholders. At this point the slaves set free by Brown would be able to incite their fellow bondsmen into general rebellion against their slave masters. Like a chain reaction, this process was supposed to continue till all of the slaves would be set free. A simple scheme? Yes. But from the beginning it was beset with difficulties. There was dissension among the ranks of his small band of twenty-two (seventeen white, five black) which caused Brown to resign his leadership temporarily. Later, fearing a traitor among his party, he was forced to move forward the date on which the armory was to be assaulted. Instead of October 24, an earlier date had to be agreed upon. Therefore, on Sunday evening, October 17, 1858, without prior warning Brown, with a party of eighteen, seized the United States Armory and made prisoners of the three night watchmen on duty. Every male who ventured into the street was made prisoner. During the night, a contingent of Brown's men under Captain Stevens had visited the house of Colonel Lewis W. Washington, a great-grandson of George Washington's brother, taken him prisoner, and set his slaves free. Similar events took place throughout the night at the homes of neighboring slave-owners. By eight o'clock the next morning, Brown had captured over sixty hostages.

The news of the event leaked out when Brown permitted a westbound train that he had confiscated to continue its journey toward Washington. When the people of Harper's Ferry awoke to find their town under siege, fighting began. By midday, with the exception of those who had fled or the six barricaded within the armory, his entire army had been either killed or captured. Listed among the dead were a town grocer named Boerly and Brown's son, Walter. His other son Oliver would be killed later that afternoon. A militia force of one hundred men arriving from Charleston at noon took up positions at every available exit. Brown retreated to the engine room killing two and wounding six, but by evening his forces had been whittled down to four unwounded, himself included.

Of the rest, eight had died, one was dying, and three had been captured. Another group sent out to free slaves that day had fled through Pennsylvania. However, it was not until the next morning that a group of marines under Colonel Robert E. Lee and Lieutenant J.E.B. Stuart stormed the engine room and captured Brown. In the process two of their men were wounded. Brown, struck in the face with a saber, reeled to the ground and received two bayonet thrusts from an irate soldier. John Brown was hanged at the end of a rope on December 2, 1859 at Charleston, Virginia (now Charles Town, West Virginia). The remnants of his small band received the same fate—death at the end of a hangman's noose.

Along with the publication of a book entitled *The Impending Crisis of the South,*[12] John Brown's inspired foray into Virginia threatened to produce severe political repercussions for the Republican party. The issuance of the book, endorsed by Galusha Grow and John Sherman, was partly responsible for the election of ex-New Jersey Governor William Pennington to the House Speakership on the fortieth ballot. In an effort to link the Republican party to the abolitionists and John Brown's Raid, Grow and Sherman were singled out during their battle for the Speakership for having approved the book. John B. Clark of Missouri offered a resolution during the Speakership debate stating the book to be "insurrectionary and hostile to the domestic peace and tranquility of the country, and that no member of this House, who had endorsed and recommended it or the Compend from it, is fit to be Speaker of the House." In the Senate Jefferson Davis referred to Brown's raid as "the invasion of a State by a murderous gang of abolitionists." Douglas was outspoken in his "firm and deliberate belief that the Harper's Ferry crime was a natural, logical, and inevitable result of the doctrines and teachings of the Republican party." Senator Mason of Virginia, sensing the possible northern political potential, maneuvered a motion through the Senate for an investigative committee to look into the events leading up to the raid. A deputy of the committee arrested Charles B. Sanborn, of Concord, New Hampshire for failing to appear before the committee to testify. However, he never left town as his release was effected by a group of his neighbors through a writ of habeas corpus. In the end attempts to fasten responsibility upon the Republican party for John Brown's raid failed. The Senate committee, operating on the basis of the conspiracy theory, could not show that the origin of the scheme extended beyond John Brown's immediate followers. The effects of the Harper's Ferry incident upon the Democratic party served to widen the gulf between Douglas and the southern-controlled organization and to hasten the complete disruption of the nation's oldest political party.

Outside the sphere of Democrat–Republican party politics, John Brown's Raid inadvertently destroyed a new political movement sponsored by the conservative Unionist aimed at preserving the Union by removing the spector of slavery from national political debate. Led by John Crittenden, a Kentuckian, and William C. Rives of Virginia, the notion caught on in the border states during 1858 and 1859. Its appeal was to the nativists, Whigs, and other displaced northern voters who normally make up the great center of American politics.

The Republican party, not yet safely out of deep water on the slavery question, was now looking forward to 1860–the next Presidential campaign. While none other than Ralph Waldo Emerson was calling Brown "a new saint awaiting his martyrdom," the party leadership adopted a most conciliatory stance in order to retain the more conservative element. They knew that to lose the forthcoming national election would be to suffer the fate of the Know-Nothings's–political oblivion. Lincoln, who like many others was working to build a strong national organization, endeavored feverishly to discourage party leaders from taking extreme positions on the slavery issue. John Brown's Raid, while not achieving its goal of freeing the slaves, had brought the nation one step closer to war. But in spite of a "higher law" and the "irrepressible conflict" or even the "house divided," the people of the nation were not ready to shed their blood. At least, this is how the leading Republican spokesmen saw it.

The year 1860 was a time of heightened political activity. Several national political conventions were held and it is the account of these events and the subsequent campaign which fashioned the political history of that year. On April 23 the Democratic Convention met in Charleston, South Carolina, as decided four years earlier. The purpose of the meeting was to adopt a platform and to choose Presidential and Vice-Presidential candidates for the forthcoming election.

When the convention opened, full delegations from every state in the Union were present. New York and Illinois were represented by contesting delegations for and against Senator Douglas. From New York the delegation opposing his candidacy had been elected by districts and were led by Fernando Wood. They were called "Hards." The "Softs," elected by convention in Syracuse, favored the nomination of Douglas. As all the tickets of admission had been given to this Douglas's slate, a row developed in the Convention over the seating of delegations. When Francis B. Flournoy, the temporary presiding officer, relinquished the gavel, the contested seats were decided in favor of the Douglas men.

Caleb Cushing of Massachusetts, a staunch states' rights advocate, was elected permanent Chairman. Charleston was the stronghold of the Slave

". . . AS AMERICAN AS CHERRY PIE"

Power and the extreme faction of the Democratic party known as "Fire-Eaters." This group was led by William Lowndes Yancey of Alabama. Every advantage that could be accorded the South by virtue of the Convention site and choice of presiding officer was made full use of. But more importantly, the thirty-three-member Resolution Committee composed of one delegate from each state was under southern control.[13] After several days, the Committee issued two reports. The pro-South majority report unequivocally asserted the right of slaveholders to settle in the territories with their slaves—"a right not to be destroyed or impaired by Congressional or Territorial legislation." In another declaration the report emphasized that it was the responsibility of the Federal Government "to protect slavery in the Territories and wherever else its constitutional authority extends."

Recognizing that to acquiesce to these Southern demands would mean to court self-destruction, the northern pro-Douglas minority issued its own report declaring that "in as much as differences of opinion exist in the Democratic party as to the nature and extent of the powers and duties of a Territorial Legislature, and as to the powers and duties of Congress under the Constitution of the United States over the institution of slavery within the Territories the Democratic party will abide by the decisions of the Supreme Court of the United States upon questions of Constitutional law." This was the first time in the history of Democratic conventions that northerners refused to yield to southerners on the question of slavery. A second minority report, the unmodified platform of 1856, presented to the Convention by General Benjamin F. Butler of Massachusetts on Monday, May 30, was rejected 105 to 195. The original minority report submitted to the Convention by delegate Samuels of Iowa replaced the majority resolution by a vote of 165 to 138.

Being outvoted the southern delegates refused to abide by the rule of the majority. Delegations from seven southern states—Alabama, Arkansas, Florida, Louisiana, Mississippi, South Carolina, and Texas—immediately left the Convention. They convened in St. Andrew's Hall in Charleston and elected Delaware Senator James A. Bayard as Chairman. The platform adopted by this group was the just-defeated majority report of the regular convention. The Convention then adjourned to reconvene in Richmond on June 11. At that time they again adjourned setting June 28 as the day of re-convention. John Edwin of Alabama was elected Chairman. Meanwhile, at the regular Democratic Convention Douglas failed to get the two-thirds vote (202 delegates) necessary for nomination. Fifty-seven ballots took place. His total number of delegates rose to 152½ at one time but remained at 151½ for the last twenty ballots. The Douglas-controlled convention, hamstrung by the two-thirds rule adopted in full convention, adjourned to Baltimore to allow filling of the empty delegations.

When the regular Convention reassembled in Baltimore on June 18, Douglas delegates had been named to replace the seceders from the South. Bypassing the two-thirds rule of the earlier conventions Douglas received the party's nomination with 181½ votes. His Vice-Presidential running mate was Herschel V. Johnson of Georgia. At this convention a second secession occurred. Caleb Cushing resigned the chairmanship and was replaced by Governor Tod of Ohio. Cushing, along with the rest of the southern delegates, reassembled and adopted the minority report of the Charleston Convention. They then proceeded to the nomination of John C. Breckinridge of Kentucky for President and Joseph Lane of Oregon for Vice-President. This ticket had also been put forth by the seceding convention meeting in Richmond that same day, June 28, 1860.

A third political party aligned against the Republican in the forthcoming election was the newly formed Constitutional Union party. This fusionist group of southern Americans and northern Whigs had John J. Crittenden as its chief spokesman. They met in Baltimore on May 9 and chose Washington Hunt of New York as Convention Chairman. On the second ballot John Bell of Tennessee and Edward Everett of Massachusetts were respectively nominated for the Presidential and Vice-Presidential slots. The party platform composed of a single plank called for the recognition of "no political principles, other than the Constitution of the Country, the Union of the States and the Enforcement of the Laws." Recalling Fillmore's effect upon the candidacy of Fremont in 1856, the threat of competition from a political party that would siphon off normally Republican votes momentarily caused a certain degree of consternation among the Republican hierarchy. However, their fears were completely allayed when it became evident that the response to the new party was lukewarm. Ten states, eight northern and two southern, failed to send delegates to the convention. Only two of the twenty-one member Whig national committee were present and half of the American hierarchy remained aloof wishing to keep their options open.

With the Democratic party hopelessly in shambles and the Constitutional Unionist too feeble to be of any import, all eyes turned toward Chicago, the site of the Second National Republican Convention. Chicago had been chosen as a compromise location for the convention by the Republican National Committee. On the suggestion of Norman Judd, national committeeman from Illinois and Lincoln's former campaign manager, Chicago was selected as neutral ground since Illinois had no

". . . AS AMERICAN AS CHERRY PIE"

favorite-son candidate.

Having no hall large enough to hold the turnout of guests expected, Chicago had only recently put the finishing touches on a building constructed to house the convention. Known as the Wigwam, the structure, standing at the southeast corner of Lake and Market streets, had been built at a cost of 5,000 dollars. The city had raised most of the money through public subscription but at convention time the 2,000-dollar debt that remained had to be collected by a twenty-five-cent admission charge. The Wigwam was a rectangular structure measuring 180 by 100 feet that held, depending on who did the estimating, anywhere between 6,000 and 15,000 people. The delegates' stage, located alongside one wall, seated 600. Around the other three walls, the galleries held 1,200.

The scent of victory filled the air. Prominent Republicans and agents for prospective candidates began pouring into the city a week before the Convention was scheduled to begin. The "Wide Awakes" were busy greeting each arriving delegation and hustling it off among a variety of loud noises ranging from cannon fire to blaring brass bands to its headquarters. At the average rate of two dollars per day, Chicago's hotels were soon filled to capacity. In the spirit of the event private homes opened their doors to visitors. By May 16, the first day of the Convention, it is estimated that Chicago's population had doubled.

Before the Convention began, it was a foregone conclusion that William Henry Seward of New York would be the party's Presidential candidate—the convention serving merely to ratify what everyone already knew to be. For the past two years he had labored diligently in the vineyard of Republicanism. The party nomination for the nation's highest office would be just reward for his services. Fully two-thirds of the delegates were with this point of view. With Governor Morgan of New York presiding over the Convention and Thurlow Weed peerless in his role as campaign manager, how could he miss being nominated? It was almost an impossibility.

Two men who played an important role in Seward's candidacy arrived Saturday, May 12, and began setting up shop. One, Thurlow Weed, his campaign manager, began in earnest shoring up his delegate support. The other, Horace Greeley, his ex-business partner on the New York *Tribune,* arrived as a delegate from Oregon and immediately went to work undermining the Seward candidacy. At this point it was not generally known that the business partnership had been dissolved as a result of the bad blood that existed between Greeley, on the one hand, and Seward and Weed, on the other, brought about by the failure of the latter to support the political aspirations of the former in the New York campaign of 1854.

Of the two, Weed's task was the more formidable. He had to unite the extremities of the party—at one end the Abolitionists, at the other Know-Nothings and Whigs—around his candidate. To oppose Seward, Greeley had pledged his support to Edwin M. Bates of Missouri, a Whig who was backed by the Blairs. Frank Jr. and Montgomery, the sons of Frank P. Blair, had proposed a scheme for colonizing slaves. They considered this approach a logical solution that would surely pick up Whig support in the Border States and in the North. Schuyler Colfax, Republican Senator from Indiana, and Lincoln's close associate, Orville H. Browning of Illinois, joined in the sponsorship of Bates.

The convention which opened officially on Wednesday, May 16, was presided over temporarily by David Wilmot of Pennsylvania who gave the keynote address. On paper the Republican strategy boiled down to the selection of either of two courses. To win in November, they would need 152 electoral votes. They could count on 54 of these coming from the northern tier of states extending from Iowa to New England. New York with 35 and Connecticut with 6 could also be counted on to go Republican. The remaining 57 votes would either have to be picked up in the Border States and Delaware which contained 59 or else in Ohio, Pennsylvania, Indiana, and Illinois with a total of 74. Regardless of the choice, the conservative political element would have to be considered in the selection of any candidate. Greeley and several other managers of dark horse candidates recognized this simple fact of life that in the end would determine the party's nominee.

Northerners, though understanding Greeley's strategy, could not accept a candidate who had not completely taken up the Republican banner. If they were going to elect a President, certainly they wanted him to be a full-fledged Republican. Besides, the border campaign was fraught with the greater peril. Therefore, many among the party leaders decided that it would be wiser to go after Ohio, Pennsylvania, Illinois, and Indiana. This was the combination of states that the candidate would have to carry to insure election. Many thought Seward could not do it. His reputation as a radical would be too damaging to the Republican ticket in several states. W.A. Buckingham, a conservative Republican, had just been elected Governor of Connecticut by a paltry 541 votes. Had he been less conservative, it was agreed that he would have lost. Similarly in two of the crucial states, Indiana and Pennsylvania, the gubernatorial candidates, Henry S. Lane and Andrew G. Curtin, thought they would lose with Seward leading the ticket. Illinois and New Jersey were equally reticent.

Over in the Richmond House on Wednesday evening on the first day of the Convention frolic prevailed, champagne poured freely, and the

New York delegation boasted of Seward's imminent nomination. But behind the scene in other parts of town, men of a different point of view were meeting. John A. Andrew, Governor of Massachusetts, had taken a committee from New England to discuss with the wavering states' delegations the possibility of a dark horse candidate. Seward was his man, but Seward could not carry the doubtful states. The party would have to unite behind a winner. He was ready to throw his support and that of the New England delegation behind a single candidate agreed upon by the joint Indiana, Illinois, Pennsylvania, and New Jersey delegation. The success of the party was too important. The best man must be sought out and nominated.

At first no candidate could be agreed upon. A meeting held at noon Thursday, attended by Lane, Curtin, and several others, and presided over by Governor Reeder of Pennsylvania, produced no tangible results. They agreed to appoint a committee, four from each doubtful state, to meet in David Wilmot's quarters at six o'clock that evening. Accordingly, this meeting took place but by ten o'clock no single candidate had been agreed upon. However, of the three names being bandied around—Cameron of New Jersey, Dayton of Pennsylvania, and Lincoln of Illinois—Lincoln was by far the strongest. By midnight no detailed agreement had been reached but New Jersey had promised to drop its favorite son in favor of Lincoln after the first ballot if Pennsylvania would follow suit. After the inducement of a Cabinet post for Cameron by Lincoln's floor manager David Davis, Pennsylvania agreed the following morning to throw its support to Lincoln after the first ballot.

When the third day of the convention began that Friday enthusiasm for Seward still ran high. The New York delegation was peerless in devotion to their candidate. Led by Thurlow Weed and William M. Evarts they marched toward the convention site as though celebrating a *fait accompli*. In their enthusiasm they tarried a bit longer than perhaps they should have. They arrived to find that with the exception of the delegates' seats every seat was taken and every inch of standing room was occupied by Lincoln supporters.[14]

The balloting which began late in the day was completed by noon. Presided over by George Ashmun of Massachusetts, the permanent Chairman, the convention began receiving nominations for President of the United States. A prominent feature of the nominating speeches was their brevity. Seward's name was placed before the body by William M. Evarts with only twenty-six words. Lincoln's was put forth by Norman Judd using only twenty-seven. With the announcement of each name a wave of applause was let loose that completely filled the room. After the names of several other favorite son candidates (Simon Cameron, Salmon Chase, Edward Bates, William Dayton, and Jacob Collamer) were placed in nomination the balloting began. In order to be nominated, 233 votes were required. If Seward were to win, he would have to do so early in the balloting before the favorite sons' delegations began shifting. On the first ballot, Seward had 173½ votes, Lincoln 102. Cameron of Pennsylvania led the favorite son candidates with 50½. Close behind him were Chase of Ohio with 49 and Bates of Missouri with 48. Dayton of New Jersey and Collamer of Vermont received 14 and 10, respectively. There was a scattering of six. Bates's poor showing meant that he was out of the race and that the contest was between Seward and Lincoln. It also indicated that the Republican strategy of going after the four northern states in preference to the border states was a wise decision since Bates could not carry the latter anyhow. They represented a potential bonus for Lincoln. On the second ballot Lincoln picked up 79 votes while Seward gained only seven. Of the votes secured by Lincoln, 44 came from Pennsylvania, 10 from Vermont and 6 from Ohio. When the third ballot began, Lincoln had 181 votes to Seward's 184½. The third ballot did it. The carefully arranged plan was put into operation. New Jersey shifted eight votes from Dayton to Lincoln. Maryland contributed 9 of its 11. By the end of the third ballot Lincoln at 231½ votes had climbed to within 1½ votes necessary for nomination. Seward had dropped 4½ to 180. Before a fourth ballot could even be considered, David K. Cartter of Ohio climbed onto a chair and announced that Ohio was shifting four votes to Lincoln. It was all over. Abe Lincoln "the man who could split rails and maul Democrats" had won the Republican nomination. In an unprecedented show of party unity, the motion to make the nomination unanimous was made by William Evarts of New York and seconded by John A. Andrew of Massachusetts.

While not in attendance at the convention, Lincoln had been nominated to run on a platform which among other things denounced disunion, the reopening of the African slave trade, and squatters' sovereignty. The platform which considered freedom the natural state of affairs denied the authority of Congress, of a territorial government, or of an individual to give existence to slavery in any of the territories. His running mate as Vice-President would be Hannibal Hamlin, Senator from Maine. Hamlin had separated from the Democratic party on the basis of his opposition to the repeal of the Missouri Compromise. He had in 1856 gained the Governorship of the state of Maine in spite of his being opposed by the State Democratic party.

In a letter to George Ashmun dated May 23, 1860, Abraham Lincoln formally accepted the party's nomination for the Presidency. His statement consisted of three short paragraphs of four sentences and was an affirmation of his adherence to "the declaration of principles and sentiments" contained within the platform. The physical absence of the candidate was as marked during the campaign as it had been during the convention. Unlike Douglas who took the stump in his own behalf, Lincoln remained behind in Illinois completely aside from the battle. He moved to the Governor's suite in the Capitol at Springfield where daily he received correspondence and met with visitors. Throughout the entire campaign, as agreed to by him and his managers, Lincoln was to make no public commitments. The responsiblity for delivering the vote was left to the state and county committees. The national committee headed by Edwin D. Morgan of New York raised money and coordinated the affairs of the state organizations. His connections with the banking interests were of great value in the campaign. Senator Preston King of New York, secretary of the national committee, handled the correspondence and distribution of campaign literature. Horace Greeley had a booklet printed containing selections from Lincoln's previous speeches. Henry J. Raymond, editor of *The New York Times*, supported Lincoln editorially, something he had failed to do earlier. From the top of the Republican organization down to the grass roots level, in spite of many mutual personal antagonisms fostered by the Convention, the workers did yeoman's service in behalf of the Republican cause. The best of the Republican orators went to work—Chase in Ohio, Wilmot in Pennsylvania, Evarts in New York, Andrew in Massachusetts, and Curtin and Lane in their respective states. But, pre-eminent and without peer in devotion and service to the Lincoln-Hamlin ticket was William Henry Seward of Auburn, New York, the man whose own political misfortune had led to Lincoln's earlier political success.

The four Presidential candidates represented every shade of opinion on the vital topic of slavery. Lincoln and Breckinridge were at opposite ends of the spectrum. The former favored preventing its expansion by law, whereas the latter demanded legal sanction for its extension. Douglas, somewhere in the middle, stood on his principle of squatter sovereignty. Bell ducked the issue completely and ran on a platform stressing the importance of saving the Union. Notwithstanding the fact that everyone knew that slavery was the only real issue that distinguished among the candidates, the campaign was relatively free of allusion to that subject. The question of the status of the black man, the topic that had divided churches, political organizations and, indeed, the country, was hardly mentioned by Republican campaigners, their strategy being to concentrate on local issues and Administration corruption. They reasoned that a strong Republican anti-slavery campaign would only serve to reunite the already fragmented Democratic party. The Republican party needed success and that success could best be realized by an adjustment of the Party platform and principles to a given local situation. Therefore, in Pennsylvania and Indiana it was the tariff question that worked in favor of the Republicans. In the northwest it was the issue of free land. Buchanan's veto of the Homestead Bill in June had played into Republican hands and aided Lincoln in Iowa, Wisconsin, and Illinois. The abolitionists helped Lincoln by denouncing him as a hypocrite.

The Democratic campaign run by Breckinridge attempted to put fear into the voters by claiming that if Lincoln were elected the South would secede. This time this sort of approach had no effect upon the northern voters but was readily acceded to in the South and among the conservative commercial interests of the East who refused to contribute to the Republican cause. Fearful that secession would mean the loss of 200 million dollars owed them by southern debtors, the northern businessmen contributed handsomely to the anti-Lincoln fusion ticket.

The fusion ticket was brought about out of desperation to stop Lincoln and the Republican party. Led by Curtin in Pennsylvania and Lane in Indiana, the Republicans had just carried the October election by 32,000 and 10,000 votes, respectively. This alarmed Lincoln's three opponents. As a last ditch effort, the Douglas Democrats, the Breckenridge Democrats, and the Constitutional Unionists formed a fusion ticket of Presidential electors in the states of New Jersey, New York, Pennsylvania, Rhode Island, and Connecticut. Heavily financed by northern businessmen engaged in commerce with the South, the "fusionists" aimed to have the election thrown into the House where some sort of deal for the Presidency could be worked out among their representatives. But alas, these efforts were doomed to failure for lack of cooperation among the principals. The personal antagonism between Douglas and Breckinridge was too great to overcome. Only in New Jersey did the fusionists pick up any electors. There they received three of the seven. Lincoln picked up the other four.

The national election was held on November 6, 1860. Abraham Lincoln, the railsplitter from Illinois and the Republican party's second Presidential nominee, carried the day. Out of 303 electoral votes, he received an absolute majority of 180. Breckinridge, Bell, and Douglas obtained 72, 39, and 12 votes, respectively. In the popular balloting the Republican nominee collected 1.9 million votes, Stephen Douglas 1.4 million, Breckinridge 849,781, and Bell, 588,879. With the exception of 3 from New Jersey that went to Douglas, Lincoln received every electoral vote from the eighteen free states. Breckinridge carried every slaveholding state except Missouri which was carried by Douglas. Bell garnered Virginia, Kentucky, and Tennessee.

Election day of 1860 saw the country divide into two parts over the question of slavery. The southern leadership in the past had been determined to rule the Union or destroy it. Now only one choice remained. Secession! To effect their withdrawal from the Union the Convention of South Carolina met on December 20, 1860 in the great hall of the South Carolina Institute in Charleston. Attended by 170 of its members, the Governor and the Legislature, the Ordinance of Secession was adopted:

We the people of South Carolina, in Convention assembled, do declare and ordain, and it is hereby declared and ordained, that the ordinance adopted by us in convention on the 23rd of May, in the year of our Lord one thousand seven hundred and eighty eight, whereby the Constitution of the United States was ratified, and also all Acts and parts of Acts of the General Assembly of the State ratifying amendments of the said Constitution, are herby repealed, and the Union now subsisting between South Carolina and other States, under the name of the United States of America, is hereby dissolved.

Five other states—Georgia, Alabama, Mississippi, Louisiana, and Florida—followed suit and joined South Carolina in secession. On February 4, 1861, a convention of delegates from these six states met in Montgomery, Alabama. As a body, they adopted a provisional constitution for "The Confederate States of America" on February 8 and the following day Jefferson Davis of Mississippi and Alexander H. Stephens of Georgia were elected President and Vice-President. Texas ratified the action of the Convention on February 24, 1861. By June 24 of that year, Arkansas, Virginia, North Carolina, and Tennessee had joined the Confederacy. A permanent Confederate Constitution adopted March 11, 1861, took effect in 1862.

The secessionist movement was carried out by the political leadership of the South. At no time between the withdrawal of South Carolina and the entry of Tennessee into the Confederacy was an ordinance of secession ever presented to the people in any of the states. For had a referendum on the disunion been held, there is the distinct possibility that the people of the South would have voted against secession as they had done in the past election.[15]

On November 6, 1860, the people of the United States had elected the nation's first Republican President. To take up the duties of that office Abraham Lincoln left Springfield, Illinois, on Monday morning February 11, 1861. Calling upon the "assistance of that Divine Being" to aid in the task before him, he bade farewell to the place he had called home for over a quarter of a century. The trip, just under two weeks, took him through Indianapolis, Cincinnati, Columbus, Pittsburgh, Cleveland, Buffalo, Albany, New York City, Trenton, Philadelphia, and Harrisburg. Warned by his advisers of a plot to assassinate him as he passed through Baltimore, he returned to Philadelphia. There he left his entourage (which included his family and some political associates) and made the journey alone, accompanied by Allan Pinkerton and Ward Lamon. Arriving in Washington at six o'clock Saturday morning on February 23, he went to the Willard Hotel where he was joined that night by his family. In the presence of a strong military force commanded by General Winfield Scott, Abraham Lincoln was inaugurated as the sixteenth President of the United States on March 4, 1861. The following day the Senate confirmed his Cabinet nominations[16] and the first Republican Administration of the United States came into being.

The elected President was a man more radical but less disposed to precipitous action than was Charles Sumner, the man who might have been President. In his inaugural address, Lincoln attempted to reassure the South that there existed no cause for alarm on their part. He had "no purpose, directly or indirectly, to interfere with the institution of slavery in the states where it exists." This power had not been granted him. Although he considered secession illegal, his only purpose would be to execute the laws of the Union in all of the states as required by the Constitution and to "constitutionally defend and maintain" it. Neither bloodshed nor violence need be a condition of this authority. But if they were forced upon the national dominion, all of the power at its command would be used "to hold, occupy and possess the properties belonging to the Government."

Violence came on April 12, 1861, when General Beauregard under order of his Confederate superiors fired on the Union fort at Sumter, South Carolina. On April 14, Major Anderson of the United States Army evacuated the fort and boarded a government vessel outside the harbor. A divided nation was now at war with itself. At the outset the usual perfunctory reasons were seen to be the cause. But before the war ended, it would become obvious that constantly and at all times conjoined with every seeming explanation would be the issue of slavery—the status of the black man in America.

6

PACHYDERMS AND PERFORMANCE

The war that divided the Nation and consumed just under half a million lives[1] lasted four years. During this period the Union debt increased thirty-eightfold[2] and the value of Confederate currency decreased 99¾ per cent. Before the hostilities would cease, the black man, the pariah of American society, would become the symbol of the struggle—the apotheosis that consecrated the cause of Union and expunged the threat of foreign intervention. Under the leadership of Abraham Lincoln, the sixteenth President of the United States, the seeds of the American ethos would be implanted. The future of the Republican party, the two-party system and, indeed, the nation were all delicately balanced and inextricably tied to the unforeseen political anastomosis taking place between the black man and the major political parties. Therefore, having encountered the black man as a political astralyte in the preceding chapters, it is the purpose of this and the succeeding chapter to view the two major political parties in terms of their practices and performance relative to the black man as a viable political entity.

The black man as a viable political factor commences with the passage of the Thirteenth Amendment, The Reconstruction Acts, The Civil Rights Act, and the Fourteenth and Fifteenth Amendments to the United States Constitution. Prior to these events the voting power of a black electorate was nonexistent in spite of the fact that in several states (Maine, Massachusetts, New York, New Hampshire, Rhode Island, and Vermont) there existed no racial restriction placed upon suffrage.

Any understanding of the viability of the black man as a political factor must necessarily begin with the Emancipation Proclamation. For it was this document that first forced the white population of America to reconsider their view of the role of the black man in society. Prior to the issuance of this historic pronouncement on September 22, 1862, the Republican-controlled Congress, in keeping with its platform pledges of 1856 and 1860, enacted legislation outlawing slavery in all present and future territories of the United States. The second Confiscation Act signed by Lincoln in July of 1862 provided for the emancipation of all slaves belonging to rebels and abettors of treason. Abraham Lincoln, the first Republican President of the United States, was not an abolitionist in the usual sense of the word. Rather, like Jefferson, he viewed colonization either here or abroad as the ultimate solution to the question of slavery. However, forced by both foreign and domestic events, it became necessary for him to consider freeing all slaves.[3] From a domestic point of view, military emancipation and arming of the blacks would prove logistically beneficial to the Union forces. Internationally considered, emancipating the slaves and changing the cause of war from one of Union to the abolition of slavery would silence the British government and certain aristocratic elements within the society. By proclaiming to set the slaves free the pro-Confederate elements in Great Britain would be counter-balanced by the large middle class. In their opposition to slavery this group identified with the newly formulated policy of the Republican party whom they considered analogous to the Liberal elements in their own country. With the issuance of the Emancipation Proclamation to take effect January 1, 1863 (provided in the meantime the rebellious state had not laid down their arms and submitted to the authority of the National Government), the Confederate hope of formal recognition and aid from abroad vanished. In the absence of sufficient help from outside, the South would be sorely trounced in a war that lasted four years. Before the war would end, General Robert E. Lee, in a futile attempt to stave off inevitable defeat, would impress upon President Jefferson Davis the necessity of bringing slaves into the army to take up the Confederate cause. They were in return to be emancipated as a reward for their service.

The war ended April 9, 1865, when General Robert E. Lee, commander of the Confederate forces, surrendered his sword to General Ulysses S. Grant, the Union commander, at Appomatox, Virginia. At this point, the necessity of defining the role of the black man within the context of "freedom" became apparent. Since the Emancipation Proclamation would set free only the slaves held by those in rebellion, additional action on the part of the government would be required. This fact had earlier

PACHYDERMS AND PERFORMANCE

been acknowledged in the Republican party platform of 1864 which resolved:

> That as slavery was the cause, and now constitutes the strength of this rebellion, and as it must be, always and everywhere, hostile to the principle of republican government, justice and the national safety demand its utter and complete extirpation from the soil of the Republic . . . we are in favor of such amendments to the Constitution to be made by the people in conformity with its provisions, as shall terminate and forever prohibit the existence of slavery within the limits or the jurisdiction of the United States.

In the election of 1864 Lincoln was reelected President over his Democratic opponent, General George B. McClellan of the Union army. His lopsided victory saw his Democratic rival carry only three states—New Jersey, Delaware, and Kentucky. Lincoln received 212 electoral votes, McClellan 21. In terms of the popular vote, Lincoln won by a majority of 494,567 carrying 2.2 million at home and 116,887 in the field. Mc Clellan carried 1.8 million at home and 33,748 in the field. As a result of the election, the Republican strength in the House went from 106 to 143. The Democratic representation dropped from 77 to 41.

As was customary, Lincoln delivered his normal Presidential message to Congress. Speaking before the new House of Representatives, he urged the passage of the Thirteenth Amendment. Cognizant of the large Republican increase in the Congress, he urged the Democrats not to vote against the measure as they had brought about its defeat a few months earlier. Without the passage of the Amendment it would be legislatively impossible to maintain the validity of the Emancipation Proclamation when the war ended. But Lincoln was determined that the emancipated bondsmen, of whom 180,000 had served the cause of Union, would remain free. This fact he stated in unequivocal terms: "While I remain in my present position I shall not attempt to retract or modify the Emancipation Proclamation. Nor shall I return to slavery any person who is free by the terms of that Proclamation or any of the Acts of Congress. If the people should, by whatever mode or means, make it an Executive duty to re-enslave such persons, another, and not I, must be their instrument to perform it."

Responding in part to the President's wishes and to their platform promise of 1864, the Republican-dominated Congress enacted the Thirteenth Amendment to the United States Constitution. This Amendment adopted by Congress on January 31, 1865, outlawed slavery.

The action of the Republicans in adopting this Amendment is in marked contrast to their actions in 1861. At that time the leading Republican spokesmen were willing to make slavery perpetual in order to avoid war. In 1865, in order to end the war and make peace perpetual, slavery had to be abolished for all time. The ratification of the Thirteenth Amendment by two-thirds of the states removed the legal shackles that had bound the limbs of the black man since 1787.

With the adoption of the Thirteenth Amendment, the Reconstruction Period began. Divided into two phases: Presidential Reconstruction, lasting from the end of the war until 1867, and Congressional Reconstruction, lasting from 1867 until 1876, its purpose was to form new governments in the rebellious states and to afford to these governing bodies recognition and protection under the Federal Constitution. Just how this was to be accomplished became a matter of great controversy.

According to Thaddeus Stevens, a leader of the Radical Republicans who acknowledged the actuality of secession, the rebellious states were to be treated as conquered territory. In this respect, they were subject to the will of the conqueror. Therefore, if new states were to be set up where old states once existed, the entire process had to be carried out under the constitutional provision by which "new states may be admitted by Congress into this Union." Based upon Stevens' Theory of Reconstruction the Great Conflagration was not a Civil War but rather a War Between the States.

Representative Shellabarger of Ohio argued that legally speaking secession was a nullity. Neither the territory occupied by a state nor the inhabitants thereof could be taken from under control of the United States Government and the Federal Constitution. Yet, the rebellious state governments had caused them to forfeit their status as states and had placed the territory which they occupied and their inhabitants under direct jurisdiction of the Federal Government. This Federal control could only be removed when new states operating according to the United States Constitution were erected "through the cooperation of Congress with the loyal inhabitants of such territory."

The Plan of Reconstruction offered by Abraham Lincoln was basically a scheme for Executive Restoration. Since, in his view, states were actually administrative units of the national government, secession was impossible. A state could no more remove itself from the jurisdiction of the Federal Government than a county could secede from a state. What had taken place during the rebellion had been brought about by the actions of disloyal persons taking control of several state governments. Certain elements within the states had been disloyal, not the states themselves. They were impersonal entities. Therefore, when 10 per cent of

110

the loyal elements among the electorate, within a given state "lately in rebellion," had taken an oath of allegiance, they might proceed to form a new state government. The state government, if of a republican form, would receive recognition and protection under the Federal Constitution.

Sic semper tyrannis. With these words, an assassin ended the life of the sixteenth President of the United States. Lincoln's successor, Andrew Johnson, a southern Democrat who had sided with the Union, assumed the Office of President. Distrusted by northerners and despised in the South, his attempts to carry out Lincoln's Plan of Reconstruction ran headlong into conflict with Congress. Before the struggle for power would end, impeachment proceedings against the Chief Executive would be initiated by his Republican opponents in Congress. Johnson formally declared the Rebellion at an end on April 2, 1866. Every southern state possessed a legally sound constitution. In each of these states the black man was denied the right to vote and on this basis congressional representation was not extended. Angered by the Presidential Plan for Reconstruction which virtually saw the black man returned to slavery in eight of the eleven states,[4] Congress had already embarked upon its own plan. On February 20, 1866, the House adopted by a vote of 109 to 4 a resolution requiring that: "No senator or representative shall be admitted into either branch of Congress from any of said states until Congress shall have declared such state entitled to representation." This resolution passed the Senate on February 21, 28 votes to 18. The Republican-dominated Congress passed the Fourteenth Amendment to the United States Constitution on June 13, 1866. The first section of the Amendment extended the right of citizenship to the black man, whereas another portion delimited white congressional representation in situations where negro suffrage rights were denied. Connecticut was the first state to ratify the Amendment. Tennessee was the only rebellious state to do so. Accordingly, she was restored to her place in the Union and her representative admitted to Congress on July 28, 1866. In the other ten rebellious states the Amendment was rejected.

With the passage of the Fourteenth Amendment and the Civil Rights Act (passed on April 9, 1866, by both Houses of Congress but vetoed by President Johnson) the United States Congress set about the task of restoring rule to the ten dissenting states. This was accomplished via the Reconstruction Bill of Thaddeus Stevens passed March 2, 1867, which declared that "Since no legal State Government, or adequate protection for life or property now exist in the rebel states of Virginia, North Carolina, South Carolina, Georgia, Mississippi, Alabama, Louisiana, Florida, Texas and Arkansas . . . said rebel states shall be divided into military dis-

tricts and made subject to the military authority of the United States."
This measure adopted in the House 135 to 48 and in the Senate 38 to 10
was the first of the Congressional Reconstruction Acts and brought the
period of Presidential Reconstruction to an end. Growing out of this
struggle between the Executive and Legislature, Congress further limited
the authority of the President when it passed the Tenure-of-Office Bill.[5]
This Act was to figure prominently in the historical impeachment trial
of President Andrew Johnson.

On January 8, less than two months prior to its conclusion, the Republican-controlled Congress enacted the bill extending suffrage to the negro
in the District of Columbia. The act enfranchising the black man in the
territories declared: "There shall be no denial of the elective franchise
in any territories of the United States now or hereafter to be organized,
to any citizen thereof, on account of race, color, or previous condition
of servitude." Enacted on January 10, and like the previous measure, its
passage had to be secured over a Presidential veto. The thirty-ninth Congress adjourned at noon on March 4, 1867. The fortieth Congress which
speedily organized that same day was overwhelmingly Republican. As a
result of the election of 1866, they had obtained a three-to-one edge in
the House. Schuyler Colfax of Indiana was reelected House Speaker in a
Congress that was a virtual continuation of its predecessor. Having as its
main order of business the perfection of the Reconstruction Act of its
predecessor, the first session of the new Congress set about the task of
providing the practical detail essential to effective and impartial operation of the suffrage requirement. This was achieved through the two
Supplementary Reconstruction Acts passed on March 23, and on July 19,
1867. Within certain limits, these measures prescribed the make-up of the
electorate in the military districts and provided in language similar to that
of the Fourteenth Amendment that no person who had "engaged in insurrection or rebellion against the United States, or given aid or comfort
to the enemies thereof, is entitled to be registered to vote." The Acts
also provided that no one should be disqualified from voting on the basis
of race, since all males over twenty-one years of age meeting the above-
mentioned condition were eligible. Resulting from this formulation, it
has been estimated that 672,000 blacks were enfranchised compared with
a potential white electorate of 925,000. However, of this latter number
100,000 had been disenfranchised and another 200,000 were ineligible
to hold office.

With legislative sufficiency equal to the task at hand, the United States
Government undertook the task of restoring civilian rule to the rebel
states. Under the guidelines provided by the Reconstruction Acts, the

military governors were to conduct a registration of voters, thereby providing an electorate in each of their districts. In turn the electorate of these districts were to hold state conventions and adopt state constitutions. The constitutions, if acceptable to Congress, would qualify the state governments for readmission to the Union once they had accepted the Fourteenth Amendment.

During 1867 and 1868, the southern states met in Convention. In compliance with the Reconstruction Acts of the Republican-controlled Congress each state convention contained black representation (Table 2). The first of these was Alabama whose delegates assembled in Montgomery in November of 1867. For the next three years each of the southern states would hold conventions and seek admission to the Union. Arkansas was the first state to ratify the Fourteenth Amendment and comply with the provisions of the Reconstruction Acts. On a resolution of Thaddeus Stevens, offered before the House on May 7, 1868, she was admitted to the Union. The last to be admitted was Texas who entered on March 30, 1870.

The shortcoming of the Fourteenth Amendment in not making suffrage synonymous with citizenship was obviated, in the case of the black man, by the passage of the Fifteenth Amendment. This latter decree dealt directly with the question of racial discrimination at the ballot box by forbidding the denial of suffrage in any state to citizens on the basis of race, color, or previous condition of servitude. Not unlike the Fourteenth Amendment which for the first time defined citizenship on a national basis, the Fifteenth Amendment contained far-reaching constitutional implications. In securing suffrage for the negro the Republican party, led by its perennial stalwarts such as Sumner and Seward, placed a construction upon the United States Constitution that was decidedly in the direction away from the states' right document that it had been for so many years.

General Ulysses S. Grant received the Republican nomination for President in the Chicago Convention of 1868. His Vice-Presidential running mate chosen on the fifth ballot was Schuyler Colfax of Indiana. The platform adopted by the Convention congratulated the country on the "assured success of the reconstruction policy of Congress" and declared that body to be "in sympathy with all oppressed people struggling for their rights." Grant's opposition on the Democratic ticket consisted of Horatio Seymour of New York and Francis P. Blair Jr., of Missouri for the Presidential and Vice-Presidential slots, respectively.

When the results of that election of November 3 were in the Republicans would be victorious. Grant received 3 million votes to 2.7 million for Seymour, a difference of over 300,000. In the electoral college the Republican margin was much greater, Grant being the victor by a vote of 214 to 80. The importance of the black vote, some 700,000, to the Republican party was obvious. Grant's ability to carry five of the seven southern states recently admitted to the Union[6] is directly attributable to the black vote which derived, at that period, from the negroes' identification with the G.O.P. It was with this recognition of the importance of the negro vote that the Republican-controlled fortieth Congress passed the Fifteenth Amendment.

With the ratification of the Fifteenth Amendment on March 30, 1870, the black man was constitutionally accorded full voting rights in all of the states.[7] And when he went to the polls that year he elected members of his own race to represent him in local, statewide, and national offices. For the first time in the nation's history black men were chosen as members of the national legislature: Hiram R. Revel was chosen Senator from Mississippi and Joseph H. Rainey and Jefferson F. Long of South Carolina and Georgia, respectively,were elected to the House. The nation's first black electorate was undeniably Republican and the party affiliation of the men that it sent to Washington would reflect that political predilection. Between 1870 and 1901 every black congressional member would belong to the Republican party (Table 3). However, this expression of black political power, in terms of the ability to send representatives to Congress, was minuscule when compared with its effect at the statewide level.

In 1866 the voters of the Boston area elected Charles L. Mitchell and Edwin G. Walker to the State House of Representatives. History records this as the first instance in which blacks were elected to statewide office. This precedent-setting example was followed by similar action in Illinois in 1876 and in Ohio in 1881. In the former instance, J.W.E. Thomas was elected to the State House of Representatives. Five years later John P. Greene received a similar mandate from the voters of Ohio. After serving two terms in that state's Lower House, he went on to become the first negro north of the Mason–Dixon Line to be elected to a state Senate. Both men were Republicans. The importance of these actions, based on their historical significance, is without parallel. What's more, they give primary evidence, since the black vote in the state was politically insignificant (less than 1,000 in Boston), that white people would elect black officials to represent them. But in 1868 the situation differed markedly. Through the aegis of their newly acquired political franchise, when blacks went to the polls to cast their ballots in state elections they elected members of their own race to represent them. The unprecedented proliferation of black elected officials at the state level continued for several years and has not been duplicated since. Although information on biographies of the men involved and documents from that period are difficult to come by, Table 4 in the Appendix gives clear indication of the presence of black representatives in the state legislative assemblies of the nation. And not unlike the men sent to Congress, the black representatives at the statewide level were categorically Republican. The fact that the black vote formed a natural constituency for the G.O.P. is amply evidenced by the Republican party affiliation of the ninety-two black legislators in South Carolina for the year 1868.

At the Executive level black Republicans in the state occupied several important offices. Alonzo Ransier served as Lieutenant Governor between 1870 and 1872. He was succeeded in that position by Richard H. Gleaves who remained in that post until 1876. Francis L. Cardozo was Secretary of State and occupied that office for four years between 1868 and 1872. Following that he became State Treasurer for four years. At his departure to fill that position in 1876 the Secretary of State's Office was taken over by Henry E. Hayne who remained there until 1876. Henry W. Purvis became Adjutant General in 1872. At the Judicial level J.J. Wright was an Associate Justice of the State Supreme Court for seven years beginning in 1870. In Louisiana P.B.S. Pinchback held a number of elective offices. He served as Lieutenant Governor and Acting Governor of the state in addition to being its Senator-elect.[8]

Dozens of black men of the caliber of those referred to in the preceding paragraphs served with greater or lesser distinction in the governments of the southern states. In addition to their roles as legislators, judges, and administrators they served as Republican party officials. And it was in the last role that they had their greatest effect upon the national as well as the statewide and local political scene. Through their influence in and identification with the Republican party the newly enfranchised black electorate was swept en masse into the party of Lincoln. The black man, as a viable political factor, appeared on the scene to the benefit of the Republican party and drastically altered the political complexion of the South for some time to come.

Once the Fourteenth Amendment had been ratified, the black man—at that time the natural constituency of the G.O.P.—became the *sine qua non* of the Republican party in the South. What was true in the case of South Carolina was generally applicable throughout the South. The black man voted the straight Republican ticket. In so doing, he elected both black and white officials to represent him. On the other hand, the white electorate voted for Democrats. Any office-holders elected on that party's

115

ticket would have to be white. It was this sort of policy practiced by the white electorate that would eventually bring to an end the original era of black political power.

George H. White, Congressman from North Carolina, was the last black Republican elected to national office until 1929. Elected in 1897, he served a total of four years as member of the 55th and 56th Congress. At the state level there were black Republican members of the North Carolina Legislature (2) until 1899, and of the Virginia Legislature (4) until 1891. Throughout the South disenfranchising amendments were adopted by the State Legislatures in the following order: Mississippi, 1890; South Carolina, 1895; Louisiana, 1898; North Carolina, 1900; Alabama, 1901; Virginia, 1901; Georgia, 1908; and Oklahoma, 1910. By the end of the first decade of the twentieth century the 7.9 million blacks living in the South—90 per cent of the race—had been reduced to political peonage. With the exception of the Illinois State Legislature where an unbroken line of succession existed beginning in 1882, black representation at the national and state levels was taken into eclipse. In Illinois, absolute black Republican control of statewide elective office lasted until 1937 when the first black Democrat was elected. Chicago became the hub and focus of identity for future black urban political movements north of the Mason—Dixon Line. Following the example in Illinois, blacks were elected to state legislatures in other parts of the country. Between 1925 and 1929 blacks were elected members of the state legislatures in the following states: California (F. M. Roberts, Senate); Kansas (W. M. Blount, House); Missouri (G. M. Allen, J. A. Davis, L. A. Knox, W. M. Moore, all to House); New Jersey (J. L. Baxter and F. S. Hargrave, both to House); Nebraska (T. L. Barnett, A. A. McMillan, and J. A. Singleton, all to House); New York (L. Perkins and F. E. Rivers, both to House); Ohio (E. W. P. Curry and P. B. Jackson, both to House); Pennsylvania (W. H. Fuller, House); West Virginia (H. J. Capehart, E. H. Harper, and T. E. Hill, all to House).

In 1929 Oscar S. De Priest, a Republican, became the first black elected to Congress in the twentieth century. Elected out of Chicago, he served for six years. Currently, there are eight black Republican state representatives and no black Republican members of Congress. Edward Brooke, Republican of Massachusetts, is the only black senator.

The holding of elective office by blacks represents but one aspect of involvement in the affairs of the republic based upon the role of the former bondsmen as a viable political entity. The American political process as exemplified by the political party system requires a body of participants to elect those candidates who will seek office in areas unbounded

PACHYDERMS AND PERFORMANCE

by district jurisdictional limits. At the national level this group of people so convened is called the National Party Convention and dates back to Andrew Jackson's first term as President. Since its inception it has met once every four years to formulate and adopt a set of principles, called a platform, and to choose candidates to run for nationwide office. By virtue of its natural distinction it is the supreme governing body of the party. Blacks have been members of the Republican National Convention, the highest of party councils, since 1868.

From its beginning the Republican party emphasized the principles of universal civil and political rights for all oppressed people. The recently emancipated bondsmen were extended the hand of friendship and welcomed into the fold. During the 1868 party deliberations in Chicago leading to the nomination of Ulysses S. Grant, James Harris of North Carolina and P.B.S. Pinchback were among the black delegates in attendance. A greater number of black delegates were present in the convention of 1872 that renominated Grant for the Presidency. Between 1872 and 1900 blacks were extremely active at the Republican National Convention. During the intervening years a partial list of those delegates taking part in the quadrennial events reads like a *Who's Who* of America's first black political movers. The following is a registry of names of prominent black Republicans who participated in the National Conventions between 1872 and 1900: James T. Rapier and Benjamin P. Turner (Alabama); William H. Grey and M.W. Gibbs (Arkansas); Josiah T. Walls, William H. Gleason, and John Long (Florida); Judson Lyons (Georgia); Walter Cohen and S.W. Green (Louisiana); B.K. Bruce and John R. Lynch (Mississippi); John C. Dancy, H.P. Cheatham, James E. O'Hara, and George C. Scurlock (North Carolina); E.H. Deas, A.J. Ransier, Robert Small, and C.M. Wilder (South Carolina); J.C. Napier (Tennessee), N.W. Cuney (Texas); John M. Langston (Virginia); C.H. Payne (West Virginia).

The majority of black delegates at the Republican National Conventions were always from the South. Beginning in 1916 a trickle of northern representatives began to appear. That year W.F. Cozart of Atlantic City was a delegate from New Jersey. He was succeeded in 1924 by Dr. George E. Cannon of Jersey City who was in turn replaced in 1928 by Dr. Walter A. Alexander of Orange. In 1920, Oscar De Priest represented the first district of Illinois. This district sent Louis B. Anderson to the Convention in 1924 with De Priest and Robert Jackson as alternates. In 1928 De Priest again became a delegate as did Dan Jackson. That same year Leroy N. Bundy, popular Cleveland Alderman from Ohio's twenty-first district, came as a delegate from the Buckeye State. Having reached a low point of twenty-nine in 1920, the number of black delegates increased to thirty-nine in 1924 and to forty-nine in 1928. One alternate delegate was in attendance in 1924. In 1928 there were fifty-five black alternates. At the twenty-first Republican Convention held in Philadelphia beginning June 24, 1940, eighty-five black delegates and alternates registered. Both black National Committee people, Perry Howard and Mrs. Mary C. Booze, were from the state of Mississippi. Four years later at the Chicago Convention eighteen black delegates from eighteen states and the District of Columbia were present, accompanied by twenty-seven alternates. Robert R. Church of Memphis was a delegate to the National Convention from 1912 to 1924.

Beginning in 1868 blacks, mainly from the South, have been present as delegates at the National Convention of the Republican party. Since 1916 they have represented districts in northern states with large black populations. Therefore, most of them came as district representatives and not as at-large delegates. At the Convention of 1952, black delegates held roughly 2.6 per cent of the voting strength. There were thirty-two black delegates and fifty black alternates in attendance. The delegations from the South—Arkansas, Georgia, Louisiana, Mississippi, Oklahoma, and Tennessee—included eleven delegates and thirteen alternates; black representation was also present from the North. At least thirteen non-southern states selected a minimum of one black delegate each. In the 1972 Republican National Convention approximately 5 per cent of the delegates in attendance were black.

Organizational-wise, the burden of responsibility for carrying out the work of the Convention is done by four committees. They are the committee on: 1) Permanent Organization; 2) Credentials; 3) Rules and Order of Business; and 4) Resolutions. In addition to these bodies which function at the quadrennial gathering there is the Republican National Committee. Like the others, it is chosen at the Convention. However, unlike the others, it remains in existence until the next Convention. It functions as the executor of the Convention's will. It is therefore responsible for conducting the campaign of the Presidential and Vice-Presidential nominees. Its additional responsibilities include keeping the party's records, arranging the inaugural ceremonies, issuing calls and making arrangements for facilities in the next convention, determining contests, preparing temporary rolls and naming temporary officers such as Chairman Pro Tempore.

During the heyday of black Republicanism powerful negro leaders within the party played important roles at the National Convention and also as members of the National Committee. As to the latter office blacks have been chosen by their state delegations and subsequently ratified in Convention as members of the National Committee since 1872. That year William A. Gleason of Florida was a member. In subsequent years the following individuals were listed as members of the Republican National Committee: P.B.S. Pinchback and Jeremiah Haralson, 1876; J.H. Devaux and J.R. Lynch, 1880; Perry Carson, 1884; P.B.S. Pinchback and Perry Carson, 1888; N.W. Cuney, James Hill, J. Long, and Perry Carson, 1892; J.G. Long, James Hill, and Judson Lyons, 1896; Judson Lyons, 1900 and 1904. There were no negro members between 1912 and 1920. In 1924 two black women, Mrs. E.P. Booze of Mississippi and Mrs. George N. Williams of Georgia, were appointed to the committee. They were reappointed at the 1928 Convention. In the 1928 Convention another black delegate from Mississippi was appointed to the Committee.

At the National Convention, blacks carried out their responsibilities as members of committees. For example, John R. Lynch and Robert B. Elliott were members of the Resolutions Committee in 1872 and J.G. Long served on the Rules Committee in 1876. The highest position held by any negro to date in any of the parties was that attained by John R. Lynch in 1884. That year he served as Chairman Pro Tempore of the Chicago Convention. At the previous Convention he had been nominated for the office of Vice-President. Had he and his supporters, both North and South, not yielded in the interest of party unity, there is the distinct possibility that the Senator from Mississippi might have been the Vice-Presidential running mate of James A. Garfield.

The selection of Lynch as Temporary Chairman in the Convention of 1884 was neither a token nor a gratuitous appointment on the part of the Republican Convention. Actually there was a floor fight for the position. In the contest John R. Lynch was pitted against Powell Clayton, a white Republican from Arkansas. Lynch's main backers were Henry Cabot Lodge and Theodore Roosevelt. When the balloting was completed Lynch had won the Temporary Chairmanship by a vote of 431 against 387 for Clayton. The keynote address at the Convention that nominated James G. Blaine for the Presidency was also delivered by Lynch who became the first black man ever to deliver the address before either party. The feat was never again repeated until 1968 when Edward Brooke fulfilled the same role in the Republican Convention that nominated Richard M. Nixon for President. The fight for the Chairmanship was indicative of the black politicians' lot within the American party system.

As we shall see, America's first black politicians were not only subject to the resentment from those in the opposite party, they also lacked any special immunity to attack from within their party. The object of their assailants within the party was to take control of the political machine put together by these political pioneers and to replace the latter as members of the Republican councils. Most often the challenges would end up before the National Convention in a struggle for delegate recognition. The significance of these intra-party political battles lay in their interest as examples of the ability of the early black political leaders to hold their own in the midst of growing opposition to black leadership. The willingness to engage in battle is of itself apt testimony to the courage and self-confidence of the leadership of the recently manumitted bondsmen. Certainly, their victorious results in most of the struggles are witness to their skill and dexterity as political movers.

Without the presence of the black man there would have been no Republican party in the form that it began, developed, and evolved. Therefore, it is not surprising that the party platform, that group of statements issued once every four years by the National Convention, has from the beginning continuously contained some sort of resolution relating directly to the status of the black man (Table 5).

As conspicuous as were blacks in their roles as elected officials since 1866, they were equally as visible performing the duties required of appointed positions. The highest level appointments, those of federal stature, were usually bestowed upon black Republicans of statewide and national reputation. Ebenezer D. Basset, the first recipient of a prestige appointment, was named Minister Resident and Consul General to the Negro Republic of Haiti in 1869 by President Grant. At that time the position carried a salary of 7,500 dollars.[9] Following Basset, the office was held in succession by a series of prominent black Republicans. John Mercer Langston, who was appointed in 1877 by President Rutherford B. Hayes, was paid only 5,000 dollars per year, the reduction in salary being brought about by the Chairman of the Appropriations Committee in the Democratic-controlled House. Langston served until 1885 at which time he returned to the United States and presented the United States Court of Claims a demand for 7,700 dollars. His claim, sustained by that court, was resustained over appeal by his opponents in the Supreme Court of the United States. The Democratic Administration of Grover Cleveland appointed a white man to head the Haitian Ministry and it was not until 1889 when another black was named to that post by Republican President Benjamin Harrison. Chosen at that time was Frederick Douglass, a black Republican of international reputation. He served for a short time and was replaced by Henry M. Smythe, a Virginian. President McKinley picked William F. Powell as his Envoy Extraordinary and Minister Plenipotentiary to the island republic. The last black official to hold the post prior to the American occupation of the island in 1915 was Henry W. Furniss of Indiana. He was appointed by President Theodore Roosevelt at an annual salary of 10,000 dollars. During the early days of its existence the Republican party maintained a straightforward policy regarding Federal patronage and the negro. Whenever the party came into power at the national level "the spoils of the enemy" were shared with its black constituency. Beginning with President Grant and his appointment of Basset through to President Roosevelt and his retaining of Booker T. Washington as personal adviser, black Republicans received eminent Federal appointments under Republican Presidents. At various times the following blacks held high-level Federal positions: Postmasters at Charleston, Columbia, Chester, Florence, Beaufort, and Barnwell—Dr. B.A. Bosemon, Charles M. Wilder, John Lee, Rev. J.E. Wilson, S.J. Bampfield, and Fred Nix Jr., respectively; Registrars of the Treasury—W.T. Vernon and J.C. Napier; Recorder of Deeds for the District of Columbia—Frederick Douglass and Henry L. Judson; Assistant Attorney General of the United States—William H. Lewis; Auditor for the Navy Department—Ralph W. Tyler; Collector of Customs for the District of Columbia—Winfield McKinley; Collector of Internal Revenue, New York City—Charles W. Anderson; Special Assistant, United States District Attorney at Chicago—S.L. Williams; Collector of the Port at New Orleans—Walter Cohen; Postmaster at Savannah, Georgia—Judson Lyons. This list is by no means complete, however it clearly indicates the nature and responsibility of Federal posts held by negroes through the Roosevelt Administration. It should also be recognized that each of the appointments mentioned above was made by a Republican President and terminated when a Democrat came to power.

As did Presidents Coolidge and Hoover in later days, three earlier Republican Chief Executives favored Federal aid for the education of blacks. Rutherford B. Hayes was of the opinion that the state governments of the South should make permanent provisions to liberally support free education for its black citizens. To insure the attainment of that goal, he felt that the efforts of the South should be augmented by Federal support. In furtherance of this position, his Republican chance-successor, Chester A. Arthur, aware of the immense responsibilities placed upon the black man by virtue of his geography and previous condition, recommended that "all that can be done by local legislation and private generosity should be supplemented by such aid as can be constitutionally afforded by the National Government." Benjamin F. Harrison, more outspoken in this respect than either Garfield or Arthur, demanded that the remedy be co-extensive with the ill. Since centuries of slavery were responsible for the negroes' present lot the education required to rectify the situation should be of sufficient intensity and duration based on "the need that suggested it." In keeping with his philosophy, he was prepared to aid the South in its responsibility to educate the negro to the extent that the former could ultimately be expected to assume on its own. The responsibility for educating former slaves was placed at the doorstep of the former slave-master.

Expecting the former slave-master to be concerned with the educational uplift of the former slave was a bit much in most circumstances. For example, in 1928 there were no negroes in the state of Mississippi attending a public institution of four-year college grade. Based on the black-white population figures for the state, whites received 234,649 federal education dollars. Based on these percentages, blacks should have received 258,035 dollars since there were more blacks in the state. Instead blacks received only 39,592 dollars—the amount of money appropriated by Mississippi from federal and state resources for black education. Seventeen other southern states had no negroes registered in a public institution of four-year college grade. The facts formed the basis for two Presidents—Coolidge and Hoover—favoring increased federal funds for Howard University.

In order to receive a college education, 259 black students from eleven of those states traveled to the nation's capital where they attended Howard University. Another 316 of the students from eleven of those states were enrolled in medical courses outside of their home states since none of the states except West Virginia made provisions for that course of study. The white schools in the seventeen states received a total of 5.3 million federal education dollars compared to a paltry 282,275 dollars shared by the black schools (junior college level) which in reality should have received 2.1 million dollars. From both federal and state sources whites in the seventeen states received 31.7 million dollars compared to 1.9 million for blacks. The Republican Administrations of Coolidge and Hoover attempted to correct the educational dollar inequity by calling for increased congressional appropriations for Howard University, a federal institution. In spite of Democratic opposition, Hoover was able to get the 1929 appropriation of 650,000 dollars through Congress. In 1930 under the Hoover Administration 1.2 million dollars was set aside by Congress for the operation of the school.

The policy of early Republican Presidents regarding appointments of blacks to high positions varied. It can be stated that none of the Chief Executives opposed prestige appointments for blacks. However, the number and responsibility of appointments for blacks differed depending mainly upon the political and social climate of the time. Grant, Garfield,

PACHYDERMS AND PERFORMANCE

Hayes, Harrison, and McKinley appointed many negroes to high governmental positions. A survey conducted by Frederick Douglass in 1872 reported that negroes were to be found in all governmental departments in goodly numbers. In the *Republican Campaign Text Book* of 1900, a partial list of fifty-eight federal appointments given to blacks was published. Included in the list were eleven major foreign service appointments to places such as Brazil, France, Santo Domingo, Russia, and Paraguay, President McKinley issued out seventy federal appointments to black Republicans and Theodore Roosevelt, according to C.F. Adams, Assistant Registrar of the Treasury, passed out more patronage to blacks than any preceding Administration. President Roosevelt's policy toward appointing blacks to federal positions was based solely on the qualifications of the individual to do the job and upon his power as Chief Executive to bestow the appointment. This course of action occasionally caused difficulty for the Administration. Two cases that come to mind immediately involved the appointment of Dr. W.D. Crum as Collector of the Port of Charleston and the resignation of Mrs. Minnie Cox, the black postmaster at Indianola, Mississippi. Both individuals were eminently qualified and the President would acquiesce in neither instance. In the latter case, Mrs. Cox sent a letter of resignation to the President following threats on her life by the whites who did not wish to see a negro in that position. Rather than accept her resignation and yield to the whites of the town, President Roosevelt closed the post office facility and ordered all mail sent to the post office in Greenville, twenty-five miles away. A few days after having taken this action he sent the name of W.D. Crum, a negro physician, to the Senate for confirmation as Collector of the Port of Charleston. Immediately, disqualifying charges were lodged against Crum which ultimately proved to be false. When these could not stand up, opponents presented charges based "on account of color" of the appointee. The President maintained his firm position regarding the appointment of officials to federal posts and in the end Dr. Crum was confirmed. In a statement clarifying his position on the matter of black appointments he declared:

I do not intend to appoint any unfit man to office. So far as I legitimately can I shall always endeavor to pay regard to the wishes and feelings of the people of each locality, but I cannot consent to take the position that the door of hope—the door of opportunity—is shut upon any man, no matter how worthy, purely upon the grounds of race or color. Such an attitude would, according to my convictions, be fundamentally wrong.

Taft's policy on appointment of black officials differed markedly from that of Roosevelt and can best be appreciated in the former's own words. In an effort to placate the Democratic party of the South as to the appointment of black officials he declared:

What I have done in this line of recognition of the democracy of the South, has been without sacrifice of any interests of my own party. . . . I have appointed many Negroes to office and have given some of them like Lewis, Johnson and McKinley, offices of essential dignity at Washington. What I have not done is to force them upon unwilling communities in the South itself.

Taft during his tenure in the White House appointed nineteen negroes to prominent positions. Included in this list was William H. Lewis of Massachusetts whom he appointed as Assistant Attorney General of the United States and Winfield McKinley as Collector of Customs of the District of Columbia.

During his Presidency Warren G. Harding's major appointment of a black to office was Perry Howard of Mississippi as an Assistant District Attorney. In this position, Howard was responsible for all railroad suits brought against the government. The twenty-ninth President viewed the South in much the same fashion as did his predecessor, Woodrow Wilson; in other words he felt that white leadership was best for the South.

Coolidge, in addition to his interest in Howard University, appointed Walter Cohen to the position of Comptroller of Customs at New Orleans. He named a black member to the Board of Mediation and Conciliation and also appointed several high-level Assistants in the following Agencies: the Veterans' Bureau, the Alaskan Railway Engineering Commission, and the Railway Mail Service. This last position was, at that time, the highest ever held by a black man in the Post Office Department. Coolidge appointed a black staff to the large Veterans' Administration Hospital in Tuskegee, Alabama, and named a Commission of five to recommend economic, political, and social changes necessary to the well-being and advancement of the people of the Virgin Islands.

The Hoover Administration appointed W.C. Hueston of Gary to the position of Assistant Solicitor at a salary of 7,500 dollars and named Charles Johnson liaison with the League of Nations and the Liberian Government. He also raised the salary of the Minister to Liberia from five to ten thousand dollars.

Not all positions held by blacks were high paying jobs with fancy-sounding titles. Most were at the lower end of the economic ladder. Between 1910 and 1928 the number of black federal employees increased from 22,540 to 52,882. During that same period the salaries rose from 12.5

million to 64.5 million dollars. The largest number, 25,390, were employed in the Post Office; the smallest number, 143, were in the General. Accounting Office. The average salary was 1,243 dollars a year. As of June 30, 1928, negroes (as 9.9 per cent of the population) held 9.1 per cent of the positions in the Federal Executive Civil Service.

On January 21, 1953, Dwight D. Eisenhower was sworn in as the thirty-second President of the United States. A period of twenty years had elapsed since the last Republican Chief Executive had been in office. Under Eisenhower a large number of blacks were appointed to top jobs in the Administration. Table 6 is a list of Eisenhower's major black appointees. In addition to these ranking appointments over 6,000 negro employees were added in jobs ranging from laborers to clerks in various departments of the Federal Government.

At the outset the Eisenhower Administration took the position that it would do all within its power to eradicate second-class citizenship for blacks. Where possible the Executive Order would be used to accomplish that goal. What could not be realized in that manner would be attempted through legislation. Via Executive fiat, he created a New Government Contract Committee under the Chairmanship of Vice-President Richard Nixon and established the President's Committee on Government Employment Policy. On January 12, 1954, he ordered the Secretary of Defense to end segregation in military post schools by September 1, 1955.

Through the efforts of the Nixon-headed Committee on Government Contracts the packing house industry was induced to begin employing blacks in white collar positions for the first time and public utility companies were made to change discriminatory personnel policies. White-collar and clerical jobs were opened up in the Federal Reserve System. In the oil industry, jobs were opened up on a competitive basis and separate contracts, one for blacks and one for whites, were eliminated. This policy led to the equalization of wages in the industry since jobs would now be competed for on the basis of qualifications and not race. The executives in the aircraft industries that carried United States mail were made to realize that it was in everyone's best interest to comply with President Eisenhower's non-discrimination policy. Their compliance led to jobs for blacks as mechanics, clerks, typists, etc. in the aircraft industry.

The segregation practices of Washington, D.C., the nation's capital, had always been a thorn in the side of any Administration. Prior to Eisenhower's first term of office no Administration had moved in a concerted manner to end the Jim Crow practices of the city. Nevertheless, the Administration kept its campaign pledge to take "appropriate action to end segregation in the District of Columbia." For the first time in history the doors of all hotels, theaters, and amusement centers were flung open to all races. The Nixon Committee broke down the race barriers in the Capital Transit Company which began employing blacks as bus and trolley operators. The Chesapeake and Potomac Telephone Company was persuaded to integrate its clerical and switchboard help. Schools were integrated with minimum upheaval. And finally, under the Eisenhower Administration, the color barrier in White House social affairs was removed. President and Mrs. Eisenhower began inviting blacks to all types of social events, such as lawn parties, state dinners, and stag dinners given by the occupants of 1600 Pennsylvania Avenue.

When the Eisenhower Administration took office in 1953, over half of the black units in the Armed Forces were still segregated. As of October 1956, all units were totally integrated. Under his Executive Order all schools[10] located on military installations had been integrated prior to the Supreme Court decision of May 17, 1954. Segregation ended in all veterans' hospitals throughout the South. Separate cafeterias, drinking fountains, restaurants, and recreational facilities that existed on naval installations when Eisenhower took office in 1953 were eliminated during his first term as President.

What the Republican Administration under Dwight Eisenhower could not accomplish through Executive Order, it attempted through legislation. The civil rights advocacy of the Eisenhower Administration led to the enactment of the first laws in that area since Reconstruction. The Civil Rights Act of 1957 established the Commission on Civil Rights and provided for the Civil Rights Division in the Justice Department under an Assistant Attorney General. It also placed new authority in the hands of the Attorney General by allowing him to institute voting rights suits to secure injunctive relief. Through the Office of the Attorney General the Federal Government was now empowered to enter into certain types of cases to protect the voting rights of individuals.

Under the Civil Rights Act of 1960 the Attorney General was given additional powers for protecting voting rights of citizens. He was now empowered to seek a Federal Court decision regarding patterns and practices of voter discrimination as evidenced by individual court cases. This Act also permitted the federal courts to appoint referees to help them determine voter qualification.

On November 5, 1968, the people of the United States elected Richard Milhous Nixon to the Presidency. The black voter overwhelmingly opposed his candidacy—88 per cent voted against him. Only 12 per cent voted in his favor. No Republican President in history had ever received such a small portion of the black vote. Despite the almost complete lack of confidence in the Republican party and its national standard-bearer shown by the black voters, the new President remained apparently resolute in his determination to utter no high-sounding empty phrases designed to gain black voter approval. Rather, he preferred that both history and black Americans should judge him by his deeds. This he made "perfectly clear" on February 2, 1970 when he declared: "I know all the words. I know all the gimmicks and the phrases that would win the applause of Black audiences and professional civil rights leaders. I am not going to use them. I am interested in deeds."

Behind such a forthright and unequivocal declaration of intent the question automatically becomes one of performance. How did Nixon perform vis-à-vis black America during his tenure of office? What were the "deeds" of his Administration that he so emphatically alluded to early in 1970? The answer to this question can best be found by looking at some of the accomplishments of the Administration in areas that pertain to black development—Federal appointments, employment, housing, education, and business aid.

In the area of appointments, Nixon named sixteen blacks to Federal Judgeships and to the United States Court of Military Appeal—the Supreme Court of the Military. Seven black officers attained general or flag officer rank during his Administration. The first black naval officer to be promoted to Admiral received that rank under Nixon. Twice as many black women were appointed to government positions under Nixon as under either of his two predecessors. Seven black ambassadors and a black delegate to the United Nations General Assembly were named. In thirty-eight months he placed eighty-eight blacks on Federal advisory boards and commissions, including the first black to ever serve on the Federal Communications Commission. Table 7 is a list of the major black appointments made under the Nixon Administration. In addition to these, the following blacks served on the White House Staff: Lieutenant Colonel Vernon Coffey, Army Aide to the President; Sally Anne Payton, Staff Assistant to the President; Ray Gerald, Assistant to the Chairman, Council of Economic Advisers; Robert J. Brown, Special Assistant to the President; Stanley S. Scott, Assistant to the Director of Communications for the Executive Branch; William Blair, Staff Assistant; and Frank Decosta, Deputy Chief of Staff and Counselor to the Vice-President.

The employment programs sponsored by the Nixon Administration were designed to increase the number of blacks on payrolls. Between 1969 and 1970, under the President's Philadelphia Plan, the total number of working hours by minorities in federal projects increased from 2 to 13

127

per cent. This project, devised to increase the opportunities for blacks in the construction industry and to prohibit discrimination, includes twenty-five "city-wide" plans in which 28,000 more blacks were hired. The Labor Department Manpower Programs were increased 40 per cent between 1970 and 1971—from 700,000 to over 1 million. Youth training and summer jobs were augmented. Despite an overall decrease in federal employment from November 1969 to May 1971, minority hiring increased to 19.5 per cent of the federal civilian work force. Employment of blacks in the 16,000 to 24,000 dollar level rose 21.4 per cent. For the 22,000 to 33,000 dollar bracket, the increase was 33.6 per cent. In the supergrade, i.e., positions paying over 28,000 dollars a year, the increase was 55.7 per cent. The number of blacks placed in policy-making positions (supergrade and above) by Nixon was eighty-seven.

To enforce non-discrimination on jobs held by Federal Contractors is the task of the Equal Employment Opportunity Commission. The budget of that office was increased fivefold and between 1969 and 1973, the annual funding jumped from 2.2 to 18.9 million dollars. This was expected to produce an additional 300,000 jobs in 1973. Along these same lines the federal budget for civil rights activities went from 0.9 billion dollars in 1969 to 2.6 billion for 1973. Of this latter figure 600 million was earmarked for enforcement. The equal opportunity program budgets of the military services increased by 38 per cent to 28.3 million dollars. The 1971—72 school year's freshman class in service academies included 216 blacks—more than the number of minority graduates in the last ten years. The black student enrollment in 1971 was 299 as contrasted with 128 in 1969.

In the field of education, southern segregated all-black schools decreased from 68 per cent in 1968 to 9 per cent in 1972. The nationwide figure of 40 per cent in 1968 has dropped to 12 per cent. To achieve this, 150 million dollars were made available to help local schools affected by court desegregation cases. In 1973 Nixon asked Congress for 2.5 billion dollars per year for continued aid to these schools and to upgrade the quality of education in disadvantaged schools in all areas of the country. The nation's black colleges received more than 200 million in 1973. This figure, more than double the total spent in 1969, was at 400 million for 1974.

To enforce fair housing practices and to eliminate housing discrimination, the Justice Department filed 100 suits against 300 defendants in twenty-four states and the District of Columbia. The funds to administer the Fair Housing Programs were budgeted at 10.9 million dollars. In 1967 only 20 per cent of the military housing units were classified as non-discriminatory. In 1971 this figure had climbed to 98 per cent under the Nixon Administration. In addition, the Administration improved Federal incentives to communities for moderate-income housing. Subsidized low and moderate-income housing starts have increased from 150,000 in 1969 to 650,000 in 1972. In conjunction with this, the Administration proposed a subsidized housing program that will allow rent to vary according to income.

Several projects in the business sphere were either initiated or carried through under the Nixon Administration. Generally speaking, financial undertakings have been to enhance the economic development of the black community. Under the 100-million-dollar Minority Bank Deposit Program, the purpose of which was to strengthen the lending capacity of black-owned banking institutions, the Administration placed 142 million dollars in minority-owned banking institutions. By fiscal 1973 the figure was expected to reach 300 million. The number of black-owned banks increased from 23 in 1969 to 38 in fiscal 1971. Their lending capacity increased by 33 per cent. The Minority Bank Deposit Program represents the largest single transfer of economic power into black-controlled economic institutions in the history of the country.

The Office of Minority Business Enterprise, established in 1969 to increase grants, loans, and guarantees to minority businesses and black trade associations, was originally funded at 64 million dollars. The overall spending of this office was expected to increase to 415 million dollars in 1973. A proposal for the establishment of an Assistant Secretary-ship in the Department of Commerce to deal specifically with minority enterprises was made. Forty-nine Minority Enterprise Small Business Investment Companies (MESBICS) were created to provide a private sector channel for venture capital into the black community. These investment companies were capitalized at over 15 million dollars and were expected to finance 422 new businesses by the end of fiscal 1972. It was also expected that 4,161 high quality jobs would result from the investment. Purchases by the Federal Government from minority owned businesses increased from 12.6 million dollars in 1969 to 200 million in fiscal 1973. Federal contracts to black businesses through the Small Business Administration (SBA) went from eight in 1968 to 812 in 1971. SBA loans increased from 41.3 million dollars to 195 million during this period and black businessmen received 18 per cent of it—double the figure for 1968.

Today, 1974, the black man is no longer as Republican as he was a hundred years ago. At the national level there is only one negro Republican elected official—Senator Edward Brooke of Massachusetts. Out of 204 elected black state legislators in 1971, eight were Republicans. Their names and the legislatures in which they sit are: Genoa Washington, Illinois; Mrs. H.B. Conn, Ray P. Crowe, and Choice Edwards, Indiana; Dr. Artis T. Allen, Maryland; W. Wilson, Nevada; David D. Albritton and John W.E. Bowen, Ohio.

7

DAWDLING DONKEYS

The Democratic party is the older of the two major political organizations now in existence. Its history under its present sobriquet can be traced back to the first term of Andrew Jackson as President.[1] Traditionally, the political base of the Democratic party has been the "Solid South." Historically, the Democratic party is the party of the former slave master. This is not to say that there has been no northern wing of the party. On the contrary, there has always been an alliance between the southern Democracy and its nothern constituency. In the days of Thomas Jefferson, and for some time thereafter, there was the New York–Virginia axis–a coalition between the agrarian interests of the South and the urban political machines of the North. This compact figured prominently in the early history of the Democratic party and, in fact, still operates today, albeit in a somewhat modified form.

As we have seen in the earlier chapters, the partnership arrangement between the Democracy of the North and the Democracy of the South has always been dominated by the latter. Within the party itself, this southern orientation has made itself visible in the practices, pronouncements, and Presidential candidates of the organization. On the question of slavery, the first Democratic party platform said in 1840:

The Congress has no power under the Constitution, to interfere with or control the domestic institution of the several states; and that such States are the sole and proper judges of everything pertaining to their own affairs; not prohibited by the Constitution; that all efforts, by abolitionists or others made to induce Congress to interfere with the question of slavery, or to take incipient steps in relation thereto, are calculated to lead to the most alarming and dangerous consequences, and that all such efforts have an inevitable tendency to diminish the happiness of the people and endanger the stability and permanency of the Union, and ought not be countenanced by any friend of our Political Institution.

This Democratic party platform statement regarding the political status of the black man appeared in identical form in the party platforms of 1844, 1848, 1852, and 1856. In 1856, the year the Republican party ran its first Presidential ticket, the Democratic party platform "reiterated with renewed energy of purpose the well considered declarations of the former Conventions upon the sectional issue of Domestic slavery." The party platform of that year included, in addition to the previous proposition, the following additional resolutions regarding slavery:

That the foregoing proposition covers, and was intended to embrace the whole subject of slavery agitation in Congress; and therefore, the Democratic party of the Union, standing on this national platform, will abide by and adhere to a faithful execution of the acts known as the compromise measures, settled by the Congress of 1850; "the act for reclaiming fugitives from service or labor," included; which act being designed to carry out an express provision of the Constitution, cannot, with fidelity thereto, be repealed, or so changed as to destroy or impair its efficiency.

That the Democratic party will resist all attempts at renewing, in Congress or out of it, the agitation of the slavery question under whatever shape or color the attempt may be made.

That the Democratic party will faithfully abide by and uphold, the principles laid down in the Kentucky and Virginia resolutions of 1798,[2] and in the report of Mr. Madison to the Virginia Legislature in 1799; that it adopts those principles as constituting one of the main foundations of its political creed, and is resolved to carry out in their obvious meaning and import.

And that we may more distinctly meet the issue on which a sectional party, subsisting exclusively on slavery agitation, now relies on to test the fidelity of the people, North and South, to the Constitution and the Union.

RESOLVED, That claiming fellowship with and desiring the cooperation of all who regard the preservation of the Union under the Constitution as the paramount issue—and repudiating all sectional parties and platforms concerning domestic slavery, which seek to embroil the States and incite to treason and armed resistance to law in the Territories; and whose avowed purposes, if consummated, must end in civil war and disunion, the American Democracy recognize and adopt the principles contained in the organic law establishing the Territories of Kansas and Nebraska as embodying the only sound and safe solution of the "slavery question" upon which the great national idea of the people of this whole country can repose in its determined conservatism of the Union—NON-INTERFERENCE BY CONGRESS WITH SLAVERY IN STATE AND TERRITORY, OR IN THE DISTRICT OF COLUMBIA.

In 1860 there were two factions of the Democratic party that ran Presidential candidates. Both the Douglas Democrats and Breckinridge faction adopted identical platform resolutions on slavery. The platform resolutions stated: "That the enactments of the State Legislatures to defeat the faithful execution of the Fugitive Slave Law, are hostile in character, subversive of the Constitution, and revolutionary in their effort." During and after the war there was no platform proposal directed specifically at the negro until 1940 (Table 5).

For the greater portion of its existence the Democratic party has been the "white man's party." By means both legal and extra-legal, the negro has been barred at all levels from participation in the affairs of the organization. However, the pioneering spirit did exist in a few hearty souls. In New York City, John A. Nail had organized a negro Democratic Club as early as 1868. This organization, unique for its time, remained under his guidance until 1900 when it was taken over by Ferdinand Q. Morton. He was succeeded at the organization helm by Mrs. Bessye Bearden in 1920.

Prior to 1924 there were two notable attempts to get negroes to look away from the Republican party, i.e., in the direction of the Democrats. The first of these took place in 1905 as part of the Niagara Movement.[3] Under the combined leadership of a number of influential whites and negro leaders including W.E.B. Du Bois, Kelly Miller, William M. Trotter, J.H. Summers, W.C. Payne, and T.H.A. Moore, the Movement condemned the Republican party for having obtained black support under "false pretenses" and recommended a future modification in the political alignment of the negro.

The second appeal of note made in an effort to entice negroes away from the Republican party into the Democratic organization took place on May 17, 1911, in Indianapolis, Indiana. On that occasion a group of "Negro Democrats" calling themselves the National Negro Democratic Convention met and issued the following appeal:

We, the Negroes in National Democratic Convention assembled, this 17th day of May, 1911, desire to appeal to the colored voters of the United States to open their eyes to the conditions surrounding us as a race, and suggest that it is wisdom's way that the Negro should no longer blindly follow any one party to his own harm and detriment, as he has heretofore followed the Republican party. We believe that the American Negro

should divide his vote the same as the white man and be found in all political parties for precisely the same reason that the white man is found
in all parties.

In concluding its business prior to adjournment, the body reaffirmed
its allegiance to the Democratic party and called upon the "intelligent,
honest, law-abiding colored citizens of the United States of America to
organize and bind themselves together in Democratic clubs, preparatory
for the war of the ballot in 1912." In September the National Independent Political Rights League met in Boston. Under the leadership of William Monroe Trotter, black editor of the *Boston Guardian,* personal
friend, confidant, and political cohort of W.E.B. Du Bois, the group
would support, work for, and urge blacks to vote for Woodrow Wilson,
the Democratic standard-bearer in 1912.

When Woodrow Wilson, former president of Princeton University, ran
for office in 1912, the Democratic party platform of that year contained
no specific reference to the negro. However, based upon his campaign
pledge stated in a letter of October 1912 written to Bishop Alexander
Walters of the A.M.E. Zion Church, he received the support of several
prominent negro leaders. Candidate Wilson's "earnest wish to see justice
done the colored people in every matter" earned for him the support of
Bishop Walters, Reverend J. Milton Waldron, Kelly Miller, William Trotter,
and W.E.B. Du Bois. Du Bois, then editor of *The Crisis*, the national organ of the National Association for the Advancement of Colored People,
called attention to the fact that Wilson was a "cultivated scholar who
has 'brains.' " He added (in the August editorial of the magazine), based
upon his conviction and that of Wilson's other black supporters, that
"Mr. Woodrow Wilson will treat black men and their interests with far-
sighted fairness. . . . He will not advance the cause of the oligarchy in the
South, he will not seek further means of 'Jim Crow' insult, he will not
dismiss black men wholesale from office, he will remember that the
Negro in the United States has a right to be heard and considered."

To direct the Democratic party's first political foray aimed at the Re-
publican-entrenched black electorate, a negro bureau was established at
Democratic headquarters. The party sponsored the organization of the
National Colored Democratic League under the leadership of Robert N.
Wood and Bishop Walters. In like manner, the National Independent
Political League led by William Monroe Trotter and Reverend J. Milton
Waldron carried the Democratic message into the black communities
throughout the nation. To swing the negroes away from the Republican
party, these organizations advertised in negro papers and sent speakers

to address black groups. All in all, 52,256 dollars were spent that year, 1912, in an effort to gain the black vote. In the outcome of the three-way race[4] that saw Wilson winning with a minority of the popular vote, Du Bois estimated that Wilson garnered 100,000 black votes.

If at the outset Du Bois and his associates were unaware of the risk involved in supporting the southern-dominated Democratic party, they would shortly be apprised of the fact. To the black leaders who had cooperated in his election to the Presidency,[5] Woodrow Wilson was a tearful disappointment. Henry Lee Moon, political analyst and editor of *The Crisis* (official N.A.A.C.P. publication), states that "within six months Wilson's fine words to Bishop Walters were junked, segregation was introduced into Federal agencies where it had not previously existed, Negro appointments and promotions were curtailed and highly qualified black civil servants were dismissed." Even the Republican-appointed black Minister to Haiti was replaced by a white appointee. Under the Wilson Administration the bureaus and departments of government failed to develop any constructive policies relative to the needs of the negro. Wilson did appoint Emmett J. Scott, Booker T. Washington's former secretary, to the office of Assistant Secretary of War. During the Taft Administration, Scott had served as a member of the Liberian Commission. Dr. Joseph D. Johnson, prominent physician of Columbus, Ohio, was made Minister to Liberia. In the campaign of 1916, Wilson reiterated his assurances of the previous election and pledged to stand behind them. But it was too late, that year the negro returned to the Republican fold.

By 1922 it had begun to appear in some quarters that the negro was no longer enchanted by the theology of the Republican party. That year the black voters of Harlem sent a Democrat to Albany to represent the Twenty-First Assembly District. Two years later, Harlem's black voters elected Henry M. Shields, a black Democrat, to represent the Twenty-First District. Many of the black wards in Kansas City, Missouri, went Democratic in the Mayoralty race held in April 1924. These events signaled the incipient detachment of the black voters' moorings from its Republican party base. At the national level the Democratic party began preparing to take advantage of the situation. During the Presidential elections of 1924 and 1928, the Democratic organization launched its most earnest effort ever witnessed in the party's history to attract black voters. In 1924 a negro division was established under Ferdinand Q. Morton, the Harvard-educated, black political boss of Harlem.[6] Lester A. Walton was the division's Secretary and Director of Publicity and Alice Dunbar Nelson was named Women's Director. In the campaign of 1928 the division was headed by Julian D. Rainey of Boston with Walton as Publicity

Director. The finances of the division were managed by a committee which included black members such as Bishop Reardy C. Ranson, J. Finley Wilson, Grand Exalted Ruler of the Colored Elks, and Ferdinand Q. Morton, Chairman of the Municipal Civil Service Commission of New York City. Adequately financed and supported by the national Democratic organization, the negro division was able to provide speakers and establish negro voters' clubs supporting Governor Smith of New York in Arkansas, Georgia, Florida, Kentucky, Maryland, Missouri, North Carolina, Oklahoma, Tennessee, Massachusetts, Connecticut, New York, Ohio, New Jersey, Indiana, Illinois, Pennsylvania, Kansas, Nebraska, Colorado, Arizona, Texas, and Minnesota.

By 1924 the urban negro was beginning to hear other political voices. He was willing to look elsewhere, away from the Republican party, for political consideration. What had occurred in New York and in Kansas City were by no means isolated instances of a new political awareness. To advance himself politically and demonstrate his independence of party labels, the negro was prepared to vote for the man and not the party. This he did in Cleveland in 1927. That year the black voters of the city elected three black candidates to represent them—one on the Democratic ticket, a second on the Republican, and a third on an Independent slate. The Presidential elections of 1928 saw Hoover receive some 15 per cent less of the black vote than had Coolidge in 1924. The negro's new political awareness brought about by his first significant fling with the National Democratic party politics was short-lived and in 1932 he was seen voting for Hoover in much the same way as he had in 1928. Politically speaking, the black man was like a caged bird. At worst he could go nowhere; at best he possessed limited political mobility. The Republicans took his vote for granted and the Democrats really didn't want it. In spite of the Democratic Presidential candidates wishing "to see justice done to the negro," it was a fact of life that the black man was as much out of the Democratic party in 1932 as he had been during the entire history of the party.

The defection from the political ranks of the Republican party that had begun in 1928 and sustained itself in 1932 was mainly at the top of the black electorate. By and large the majority of black voters were to remain snugly nestled in the arms of the G.O.P. In spite of Hoover's disastrous economic policies that affected them most, negroes as a group were unwilling to switch their vote to the Democratic party. In 1932 they saw no compelling reason to vote for Franklin D. Roosevelt who till then had been relatively undistinguished in his political view concerning the negro. His racial attitudes were fairly conventional; back in 1911 he had found nothing offensive about punctuating the text of a speech with a "nigger story." Had he not been quite comfortable as Assistant Secretary of the Navy under Woodrow Wilson? As Governor of New York, he demonstrated no special interest in the negro either in appointments or legislation. And not unlike Wilson, was he not courting southern support in his selection of John Nance Garner[7] of Texas as his running mate? In spite of what the black leaders were saying, and in spite of the depression of 1929, the vast majority of the black electorate were not willing to take a chance on Franklin Delano Roosevelt in the Presidential election of 1932. They chose to stick with the Republican party—the party of Lincoln.

As usual the Democratic party platform, in deference to the organization's southern constituency, made no mention of the negro. Nevertheless, Roosevelt was triumphant in the election of 1932. In so doing, he carried forty-two states and picked up 472 electoral votes out of a possible 531. His popular vote total was 22.8 million compared to Hoover's 15.8 million. In his inaugural address given March 4, 1933, the thirty-second President of the United States made no mention of the negro. His entire address was devoted to the economic ills of the nation. Roosevelt promised the nation "action" and action he delivered.

During the first hundred days of this Administration, Roosevelt took the steps he deemed essential if the nation were to recover from a steadily worsening economic and moral crisis. The present state of affairs which earlier had been highlighted by the stock market crash of October 1929 was currently accentuated by 13 million unemployed men. To begin the process of "restoration"—putting the nation back on a sound economy, cutting down unemployment, and encouraging the people once more to believe in the soundness of their government, Roosevelt took a series of Presidential actions and brought the power of his office to bear directly on the situation. On March 3, 1933, the Civilian Conservation Corps (CCC) would be created by the Reforestation Unemployment Act to ease unemployment. On March 3 he made plans for a special session of Congress; on March 6 Congress passed legislation forbidding the export of gold, except when authorized by the Treasury. Accordingly, he closed all banks and prohibited all gold payments and exports. And finally, on March 12, he did what all American Chief Executives must do if they are to earn the title of leader. He went to the people with his program for their approval. In the first of his famous fireside chats he embraced the people of the nation and reminded them that "Confidence and Courage are the essentials of success" in any endeavor; that if, in the current crisis, both the people and the government remained firm in their mutual resolve to overcome, "Together, we cannot fail." The rest is history. The thirty-second President of the United States knew and believed in his people and they responded in kind. Most men, be they President or pauper, king or knave, live in their own time. But occasionally events produce a leader who can rise above the moment and endear himself to future generations. In this respect Franklin Delano Roosevelt was like Lincoln and not unlike Jefferson.

The Agricultural Adjustments Acts (AAA) became law on March 12. To implement the legislation and the President's wishes a number of agencies would be created.

The central theme of the early New Deal, as the President's recovery programs were called, was economic readjustment to be realized through agricultural and industrial planning. Two agencies, the AAA and the NRA, were charged with overseeing the project. It is important to recognize that the New Deal was not a program aimed directly at the needs of the negro. The New Deal was an economic recovery program, not a program for blacks. As such, the New Deal offered nothing new to the negro. It is a fact, as Arthur Schlesinger has written concerning the New Deal in its infancy, that:

Under AAA, Negro tenant farmers and share-croppers were the first to be thrown off farms as a consequence of the crop-reduction policy. Under NRA, Negroes either had to accept racial differentials in wages or run the risk of displacement by unemployed white men; in the case of jobs still reserved for Negroes, a complicated system of exemptions minimized the application of the codes; and local control of compliance machinery made it almost impossible for the Negro to seek effective redress.[8]

It is to the credit of the Roosevelt Administration that for the first time in history a Democratic Administration began to move against racial discrimination. Under the leadership of Harold Ickes, Secretary of the Interior, the Administration launched an oblique assault on discrimination in the New Deal agencies. It was through his efforts that segregation in the Department of the Interior was ended and negroes were hired as architects and engineers in PWA projects. The former president of the Chicago chapter of the N.A.A.C.P. saw to it that William Hastie was hired as assistant solicitor in the Interior Deparment. Later, he backed Hastie for appointment to a federal judgeship in the Virgin Islands. Another approach used by Ickes consisted of establishing an inter-departmental committee to delve into the problems created for the negro by NRA-minimum wage and AAA-crop reduction policies. Out of funds contributed by the Julius Rosenwald Fund, Clark Foreman,[9] a young white liberal from Georgia, was appointed to head the committee. Foreman who was former Director of Studies for the Fund, although based in the Department of the Interior, was expected to function through the entire Administration. As his assistant, Foreman brought in Dr. Robert C. Weaver, a black Harvard graduate with a Ph.D. in economics. In the Commerce Department, headed by Daniel C. Roper of South Carolina, Eugene Kinckle Jones of the Urban League was appointed Adviser on Negro Affairs.

The committee headed by Foreman and supported by Eleanor Roosevelt, was successful in its campaign to use negroes as advisers in CCC camps. When Foreman resigned, he was succeeded in that post by Robert C. Weaver. In the following years, with Weaver at the center, the committee was expanded to include negroes in professional, technical, and administrative fields. The "Black Cabinet," as the enlarged group came to be known, included at various times a number of prominent negroes (Table 8). Unofficially headed by Mary Mcleod Bethune, this advisory committee functioned to get negroes into government service and to break down established patterns of racial exclusion in government.

The effects of administrative policy upon discrimination against blacks were readily acknowledged by representatives from the NRA and the AAA. NRA officials admitted to the committee that the agencies' effort to decrease "the spread between the wages of white and colored laborers had been nullified to an undetermined extent by discrimination against negroes." Likewise, based upon their experience, AAA confessed to its failure to do justice to the negro. Their lack of success was based on the fact that the amount of authority given to the agencies' local administrative units precluded the negroes' getting a "fair shake." Neither of the main New Deal agencies could come up with a satisfactory solution that would safeguard the rights of the negro within the program without, at the same time, threatening the essential aims of the program. It was at this juncture that the inter-departmental committee acquiesced in deference to a relief program for salvaging the economically displaced blacks. As a direct result of this decision, 43.4 per cent of the negroes who earned a living and supported their families based on their earnings as domestics, were thrown out of the labor market. In May 1934, out of a total 278,338 blacks in the domestic industry, 121,044 were on relief (Table 9). Notwithstanding the level of performance of their programs, the Roosevelt Administration was interested in the black urban voter. When speaking before large negro audiences, Secretary of Interior Ickes repeatedly listed the benefits of the Administration program as: 1) large sums of relief money made available; 2) work relief jobs and federal farm aid without discrimination; 3) employment of negro architects and managers in nineteen federally constructed low-income housing projects; 4) PWA grants to Howard University and aid to negro schools throughout the country; 5) 3,050 additional beds in negro hospitals; 6) the Social Security Act.

The black vote came cheap to the Democratic party—a few jobs for the black intelligentsia; for the black politicians, a little patronage here and there; and for the masses of black folk, a whole lot of welfare. Roosevelt carved a niche for himself in the minds and hearts of black folk, not because of what he said, nor because of any derived political benefits secured by the race. By any reasonable standard, the thirty-second President's views on race differed not markedly from those of his contemporaries. Roosevelt is remembered among black folk for one simple reason. He fed us when we were hungry. When we had no food, he saw to it that we ate. That elemental fact alone was enough to make any hungry man forget about Abe Lincoln.

In November of 1934, Democrat Arthur Mitchell was elected by the blacks of Chicago. He defeated incumbent Republican Oscar De Priest and became the first black Democrat in the history of the nation to be elected to Congress. That same year 170,000 Pennsylvania negroes voted the Democratic ticket. Negroes in Pittsburgh sent their first black representative to Harrisburg. The handwriting was on the wall. The urban negro had become unglued from the Republican party. Where he had previously voted for Lincoln and liberation, he was now prepared to vote for Roosevelt and relief. All that it would require was a little coaxing. To this end, the Democratic party and the black Democrats were well organized. Going into the campaign of 1936, the Democrats put on the slickest and best organized drive for the negro vote theretofore witnessed in the history of the party. Congressman Mitchell declared that "Mr. Roosevelt has appointed more negroes to responsible government positions than the last three Republican administrations taken together." He charged that the Republican party, instead of doing something for the negro, had really led him "dumb and hopeless" up another blind alley. Praises for Roosevelt came from all segments of the black establishment. Robert L. Vann, editor of the *Pittsburgh Courier,* put the weight of his paper (estimated circulation, 178,000) behind Roosevelt. J.E. Spingarn, the white president of the N.A.A.C.P., himself a lifelong Republican, came out in behalf of Roosevelt. Former secretary to Booker T. Washington, Emmett J. Scott, added that "the Republican Party since the days of the administration of President Taft, has been most negligent of the Negro."

DAWDLING DONKEYS

To help the negro make up his mind, Democratic party organizations sprang up in urban ghettos throughout the country. In the East, for example, Julian D. Rainey, son of the Reconstruction Congressman, headed the organizational drive. The Good Neighbor League was put together by Dr. Stanley High. Millions of pictures showing Eleanor Roosevelt touring Howard University were sent through the mails and ended up in negro homes. The Democratic party was determined to capture the negro vote. That the negro was seduced by the party's efforts is borne out by the election returns of 1936 (Table 10). The Democratic campaign of 1936 did help the negro make up his mind. At the Philadelphia Convention that year no direct mention of the negro was made in the platform. There were, however, for the first time in the party's history black delegates to the National Convention. At the June 22 Philadelphia gathering, a negro minister offered the invocation and Congressman Arthur Mitchell seconded the nomination of President Roosevelt.

In 1940 the Democrats met in Chicago and again nominated Franklin D. Roosevelt for the Presidency. In his quest for an unprecedented third term he needed every vote that he could muster. Consequently, for the first time since 1860, the party platform made specific mention of the negro. This was also the first time in the history of the Democratic party that its official Presidential campaign document recognized the political aspects of the black man's existence in a positive sense. This action proved to be of great benefit to the Roosevelt campaign and helped to complete the political transformation of the big-city negro into a Democrat. When the results were in, Roosevelt had again triumphed. He defeated Wendell Willkie, the Republican candidate, by over 5 million popular votes. In the Electoral College, Roosevelt received 443 votes to Wilkie's 82.

The political transformation of the negro was also evident at the state level in urban areas north of the Mason–Dixon Line. Between 1936 and 1940 one-half of the blacks elected to state legislative bodies were enrolled Democrats (Table 11). At the national level, William L. Dawson, Democrat of Illinois, succeeded Arthur Mitchell in the seventy-eighth Congress. Elected in 1942 by 1,000 votes, Dawson became the second black Democrat to sit in Congress. He was joined in the seventy-ninth Congress by a fellow black Democrat (elected on the Democratic and American Labor party tickets) named Adam Clayton Powell, Jr. Elected out of New York City in 1946, Powell would become an uncompromising fighter for the rights of black people. Like everyone had done before him, he did his best. Like a few had done, he told it like it was. But unlike any politician before his time, he continued the fight when all the other black leaders had turned against him. As he liked to think of himself in quoting from II Tim. 4: 2, "I have fought a good fight, I have finished my course, I have kept the faith." And because he "kept the faith," black folks will remember him for generations to come. He will be the yardstick by which *all* black politicians will be measured. For not only was he a political practitioner of the highest order but he was also unstintingly committed to the freedom of his people. It is in the combination of these two attributes that he still remains peerless.

On June 25, 1941, Roosevelt reluctantly signed Executive Order 8802. He issued the Order in response to a threatened march of 59,000 negroes on Washington. The march, scheduled to take place in the spring of 1941, was to be led by A. Philip Randolph in demand of jobs for blacks in the booming defense industry. The industry which held innumerable government contracts had refused, in spite of a serious labor shortage, to employ or upgrade negro workers. In a tense meeting that took place in the White House, Randolph called for a showdown between the blacks and the Roosevelt Administration. Either the President would take the necessary administrative steps to end discrimination in employment in the defense industries and government or else the blacks would march on the nation's capital. Roosevelt attempted to prevail upon Randolph that the march was not in the best interest of the country. But Randolph remained firm. In the end, Roosevelt agreed to issue the Order according to which the President reaffirmed "the policy of the United States that there shall be no discrimination in the employment of workers in defense industries or government because of race, creed, color or national origin."

This proclamation led to the employment of large numbers of blacks in government and industry at all levels. Also, during his several administrations Roosevelt appointed blacks to comparatively high-ranking positions in the Federal Government (Table 12). The highest of those appointments went to William H. Hastie. He was first named a Federal Judge in the Virgin Islands in 1937.

By 1944 Roosevelt had served an unprecedented three terms as President. In the process he became a national hero and his party chose him to seek the nation's highest office for the fourth time. To the negro, the performance of his past Administration had left a great deal to be desired. Locked in the midst of a world war, the struggle abroad to preserve the Four Freedoms meant little to the negro at home. In the armed forces, segregation, discrimination, and humiliation still existed and was sanctioned by the government. At home, an upswing in employment in war-related industries was of great benefit. Nevertheless, there existed a widespread denial of equal opportunity in skilled, technical, and administrative jobs. The black press began to clamor about the gap between promise and performance. In response, the Administration, for fear of losing black support, took corrective action to lift some of the restrictions placed upon blacks in the armed forces. It opened the naval auxilliary (WAVES) and its Coast Guard counterpart (SPARS) to negro women on an unsegregated basis. The Navy began accepting and training black officers and nurses and the Army placed black troops in combat service. To support the FEPC, troops were ordered into Philadelphia to deal with a strike promoted by white transit workers who objected to blacks being hired as motormen and conductors. Additionally, the President did a little "jaw-boning" on his own. During the campaign, he came out in support of a permanent FEPC and for doing away with economic and racial restrictions placed on the ballot.

However, the campaign did have two serious shortcomings: the replacement of Henry A. Wallace as Vice-Presidential candidate and the weakness of the Democratic party platform. Negroes had come to admire Wallace for his willingness "to go down the line unswervingly for the liberal principles of both political and economic democracy regardless of race, color or religion." As to the racial plank in the party platform, it was so weak that Walter White, Executive Secretary of the N.A.A.C.P., denounced it as a mere "splinter." Nevertheless, due in part to the activities of the PAC[10] the negro remained in the Democratic column in 1944. The results of the 1944 election in which Roosevelt and his new Vice-Presidential candidate, Harry S. Truman, were opposed by Thomas E. Dewey of New York, saw the Democratic team win by a margin of 1.8 million popular votes. As a result of the election Roosevelt ended up with 432 electoral votes. Dewey had 99. The fact that negroes voted solid Democrat made all the difference in the election's outcome. Had the opposite been true, had negroes voted solid Republican, Dewey would have been the winner. As Herbert Brownell, Chairman of the Republican National Committee, explained in a post-election analysis: "a shift of 303,414 votes in fifteen states outside of the South would have enabled Governor Thomas E. Dewey to capture 175 additional electoral votes and to win the presidency with an eight electoral vote margin."

Henry Lee Moon explains the role played by the negro vote in the 1944 election of Roosevelt by concluding that a shift of 5 per cent or less of the total vote in twenty-eight states would have reversed the electoral votes cast in those states. In twelve of these states alone with an electoral vote total of 228, the negro voting potential was more than enough to change the state from one column to the other. He goes on to demonstrate the "decisive potential" of the black vote and to show how that vote "contributed" to the election of Roosevelt in 1944. In reference to Brownell's remarks, Moon offered the following analysis in support of his own contention:

In at least eight of the fifteen states listed by Brownell, the Negro vote exceeded the number needed to shift in order to place them in the Republican column. In Maryland the 50,000 votes which Negro citizens in Baltimore alone cast for F.D.R. were more than double his 22,500 state plurality. Negro voters of five New Jersey cities gave the President a total of 28,780 votes to assure him a winning margin of 26,540. Michigan, which Roosevelt lost in 1940 by the narrow margin of 6,926, was carried by 22,500 with the colored citizens of Detroit casting 41,740 votes for him. Negro voters in Kansas City and St. Louis accounted for 34,900 of the President's margin of 46,180 in Missouri. In Chicago, 121,650 voters in predominantly Negro districts contributed to the 140,165 margin by which the President carried the state of Illinois. The black belts of New York City and Buffalo accounted for 188,760 Roosevelt votes or more than half of his state plurality of 316,000. The combined American Labor and Liberal party tickets for which many Negroes voted gave the President a total of 825,640, enough to overcome the Republican lead over the Democratic slate and hold New York's 47 electoral votes. The President carried Pennsylvania by 105,425 votes to which Negro votes in Pittsburgh and Philadelphia contributed no less than 52,000. These seven states account for 168 votes in the electoral college and were essential to the Roosevelt victory. In addition, Negro votes contributed substantially to the Roosevelt lead in West Virginia, Kentucky and Delaware.[11]

Franklin Delano Roosevelt's fourth term of office came abruptly to an end on April 12, 1945. While relaxing in Warm Springs, Georgia, his favorite spot away from Washington, he suffered a cerebral hemorrhage. As prescribed by the United States Constitution in Article II, Vice-President Harry S. Truman of Independence, Missouri, became President. The nation's black electorate was, to say the least, apprehensive about the new Chief Executive. Had they not preferred Wallace to Truman earlier? But to the surprise of no one who knew him, Truman turned out to be a paradox. As a Senator, he had been in favor of the social reform measures of the New Deal, as well as invoking cloture in senatorial debates over legislation affecting black citizens' rights.

Although lacking the charisma of Roosevelt, Truman proved to be more forthright in his demand for equal opportunity than his predecessor. He undoubtedly played a hand in the defeat of Roger C. Slaughter, a fellow member of the Kansas City Pendergast machine, who opposed his Fair Employment Practices Commission Bill. Slaughter, the Fifth Congressional District Representative in Washington, was opposed to Truman's proposal and publicly boasted that it was his vote in the House Rules Committee "what killed it." In a district whose total electorate was composed of fiteen per cent black voters, his intransigence proved his undoing. The Fifth District which he had carried by a 5,183 vote margin in 1944 was lost to him in the next election (Primary) by 2,783 votes. There were some 7,000 negro votes cast against him. His vote total in thirty predominately black precincts was negligible—the highest vote being received by him in any precinct was 35, in two he picked up none.

Truman appointed several negroes to high offices. They were Edith Sampson, United States Alternate Delegate to the United Nations (1950–53); Channing Tobias, United States Alternate Delegate to the United Nations (1951–52); William H. Hastie, Governor of the Virgin Islands; Irvin C. Mollison, Judge of the United States Customs Court, New York City; Edward R. Dudley, Ambassador to Liberia; Anna E. Hedgemann, Assistant to the Administrator, Federal Security Agency.

In the election of 1948, Truman won a surprise victory over Thomas E. Dewey. It is estimated that the incumbent President received 69 per cent of the black vote. It was this large black vote that was responsible for his narrow margins in three key states—Illinois, 33,612; California, 17,865; Ohio, 7,107. Truman was able to further enhance his stature among negroes based on the proposals he placed before Congress. In his message to Congress on February 2, 1948, he called for legislation: 1) establishing a permanent Commission on Civil Rights, a Joint Congressional Committee on Civil Rights, and a Civil Rights Division in the Justice Department; 2) strengthening existing civil rights' statutes; 3) providing Federal protection against lynching; 4) protecting more adequately the right to vote; 5) establishing a Fair Employment Practices Commission; 6) prohibiting discrimination in inter-state transportation facilities; and 7) providing home rule and suffrage in Presidential elections in the District of Columbia. It was Executive Order 9981 signed by Harry Truman in 1948 that was directed at ending segregation in the armed forces. Unlike his predecessor, Truman did challenge Congress on issues of prime concern to negroes. It was in vain that he commented that "we must protect our civil rights so that by providing all our people with the maximum enjoyment of personal opportunity we shall be a stronger nation—stronger in our leadership, stronger in our moral position, stronger in the deeper satisfactions of a united citizenry."

In the Presidential election of 1960, John Fitzgerald Kennedy narrowly won out over Richard Milhous Nixon by a margin of 112,827 votes. In this race there were a total of 68.8 million votes cast. Estimates of

Kennedy's percentage of the negro vote nationally range from a low of 60 per cent to upwards of 80 per cent. The Gallup Poll placed Kennedy's share at 68 per cent. Harry Golden, allowing for a small discrepancy between his figures and those of the N.A.A.C.P. and the National Democratic Committee, claimed that, in contrast to Truman who received around 70 per cent in 1948 and Adlai Stevenson who averaged 50 per cent in his two runs, Kennedy carried off 85 per cent.[12]

Notwithstanding the fact that there was some disagreement over the actual percentage of the black vote received by Kennedy, it must be pointed out that because blacks voted overwhelmingly Democratic, Kennedy won the Presidency. In state after state it is evident that had the black voters pulled the Republican lever en masse, Nixon would have been elected.[13]

Kennedy's original plan for widening the participation of the negro in American life was built around additional civil rights legislation. But this approach soon ran into stiff congressional opposition by the southern members of his party. Consequently, Kennedy was forced to retreat from this tactic in favor of an Eisenhower approach consisting mainly of Executive action.

In what had by now become traditional Democratic party politics, Kennedy appointed a number of prominent negroes to prestigious governmental positions (Table 13). In addition, he went a step further and announced his intention to promote Robert C. Weaver, Housing and Home Finance Administrator, to a Cabinet position if and when an Urban Affairs Department were created.

Under the heading of Executive action taken by the Kennedy Administration on behalf of the negro, the following would be included: 1) the initiation of voting rights cases by the civil rights division of the Justice Department headed by Burke Marshall; 2) the speeding up of school desegregation in the South; 3) the dispatching of 600 United States marshals by Attorney General Robert Kennedy to protect "freedom riders" from mob attack in Alabama; 4) the deployment of United States marshals to protect James Meredith, the first known black to register at the University of Mississippi; and 5) the issuance of his "stroke of the pen" order on housing discrimination.

During the Kennedy term of office no civil rights legislation was passed by Congress. On the question of civil rights and the rights of negroes, John F. Kennedy provided the moral leadership that was essential in the world's most powerful nation. When on June 11, 1963, Governor George Wallace of Alabama defied a Federal Court order by "standing in the school house door" to prevent two negroes from registering at the University of Alabama, the President took immediate action. He ordered the Alabama national guard into federal service to protect the rights of the negroes. Three hours later Governor Wallace stepped aside and the students were permitted to enroll. Speaking before the nation in a televised address after the crisis had passed, the President established the moral framework in which future black-white relations in America must develop. As to the greater question involved and its relationship to the rights of black people, the President declared:

We are confronted mainly with a moral issue. It is as old as the scriptures and as clear as the American Constitution. . . .
    We preach freedom around the world, and we mean it, and we cherish our freedom here at home, but are we to say to the world, and much more importantly, to each other that this is a land of the free except for the Negro; that we have no second-class citizens except Negroes; that we have no class or caste system, no ghettoes, no master race except with respect to Negroes?
    Now the time has come for this nation to fulfill its promise.
    We face a moral crisis as a country and a people. It cannot be met by repressive police action. It cannot be left to increased demonstrations in the streets. It cannot be quieted by token moves or talks.

    This pointed message delivered to the nation was actually the prelude to a legislative proposal that the Kennedy Administration would soon submit to Congress. The proposed legislation, consisting of eleven bills, was designed to reinforce the proposition made during the Reconstruction era that "race has no place in American life or law." However, before any legislation reached the floor of the Congress, John Fitzgerald Kennedy, the thirty-fifth President of the United States, would achieve martyrdom. On November 23, 1963, an assassin's bullet would snuff out the life of the man whom many blacks had come to view as a second Abe Lincoln. On that fateful autumnlike day in the City of Dallas, the black man's hope for political justice was seemingly ended.
    Kennedy was succeeded in office by his Vice-President, Lyndon Baines Johnson. The new President born near Stonewall, Texas, in 1908, became the nation's second southern politician since the war of 1860 to hold that office. Once before a man named Johnson had come to the position by way of an assassin's bullet. In 1865 Vice-President Andrew Johnson, originally a Tennesseean, had succeeded Abraham Lincoln. With that event there began one of the most notorious struggles for power between the Executive and Legislative branches of government ever witnessed in American political history. With the black man positioned at the center of the contest, attempts to impeach the seventeenth President would fall one vote shy of success.

When Lyndon Johnson assumed the Presidency, it was commonly thought among black people that his southern background would lead him to use his office to stifle, if not oppose, civil rights legislation. But he fooled everybody. Once having assumed the office Johnson immediately took steps to put the nation at rest as to what course he would pursue. In a brief address to Congress on November 27 the southern-born President gave top priority to the passage of the Civil Rights Bill then tied up in the House Rules Committee. On the question of the civil status of the black man in American society, the thirty-sixth President of the United States told Congress that: "We have talked long enough in this country about civil rights. . . . We have talked for one hundred years or more. It is now time to write the next chapter, and to write it in the books of law."

These simple phrases spoken by Lyndon Baines Johnson so soon after taking office would prove to be much more than the usual political rhetoric designed to insure the loyalty of the black vote to the Democratic party. By means of these simple words the Chief Executive sounded the clarion call. For the third time in the country's history a United States President had called upon the Congress and the people to extend those civil liberties basic to the nation's existence and guaranteed by the Constitution to the black man. Congress, under the combined leadership of Mike Mansfield, Hubert Humphrey, and Everett Dirksen in the Senate and Emanuel Celler in the House, would ultimately respond in the affirmative. Historians will rank the civil rights accomplishments of the Johnson Administration in a category with those of the Reconstruction. For it was during his Administration that the most far-reaching measures in the area were advanced and realized since the period following the death of Lincoln. Under the Executive leadership of Lyndon Johnson, the omnibus Civil Rights Act of 1964, the Voting Rights Act of 1965, and the Housing Act of 1968 were enacted into law.

The passage of the Civil Rights Act of 1964 was marked by the longest debate in Senate history. Finally, after eighty-three days of filibuster, debate was cut off. For the first time in history the Senate, by a vote of 71 to 29, invoked cloture in a civil rights debate. On June 19, 1964, the bill was adopted in the Senate by a vote of 73 to 27. The House passed the Senate bill 289 to 126 on July 2. The major provisions of the bill 1) broadened the laws covering voting rights by speeding up voting suits in courts and outlawing arbitrary discrimination in registration procedures; 2) barred discrimination in public accommodations, such as hotels and restaurants bearing a substantial relation to interstate commerce; 3) authorized the federal government to bring desegregation suits against public facilities and public schools; 4) extended the life of the Civil Rights Commission and expanded its power; 5) permitted withholding of federal funds from programs practicing discrimination; 6) established the right to equal employment opportunity in business and unions with twenty-five or more members; and 7) created the Community Relations Service, headed by former Governor Leroy Collins of Florida, to help resolve local civil rights problems.

The Civil Rights Acts of 1957, 1960, and 1964 all contained provisions designed to eliminate racial discrimination in voter registration and elections. However, each suffered from an obvious drawback—their reliance on the slow-moving judicial process. Responding in part to civil rights activists led by Dr. Martin Luther King, President Johnson went before a joint session of Congress on March 15, 1965, and called for additional legislation that would overcome the shortcomings of the earlier statutes. He asked Congress to enact a law that would "strike down restrictions to voting in all elections—federal, state and local—which have been used to deny Negroes the right to vote." In response to his request and after extended debate in which cloture had again to be invoked, a bill passed the Senate on May 26 by a vote of 77 to 19. After being delayed in the House Rules Committee, a bill was adopted by that body on July 9 by a vote of 333 to 85. The slight difference in the two versions of the bill were ironed out in a House-Senate Conference Committee. The final measure was adopted in the House on August 3 by a vote of 328 to 74 and the following day in the Senate 79 to 18. Known as the Civil Rights Act of 1965, the major provisions of the statute automatically suspended literacy tests or other devices found to be discriminatory. The bill authorized federal voting examiners to register persons in any state or county that used a literacy test or similar device in the 1964 election and where less than 50 per cent of the eligible voters either registered or voted.[14] Additional provisions were made that authorized the Attorney General to: 1) test the validity of poll taxes; 2) seek court orders and appoint federal examiners where voter discrimination is alleged; 3) place restrictions on new state voting laws; and 4) provide criminal penalties for interference with rights granted in the law.

Housing has always been a difficult area in which to obtain legislative enactment. President Kennedy's Executive Order 11063 was of limited benefit in this respect, for not only did it lack sufficient statutory safeguards to render it durable, it also covered only about 18 per cent of new housing. Not covered by the Order was housing financed through savings and loan associations and commercial banks. The type of measure pushed by the Johnson Administration and its subsequent congressional enactment made possible in the aftermath of the assassination of Martin Luth-er King,[15] was designed to cover 80 per cent of all housing by 1970. The open-housing section of the Civil Rights Act signed into law by President Johnson on April 11, 1968, prohibited discrimination in the sale or rental of housing on the basis of "race, religion or national origin." It was to go into effect in three stages the first of which immediately prohibited dis-crimination in housing units owned and operated by the Federal Govern-ment and in dwellings built under Federal programs. The next stage which became law on December 31, 1968, covered most apartment build-ings and single-family housing built in real estate developments. Beginning January 1, 1970, the final stage became effective. Its coverage extended to all privately owned single family homes sold or rented through brokers. Enforcement of the law was left mainly to the Secretary of Housing and Urban Development, however, private suits could be initiated. Likewise, the Attorney General was authorized to bring suit where a pattern or practice of discrimination existed.

Another provision of the Civil Rights Act of 1968 provided criminal penalties for persons interfering with the exercise of the civil rights of others. Congress also passed a law on March 14 prohibiting discrimina-tion in juror selection in federal trials. The law required random selection of jurors from voter registration lists.

Johnson's attempt to deal with the racial problems of the nation cover-ed areas outside of what might be defined as purely civil rights. Addres-sing the Howard University class of 1965 at graduation exercises the Pres-ident frankly acknowledged the effect of poverty upon the nation's black population. In addition, he went a step further and candidly noted the distinguishing aspects of black poverty as opposed to white poverty. He said:

Negro poverty is not white poverty. Many of its causes and many of its cures are the same but there are differences—deep, corrosive, obstinate differences—radiating, painful roots into the community, and into the family, and the nature of the individual. These differences are not racial differences. They are solely and simply the consequences of ancient brutality, past injustice and present prejudice."

To the thirty-sixth President of the United States, part of the answer was to be found in jobs, welfare, social programs, poverty programs, edu-cation, training, medical care, etc. The Johnson Administration sought and obtained legislation and financing to enact programs in these areas. Under the Economic Opportunity Act of 1964 and the Elementary and Secondary Act of 1965, funds were made available to deal with many of

DAWDLING DONKEYS

the direct and indirect consequences of poverty. The 1964 Act established the Office of Economic Opportunity (OEO) and charged the Agency with the planning and coordination of Federal antipoverty efforts and
the mobilization of antipoverty resources. Community Action Programs
were created to mobilize and coordinate community resources and to expand the availability of social and educational services. Self-help, to be
achieved through involvement in planning and administration, was to be
an important aspect of the programs. Job training to improve employ-
ability and adult work relief programs were called for to facilitate com-
petitiveness in the labor market. Through the Job Corps a "last chance"
was provided for those young people ill-prepared to enter the job market
due to a lack of educational qualifications. Finally, the Act made loans
available to foster self-employment for poverty-level rural residents and
small business owners. To achieve the goals it envisioned, OEO worked
through programs such as the Migrant and Seasonal Farm Workers Assistance Programs, Community Action Programs, Head Start, Job Corps,
Legal Services, Neighborhood Health Services, Upward Bound, Volunteers
in Service to America (VISTA), and many Manpower Programs. As in
the early Roosevelt Administration, many blacks were employed in Federal programs created during the Johnson Administration. Some of these,
along with other high level black appointments are listed in Table 14.
Under Johnson the nation's first black cabinet member, Robert Weaver
(HUD), and the first black Supreme Court Justice, Thurgood Marshall,
were appointed.

Currently, the overwhelming majority of black voters are in the Democrats' column. The black vote is by all practical standards the exclusive
property of the Democratic party. This is seen in the fact that out of 204
black elected State Legislators in 1971, 195 were Democrats, one Independent, and that all fifteen black United States Representatives (Table
15) belong to the Democratic party. In 1967, Carl Stokes (Cleveland)
and Andrew Hatcher (Gary), elected on the Democratic ticket, became
the first black mayors of major American cities.

Within the party organizational structure blacks have also achieved a
number of firsts. Hulan Jack of Manhattan was elected the first black
borough president in 1954. J. Raymond Jones of New York City is the
first black to ever serve as a county chairman in the history of Democratic party politics. He headed Tammany Hall in 1964–65. At the
national level, Basil Patterson was elected Co-Chairman of the National
Committee at the 1972 Miami Convention—thus becoming the first black
to serve in that post. At that convention there were 483 black delegates.

8

GET SMART

Their cause must be our cause too, because it is not just Negroes but really it is all of us, who must overcome the legacy of bigotry and injustice.
—Lyndon Baines Johnson

America is a nation of men—black men and white men. Consequently, it is of little value to speak of the American political system if one is not prepared to accept as fact the pivotal role allotted the black man in the evolution of that system. At every major juncture, during the entire course of national development and differentiation, the black man has found himself situated at the vortex of those frequent power struggles that ensued among opposing factions of the political power structure. From the beginning, the presence of the African has been a critical element in the development of that government of laws known as American democracy that was devised by men from Europe.

Before there was even the template, when America was only a notion, there was the black man in the midst of the struggle for independence. To Thomas Jefferson, the fact that King George III supported African slavery was one of several reasons for severing political ties with England —an overt act of political self-assertion that led to war.

Once having waged a successful war of independence against British imperialism, it was left to the victors to form a new government. The task of putting together a constitution for the new nation devolved upon the combined leadership of representatives from each of the thirteen free and independent states. To accomplish this goal, they met in Philadelphia on May 25, 1787. At this Constitutional Convention that witnessed the framing of the American Constitution—the basis of ascendancy of the new government—much time was devoted to the question of the political and moral status of the black man. The resolution of these questions was essential in determining the form of document that would finally emerge. For that reason, it was of fundamental importance in defining the type and nature of any new government agreed upon by the parties involved. Above all, it was imperative, if the new rulers were to remain true to the Revolution, that the product of their deliberations recognize the rights of man as its paramount virtue.

The new form of government envisaged by most in attendance was the federal state—a practical alternative to the imperial state, considering their recent history. Through such a system of rule, the independent and free states could be brought together as an aggregate, each maintaining a certain degree of autonomy and self-control while at the same time benefiting from membership in the larger union.

Structurally and functionally, the federal form of government is, by nature, subject to internal rupture because of the two opposing forces inherent in its design. On one hand, there is the *centrifugal* tendency—the force that tends to peripheralize power in the hands of the constituent members. Opposing this, there is a *centripetal* drift—the force that tends to centralize power in the hands of central authority. Obviously, in establishing the proposed government, it became imperative that these two forces be constantly mediated. On the question of the black man's status, mediation meant compromise. In essence, that is the political basis of the three-fifths-of-a-man clause in the United States Constitution.

The compact that was finally adopted at the gathering of delegates bore heavily the mark of corruption. For it had been necessary in preparing the document that the black man be considered politically subordinate without, at the same time, usurping the authority of "their maker" and declaring him morally inferior. In simple terms, political subordination meant slavery for the black man. But was this not a paradox? Certainly there was a basic inconsistency. To Thomas Jefferson, who was not in attendance at the convention, slavery was an "abomination"—a defilement of the laws of God and irreconcilable with the basis for having waged the Revolution. In an earlier letter written to a French lexicographer, he had expressed bewilderment at the audacity of that man:

Who can endure toil, famine stripes, imprisonment and death itself, in vindication of his own liberty, and, the next moment be deaf to all those motives whose power supported him through trial, and inflict on his fellow man a bondage, one hour of which is fraught with more misery than ages of that which he rose in rebellion to oppose.[1]

The black man's presence had a profound effect upon the manner in which the Constitution was written and finally adopted. In addition to the wording of the Preamble, several other clauses (Table 16) had to be included which dealt specifically with the station of "all other persons." The political significance of the black man in the writing of the United States Constitution is further attested to by the large number of clauses that relate indirectly to his presence through the section on representation.

On September 17, 1787, the American Constitutional Convention adjourned, sine die, and the representatives in attendance returned home. As any school-child can tell you, the government provided for in the Constitution was to be made up of three branches; the Executive, the Judicial, and the Legislative. Referred to as the Presidency, the Supreme Court, and the Congress, their statutory duties were (in reverse order) to make the law, to interpret the law, and to carry out the law. These three institutions were purposely designed by the framers to be the constants of the federal system. The President (because of his constitutional powers) and the Supreme Court (because of its supposed political independence and its reliance upon the Executive branch for enforcement of its mandate), as originally conceived, were to represent the centripetal force in the government. The Congress, on the other hand, was designed to function as the centrifugal force. It was through its efforts that the rights of the individual states were to be protected against an overly-zealous Chief Executive.

The Congress of the United States met for the first time in the spring of 1789. For the next sixty-odd years, they would be pre-eminently occupied with the task of expansion—making America stretch from the Atlantic to the Pacific. Expansion meant land and to the agrarian interest of the South land meant power—economic and political. And who was to work the land that was to produce this power? Obviously, the black man. The northern industrial and shipping interests, fully aware of the overwhelming potential of slave labor contrasted with their system of free-labor, were nevertheless prone to look askance at the plantation system. After all, they were doing a great deal of business with the South. It is therefore not surprising that the political representatives of the North, in spite of a great deal of anti-slavery rhetoric, adopted a conciliatory attitude toward the South. Between 1789 and 1850, mediation was the rule-of-thumb for settling Congressional debate on the subject of new states entering the Union. The period produced a number of political leaders quite adept at the practical art of keeping men with opposing viewpoints from parting company during heated debate. It was through the leadership of men such as Daniel Webster of Massachusetts and Henry Clay of Kentucky that the Missouri Compromise was formulated and agreed to by Congress. As long as the unity ratio between slave and free states could be maintained, both sides, North and South, were prepared to let expansion proceed. To the black man, however, expansion through compromise meant more slavery—more black slavery. So it is not really surprising that between 1790 and the time of war, the number of blacks held in bondage increased nearly sixfold (Table 17). Between 1828, when Andrew Jackson was first elected President, and 1860, the Democratic party was in control of the Presidency for twenty-four years. Their stance during the entire period was unstintingly pro-slavery.

The Executive Branch first entered the slavery discussion in 1806 when Thomas Jefferson called upon Congress to enact legislation outlawing the African slave trade. Obviously his request had little impact for, as mentioned earlier, the number of Africans entering this country steadily increased. However, the importance of his plea, regardless of his motives, should not be overlooked for it added a new dimension to the debate. In effect, what Jefferson had done was to move the whole issue to a different level—a level which, by constitutional design, would ultimately be forced to offset the peripheralizing tendencies of Congress if the federal system were to survive. A good indication of what was actually involved can best be judged by the reaction of his close friend, John Randolph. The latter, no less a political sophisticate than Jefferson and well aware of the implications, recognized that such action could ultimately lead to disunion.

Jefferson's action served to force the realization on the southern members of Congress and the Democratic party that it was unrealistic to assume that they would always be the final arbiters on the slavery question. On a purely partisan basis, there existed the real possibility that an opposition party President might use the power of the office to oppose the institution. To avoid that eventuality, it would be necessary to destroy the political opposition and build a strong Democratic party under southern domination. History recalls that Jefferson was able to accomplish both tasks. Furthermore, the South realized that the only real insurance against Executive prerogative on the slavery question lay in their controlling not only the Democratic party but also Congress as well as the Presidency. To have their interests served, the man in the White House had either to be politically pro-slavery or philosophically anti-centralist. In the minds of the southern Democrats there was not that much difference between the two positions. The success of Jefferson in destroying the opposition Federalist Party and building a strong, southern-based Democratic party, led to the one-party "Era of Good Feeling." Following this period, the southern hold on the Democratic party became a permanent and durable political fact of life.

The admission of California as a free state signaled the last of the great compromises that the Southern Democracy was willing to endure. In spite of the fact that they got a fugitive slave law enacted as part of the deal, they were no longer willing to debate the political and economic interests of "their" part of the country. On the issue of the expansion of slavery, they were determined to have their way. As far as they were concerned, they would just as soon see slavery spread throughout the entire nation and even down into Cuba and the Caribbean. So as we approach the close of 1852, it is clear that compromise had become a thing of the past. For one thing, the leadership ranks on both sides of the slavery question had been depleted. Men such as Jackson, Clay, Calhoun, Adams, and Webster were no longer around. Secondly, the defeat of the Whig party in the Presidential election of 1852 had been interpreted by the Democrats as a mandate to bring to rest forever the debate over slavery. That election which foreshadowed the doom of the Whigs as a political force of any consequence also placed the southern-dominated Democracy in control of Congress. Linn Boyd of Kentucky was elected House Speaker with 143 votes out of a possible 217 and on the Senate side, the Democrats were in control 36 to 22.

In firm control of Congress and the White House, the southern-controlled Democratic party made plans to extend its vast slave domain. Led by Jefferson Davis, Stephen Douglas, and Archibald Dixon, a successful effort would be launched to rescind the Missouri Compromise. On March 3, 1854, the Senate of the United States passed a bill organizing the Territories of Kansas and Nebraska on a "Squatter Sovereignty" basis. The same legislation, which cleared the House on May 22, declared the Compromise of 1820 to be inconsistent and void on the basis of the Compromise of 1850 which recognized the rights of states and territories over and above those of Congress.

Years of political battle over slavery had ended. The South had won. The North had lost. In losing, the Whig party disintegrated, for the North—South alliance between the constituent members could no longer be maintained. This meant that from a purely political perspective the future of the nation at this point, was entirely in the hands of the Democratic party.

By 1854, the equilibrium between the peripheralizing and centralizing forces in the American federal system had shifted decidedly in the direction of the former. There existed an extreme imbalance in the power of the state relative to that of the central government. Consequently, the system of checks and balances that exists among the three branches of the national government had also been obliterated. Further aggravated by the destruction of the two-party system as a result of Whig demise, it was conceivably just a matter of time before the imbalance within the system became permanent and the center fell out. Because of the gross distortions in the relationships among the different elements of the Government, the self-correcting devices, normally expected to be effective, were no longer operative. If the balance were to be restored, a new anti-peripheralist party would have to be created. Forming an effective new party and insuring its success at the polls was a long shot, but it had to be tried. The future of the American federal system could *only* be guaranteed by the people allied in a single voice against the excesses of those in power.

Short of any drastic measures that might have been perceived, the forming of a new party seemed to hold out the most hope for political reform. Because of the circumstances, the cardinal tenets of the new organization would have to be based on a philosophy of federal government that differed markedly from that of the pro-slavery Democrats. In deference to the seeming radicalism of such an approach, this in itself was not too much to expect since, in effect, the political and philosophical arena in which the battle would have to take place had already been decided by the powerful, southern-dominated Democratic party. The party of the plantation owner was philosophically anti-centralist and politically pro-slavery. These two terms were synonymous. Therefore, based on the adversary nature of the American political process, the new party had no choice but to be anti-peripheralist which, by derivation, also meant that it had to be anti-slavery. Again, as in the previous case, there was no separating the two. This was the hard decision facing those who first met in Fond du Lac County, Wisconsin, in February of 1854. At Ripon and subsequently at many other similar gatherings throughout the country, it soon became apparent that opposition to slavery was the only viable political and philosophical basis upon which a durable new party could be built. In consideration of the charming effect of the word "Democracy," Alvan E. Bovay[2] suggested the "significant, flexible and magical [term] 'Republican.' " as "its only counterpart"—hence the name of the new party.

The northern electorate was quick to respond to the Republican call. In 1854, the new party was able to take control of the House of Representatives, elect the Speaker, and make gains in the Senate. Two years later they were able to run their first Presidential candidate. Their national ticket, headed by John C. Fremont, fared better than had any anti-slavery party in the nation's history. Sensitized by the caning of Sumner on the Senate floor and the calamitous state of affairs in "Bleeding Kansas" the electorate gave the new party a firm vote of confidence. And, although the "nigger-loving" *black* Republicans did not win, the impressive showing made by the "Pathfinder of the Rockies" offered the new party encouraging prospects for the future. Slavery, the status of the black man in America, was indeed a national issue on which a new national political organization could be built. This simple fact had always been known in the South. The North, for reasons of its own, was obviously slow in coming to that realization. However, once the demonstrated appeal of the anti-slavery posture had manifested itself politically, things began to happen.

The natural laws of the universe require that "for every action there is an equal and opposite reaction." The same sort of generally applied axiom was also found to hold true for the relationship between the anti-slavery forces of the North and the pro-slavery forces of the South. Once the North, operating through the Republican party, had succeeded in offsetting the peripheralizing tendencies of the South, the latter moved quickly to reestablish its prior position of predominance. So, as to be expected, the Democratic presidential nominee in 1856 was by no means anti-slavery. As Minister to England, James A. Buchanan had been party to the Ostend Manifesto—that foreign policy document through which the South had envisioned Cuba and Central America as additional slave territory.

Following the election of Buchanan in 1856, the slavocracy-controlled Democratic party moved to assert the last vestige of constitutional authority that would make slavery the law of the land. The Supreme Court of the United States was brought into the picture. Having neutralized the centralizing authority of the Presidency by maintaining absolute control over its occupant, the South, through the issuance of the Dred Scott Decision by the Taney Court, converted that normally centralizing body into a powerful peripheralizing force. True to the constitutional axiom that slaves were indeed property, the Democratic Supreme Court of the United States acknowledged and reinforced the control of that property to be the exclusive rights of individual states—not to be interfered with by the Federal Government.

Since the first days of the convention to form the Constitution, the North had perpetually accommodated the South on the question of the black man's status. After all, it really was too much to expect that honorable white men would ever come to blows or even part company over heathens from Africa. For it was a fact steeped in Christian theology that the "sons of Ham," cursed by God, were considered inferior. At least, this was the way that most white folks saw it. As a result, black men in the North, being in such small numbers, were, in a sense, unreal; they were more like an abstraction that occasionally abolitionists mounted their soap boxes in defense of or, as in the case of John Brown, in reverence to. But in the South, the black man was a reality. He was the base on which the past, present, and future were built. Without the black man as a slave, the South would be politically and economically destined to suffer the fate of a weak partner. So it is not surprising that after seventy years of political strife over the issue of slavery, the South would be the victor. At any cost, they had to win. They couldn't afford to lose. Their vital interests were at stake. And should it ever become necessary to secede in order to win, so be it. After all, secession was merely a *pro forma* consideration in light of the constitutional impact on the federation of the Compromise of 1850 and the Dred Scott Decision. What difference did it make to the South whether you called the government a federation or a confederation? The important thing was to insure that, in any instance, the central government would have no control over slavery. And, to the power-laden Democracy of the South, that was worth fighting for—even if it meant cutting off its northern phalanx as it did in 1860.

Opposition to slavery was the issue on which the new party rode to victory in the national election of 1860. Abraham Lincoln, the nation's first Republican President, was inaugurated on March 4, 1861. On the question of African slavery he, like Jefferson, trembled for his country when he remembered that "God is just." Both were aware of the danger to the nation of the avenging justice of God and realized that there was "a question of God's eternal justice wrapped up in the enslaving of any race of men, of any man, and that those who did so braved the arm of Jehovah."[3] Slavery, the sin against God that the European had bestowed upon the African for over two hundred years, had to be worked out in "pain and grief and bitter humiliation." The war between North and South, between kith and kin trained to separate lines of life and thought, did not end until "both had drunk of the cup to the very dregs." Those by whom the "offense" came were forced to suffer four long years of agonizing internecine war.

A house divided against itself cannot stand. I believe this Government cannot endure, permanently, half *slave* and half *free.*
I do not expect the Union to be *dissolved*—I don't expect the house to *fall*—but I do expect it will cease to be divided.

This prognostication made by Senatorial candidate Lincoln in 1858 proved accurate to the letter. Unity came by the sword. During the process of re-unionization or, in other words, Congressional Reconstruction, the whole question of the powers of the states relative to those of Congress turned upon the political status of the black man. But this time, Congress was in the driver's seat. The passage and subsequent ratification of the Thirteenth, Fourteenth, and Fifteenth Amendments to the United States Constitution by the Republican Congress was, in the first instance, a manifestation of the new relationship. In all three cases, the rights of Congress to legislate regarding the individual states was established via constitutional authority. As a result of the Thirteenth Amendment, Congress was granted the right to legislate on the question of slavery. The Fourteenth Amendment, for the first time in history, gave a constitutional definition to the term "citizen," and the Fifteenth decreed that neither "race, color or previous condition of servitude" should abridge the voting rights of those citizens. Heretofore, each of these questions had been considered to be exclusively within the domain of states' rights.

As a direct result of the Fourteenth and Fifteenth Amendments, the role of the black man in the American political system changed as did the process itself. In refusing to mitigate the broad effects of emancipation by confining the activity of the negro, the Reconstruction measures were seen at first to consolidate a new economic, political, and social status for the recently manumitted bondsmen. This new relationship between black citizens and the two major political parties can best be summed up in the words of Frederick Douglass who declared that: "The Republican Party is the ship, all else is the sea."

The 800,000 registered blacks in the Old Confederacy made up a natural constituency for the G.O.P. But fear of "negro domination" on the part of white southerners, coupled with the lack of an avid commitment to black suffrage within the Republican ranks soon rendered the negro politically vulnerable. Aided by the Congressional Amnesty Act of May 22, 1872, which, for the most part, removed all disabilities placed by the Fourteenth Amendment on those who had supported the Confederacy, the way was paved for the return of the Democratic party to control in the South. Similarly, when in order to secure the Presidency for Rutherford B. Hayes in the "disputed election" of 1876, the Republicans reversed their field and adopted a conciliatory states' rights attitude toward the South and the Democrats declared open season on the black vote. Between 1870 and 1876, the Democrats took control of the following states: Georgia, North Carolina, Tennessee, Virginia, 1870; Texas, 1873; Alabama, Arkansas, 1874; Mississippi, 1875; Florida, Louisiana, South

Carolina, 1876. The asendancy of the Democratic party in the South meant black political decline. Once returned to power, the Democrats used every means available, legal and extra-legal, to curtail the suffrage rights of the black man.

Included under the heading of extra-legal means employed by political overseers of the Democratic South would be the brute violence and intimidation practiced by the Ku Klux Klan, the clever manipulation of ballots and ballot boxes, the deliberate theft of ballot boxes, false counting of ballots, illegal arrests of black voters the day before election, and the sudden removal of polling places.

Beginning in 1890, southern states under Democratic control began adopting legal means to disenfranchise the negro. To insure white control of statewide and local politics, the following state legislatures adopted suffrage amendments as part of their constitutions: Mississippi, 1890; South Carolina, 1895; Louisiana, 1898; North Carolina, 1900; Alabama, Virginia, 1901; and Georgia, 1908. The substance of the laws restricting suffrage was that the prospective voter had to have paid his taxes in full and then, in order to register, had to own a certain amount of property, or had to pass an educational test or else come under either the Grandfather Clause or an Understanding and Character Clause.

Property Test. Ownership of real or personal property worth x number of dollars or which taxes for the preceding year have been paid.

Tax Test. Payment of a poll tax as a voting prerequisite.

Educational Test. Ability to read and write United States Constitution in English; if physically disabled from reading and writing, must possess "ability to understand and give a reasonable interpretation of Constitution."

Grandfather Clause. Permission to an individual who could not satisfy either educational or property test to continue as a voter for life if he was a voter in 1867 or was an old soldier or the lineal descendant of such voter or soldier.

Understanding and Character Clause. Permission to an individual lacking property and education to register if he was of good character and understood duties and obligations of good citizenship.

As a case in point, the legal disenfranchisement of the black man in Louisiana serves to demonstrate the techniques and effects of circumventing federal suffrage requirements. In February of 1868 a constitutional convention met in Tulane Hall in the City of New Orleans. The main object of the gathering was to frame new suffrage requirements that would legally or quasi-legally eliminate the blacks from politics, and thus obviate the continued use of "shot-gun" tactics to accomplish that end. Since the stated purpose was to eliminate the blacks alone by getting around the requirements of the Fifteenth Amendment (which outlawed voter discrimination based solely on color), the system finally adopted was a complicated one. Accordingly, an applicant for registration had to show that he could read and write, or that he was the bona fide owner of 300 dollars worth of taxable property within the state: provided however —and these are the famous naturalization and grandfather clauses—that:

No male person who was on January 1, 1867, or at any date prior there- to, entitled to vote under the constitution or statutes of any state of the United States wherein he resided, and no son or grandson of any such person not less than twenty-one years of age at the adoption of this con- stitution, and no person of foreign birth who was naturalized prior to the first day of January 1898, shall be denied the right to register and vote in this state by reason of his failure to possess the educational or proper- ty qualifications prescribed by this constitution: provided he shall apply for registration and shall have registered in accordance with the terms of this article prior to September 1, 1898, and that no person shall be en- titled to register under this section after this date.

The new system for eliminating black participation in the elective pro- cess proved most successful. As of January 1, 1867, there was a total of 294,432 registered voters in Louisiana. Of this number 130,334 (44.3 per cent) were black. In 1900, resulting from procedures provided for in the constitution of 1898, there were 130,757 registered voters. And of this number, only 5,320 (4.1 per cent) were black. Therefore, since most Republicans were black and all blacks were Republican, the success of the Democrats in disenfranchising the negro spelled disaster for the G.O.P. in the South. On the false assumption that a two-party South could be built at the expense of its black constituency, the Republicans in Washington failed to take appropriate action under the Fourteenth Amendment to check the electioneering practices of the Democrats.

By the end of the nineteenth century black disenfranchisement was virtually complete. With the departure of Representative George E. White, black Republican of North Carolina, on January 29, 1901, both Houses of Congress were again lily-white. At the time, his prediction,[4] that one day the black man would rise up "Phoenix-like" and return seemed more like the impossible dream. For viewed within the context of the Jim Crow system erected in the Democratic South, and its perva- sive pattern of discrimination rooted in law and custom and enforced by legal and extra-legal violence, the black man was totally lacking of any voice in the social,[5] political, and economic decisions affecting him.

The Democratic South relied upon two basic tactics to keep the black man away from the ballot box. Both proved most effective. Through violence such as that practiced by the Ku Klux Klan, 3,275 blacks were lynched between 1882 and 1936. During this period the Republican National Committee repeatedly opposed such practices and called for the enactment of anti-lynching legislation. The Democratic party platforms were completely silent on the matter. In the courts the Democrats were equally successful in denying the black man his constitutional rights of suffrage. In spite of the fact the The Grandfather Clause was first declared unconstitutional by the Supreme Court *(Guinn and Beal* vs *United States)* on June 21, 1915, the negro in the South was still excluded from political participation. This was accomplished under the aegis of the "white primary" based on a Supreme Court decision *(Grovey* vs *Torons-end)* that political parties are "voluntary associations for political action and not the creature of the state." And that although private persons or groups could not violate the Fourteenth Amendment, the Democratic party, as a private association, could legally exclude blacks from its primaries without violating the equal protection clause of the constitution. In reaching that decision, the Supreme Court of the United States acknowledged what everyone had long known to be. The Democratic organization in the one-party South was indeed the "white man's party" and there was no room in the political inn for the black man.

The outrageous living conditions heaped upon the negro as a result of the Jim Crow practices of the South caused many to migrate to the North. Between 1920 and 1930 over three-quarters of a million blacks left the South. In 1923 alone 478,000 were uprooted. This number exceeded the 450,000 who had left in an earlier period between 1916 and 1918. The migrants who left primarily because of intolerable economic conditions settled in the northern industrial states. By way of example, the following states showed marked percentage increases in their black populations between 1910 and 1920: Michigan, 182; New York, 108; Illinois, 80; New Jersey, 78; Ohio, 66; Pennsylvania, 52.[6]

Politically speaking the southern emigrant soon learned that what had been denied him back home was apparently accessible in the North. Geography did make a difference. And when he went to the polls, to no one's surprise, he pulled the Republican lever. For, in case after case, when a black man was elected to an important political post it occurred on the Republican ticket. The first black to serve in the New York State Assembly was Edward A. Johnson, a Republican out of New York City. Elected in 1917, he served one term and was succeeded in 1919 by another black Republican, John C. Hawkins, who served until 1923. Likewise, in New York City the first black Alderman, George W. Harris, Founder and Editor of the New York *News*, was also a Republican. He was elected in 1920. Farther west in Illinois, where blacks had served in the state legislature since 1882, the people of the first Illinois Congressional District chose Republican Oscar De Priest to represent them in Washington. Again, the attachment of the negro to the G.O.P. proved unshakable. As a matter of fact, the negro in Chicago in 1930 was more Republican than the white man. For although the black man constituted only 6.9 per cent of the total population and 8.7 per cent of the voting age population, he made up 11 per cent of the Republican vote. The black masses during the first one third of the twentieth century were doggedly attached to the party of Lincoln and anybody who was anybody in black politics was Republican. Hence, it is not surprising that William L. Dawson, who would one day become one of the most influential men on Capitol Hill, began his career in Chicago as a successful Republican candidate for Alderman.

North of the Mason–Dixon Line the black man encountered a different political dynamic. Not only was he able to cast his ballot freely, he soon discovered that the give and take of two-party politics offered added advantages. Whereas the one-party politics of the Democratic South had excluded him from political participation, both parties in the North welcomed and sought his vote. The Democratic machines of the North, in contradistinction to their southern counterpart, were prepared to challenge the Republicans at the polls for the black vote. And how well they succeeded in wooing the negroes away from the G.O.P. is seen not only in the fact that the first negro Democrat was elected to Congress in 1936, but also in the relative number of elected black officials at the statewide and local levels between 1936 and 1940. The large shift in the black vote witnessed in the national election of 1936 was not the sudden stampede into the Democratic fold that one might suspect. Rather, it was the culmination of grass roots organizing at the ward level by the number-two party trying harder to be number one. This is not to say that issues such as segregation, lynching, civil rights, and the depression were not important. They certainly were. But the actual work of getting the voters to pull the Democratic lever was done by the myriad of dedicated party operatives throughout the black enclaves of the North. On this important point, history does indeed have a way of repeating itself. In 1912 and 1932 and again in 1972[7] no group of national negro leaders or luminaries has been able to alter the voting pattern of the national black electorate. Change in party preference can only be accomplished by effective leadership at the ward and precinct level.

The negroes in the North did not leave the Republican party in one massive wave. Rather, they sauntered over to the other side in discreet and discernible packets. And, although by 1940 they had become thoroughly identified with Franklin Delano Roosevelt and the New Deal Policies of the Democratic party, a significant portion of the black voters remained steadfast in their devotion to the party of Lincoln. In fact, so great was the primal attachment that in 1956, with the aid of an active campaign aimed directly at blacks, Eisenhower was able to capture 40 per cent of their vote. But alas, the Republican party was to succumb to old age and complacency—the twin tyrants of demise. Incapable of rejuvenation from within, the G.O.P. was neither able to lead the nation into a new era nor even prepared to take political advantage of the Eisenhower record on civil rights. But the Democrats were, and during the Kennedy campaign and his subsequent Administration, they took the civil rights initiative completely away from the Republicans.

By 1964, the political metamorphosis of the negro from Republican to Democrat was complete. That year Lyndon Baines Johnson, the first southern politician to be elected President in the twentieth century, fell heir to 97 per cent of the black vote. And so, after more than one hundred years of active political participation, the black man has experienced, from both sides, the immediate and long-term effects of party policy upon his condition. From that vantage point, several things are readily apparent: 1) on a quantifiable basis, the Republican party maintains the edge in having advocated and fostered policies from which the black man derived broad-based political benefits; 2) since blacks were first enfranchised, both parties have, during the course of history, adopted policies that led either directly or indirectly to black disenfranchisement; and 3) whereas it was the Republicans who the negro once considered his "friends," today the Democrats are accorded that designation.

Considering the make-up of the national Democratic organization, every Presidential nominee has had to contend with a blatant anti-black southern constituency. And none, perhaps with the exception of Lyndon Johnson, has been willing or able to effectively promote civil rights legislation from which the negro would be the immediate benefactor. If in 1960 John F. Kennedy was wary of rubbing the South the wrong way and therefore decided to go slow on the question of civil rights, it is all the more obvious that Woodrow Wilson in 1912 would be more reticent. In return for their support, Democratic candidate Wilson had promised a group of negro leaders, including W.E.B. Du Bois and William Monroe Trotter, that if elected he would see to it that the negro obtained justice "in every matter." Once elected, however, Wilson pursued another course. The man who would become the architect of the League of Nations and who wished to "Make the World Safe for Democracy," forgot his campaign pledges and silently concurred while segregation was introduced into federal agencies and well-qualified black civil servants were dismissed. As Henry Lee Moon, editor of *The Crisis*, put it:

Despite all his vaunted idealism, his reputed world view, his oral commitment to democratic principles, Woodrow Wilson . . . was on the basic race issue as provincial as George Wallace or Lester Maddox. . . . At heart he was a bigot—an educated racist, contemptuous of black folk.[8]

The "racist" policies of the Wilson Administration that Moon described were not limited solely to the Chief Executive and his White House staff. The Democratic Congress that was elected along with Wilson contained a number of Dixie "demagogues," as Du Bois referred to them, who sponsored "the greatest flood of discriminatory bills . . . that has ever been introduced since the civil war." Teddy Roosevelt, in seeking the Presidency via the third-party route, needed southern support. In short, this meant that the Progressive party had to forego a large number of black voters to whom Roosevelt had endeared himself while President. And since the black delegates to the Republican Convention remained with William Howard Taft, Roosevelt's ideological and practical support came from the "Lily White" faction within the party.

In 1972, 21 per cent of the delegates to the Democratic National Convention were black, whereas approximately 5 per cent of the Republican delegates were black. Better than any other indicator, these figures come closer to representing the actual participation of blacks in the national political arena. The small number of black Republican delegates represents a large decrease. At one point in history, blacks were to be found solely in attendance at Republican Conventions. In fact, prior to 1928, blacks had never attended any National Democratic Convention. That year several black alternate delegates appeared at the convention in Houston, Texas. In deference to the strict segregationist policies of the southern Democrats, the blacks were fenced off from the main body at the convention by a chicken-wire enclosure.

The exclusionary measures regarding blacks adhered to in the South and acquiesced to at the national level have, on more than one occasion, been sustained by the Supreme Court of the United States. Indeed, the nation's highest tribunal has been used successfully by opponents of black enfranchisement to thwart the negroes' quest for political opportunity. In case after case, beginning with the Dred Scott Decision, Court rulings were handed down which effectively blocked black participation in the meaningful party politics of the one-party South. It was not until

1944 that the Supreme Court ruled *(Smith* vs *Allright)* that the "white primary" was basically a legal device that excluded negroes from participating in the choice of elected officials. And, as a result of this ruling, black political activity increased dramatically. While fewer than 250,000 and those mostly in the cities, had been registered in the South prior to World War II, ten years later there were more than one million registered blacks.

By the mid-fifties civil rights was fast becoming a national political issue and the advance guard of both parties knew it. Due in large part to the activities of Attorney General Herbert Brownell and several congressional Republicans, it seemed for a time during the campaign and election of 1956 that the Republican party might indeed recapture the black vote. In reference to civil rights, Vice-President Nixon told a Harlem audience that if Republicans were elected "you will get action nor filibusters." Hubert Humphrey warned the Democrats that they were "digging their own grave by inaction in the field of civil rights." This admonition proved correct. For in 1956 black votes provided the margin of Republican victory in Louisiana and Tennessee and were decisive in Eisenhower's carrying the Alabama counties containing Birmingham, Mobile, and Montgomery. Elsewhere in the South blacks voted heavily Republican—in Maryland, North and South Carolina, Virginia, Miami, Tampa, and Savannah. Up north in Adam Clayton Powell's Harlem District, Eisenhower's share of the black vote rose 17 per cent over his 1952 total, and an 11-percent increase was registered in Democrat William Dawson's southside Chicago District. In fourteen Congressional Districts having black populations greater than 20 per cent, Eisenhower averaged a gain of 6 percentage points—a figure more than double his 2.3 per cent gain nationwide.

Prior to 1956 the battle for civil rights had been more or less juridical in emphasis. Highlighted by the Supreme Court decision in the case of Brown versus the Board of Education (1954), the civil rights struggle had been waged mainly in the courts. There had been no serious civil rights legislation enacted by Congress since the days of Reconstruction. The inocuous measures of the Truman Administration, sponsored by Senator Hubert Humphrey, went no further than establishing a five-man commission to gather information, make studies, and report. It was under the Eisenhower Administration and due mainly to the zeal of Attorney General Herbert Brownell, working through Kenneth Keating's House Judiciary Committee, that the first sincere effort to obtain civil rights legislation was launched. Brownell's initial efforts culminated in the enactment of the first civil rights legislation in the twentieth century. Led by Republican Senators William Knowland and Leverett Saltonstall and Democrat Senator Lyndon Johnson, the Senate of the United States passed, 72 to 18, the historic measure on August 7, 1957. All of the Republicans present approved the bill; all of the nay votes were cast by Democrats. Five southern Senators, including Lyndon Johnson of Texas and George Smathers of Florida, voted with the majority.

In comparison with previous civil rights measures enacted during Republican Administrations, the 1957 bill was indeed mild. The "pitiful remnant of a civil rights bill," as it was called by Republican Senator Gordon Allott of Colorado, was the child of less-than-committed leadership within the Republican hierarchy and the *pro forma,* salutary respect given southerners on matters of civil rights within the Democratic party. Along with several other Democratic partisans, the influence of Roy Wilkins of the N.A.A.C.P. was probably decisive in opting in favor of a watered-down bill—the rationale being that it could serve as a base to be built upon in the future. However, the best indicator of what impact the bill would have once it became law can be deduced from the words of Democrat Richard Russell of Georgia, one of the nation's leading segregationists. He hailed the final measure that passed the Senate without the necessity of a cloture motion as "the sweetest victory in my twenty-five years as a Senator." So it is not surprising that within fifteen days after having affixed his signature, the inefficacy of the bill was made abundantly clear to the President and the nation. In order to force compliance with the decision of former Republican Governor Earl Warren's Court *(Brown* vs *Board of Education),* the Eisenhower Administration ordered troops into the South for the first time since Reconstruction. Their purpose was to insure the desegregation of Central High School in Little Rock, Arkansas.

The severe limitations of the 1957 measure were partially obviated by the second Civil Rights Act passed during the Eisenhower Administration. According to the 1960 Act, the Attorney General was given additional powers. However, not unlike its immediate predecessor, it too was a compromise and totally inadequate to the growing legions of civil rights activists. From their vantage point, not only did it deal ineffectively with voting rights; it also failed to even touch upon several vital issues, namely, employment, housing, school desegregation, and access to public accommodations.

Up to this point in history the Republican party had been the unchallenged leader in the area of black civil rights. In terms of legislative enactment, Supreme Court pronouncements, Executive fiat, and platform promises, the party of Lincoln had led the way. On this, the major question of American history, while the donkeys dawdled the pachyderms performed. Whenever civil rights legislation had been enacted, it was done so through the leadership of a Republican Administration and/or Republican congressmen. Even the outstanding liberal Democratic Presidents such as Woodrow Wilson and Franklin Delano Roosevelt were content to let sleeping dogs lie. They were unwilling to raise the ire of their southern colleagues by pushing for civil rights legislation. As a matter of fact, it was not until 1940 that a Democratic platform even made positive mention of the negro (Table 5).

In the election of 1960 civil rights was a major issue and both parties, as their platforms indicate, wanted the black vote. But somehow the Democratic strategy paid dividends while that of the Republicans fizzled. While the Republicans were content to rely on their record in the field of civil rights, the Democrats chose to step up the game. In preference to legislation, Democratic candidate John F. Kennedy chose to emphasize the responsibility of the President to provide a "moral tone and moral leadership" in the field of civil rights. And a long-distance phone call to Mrs. Martin Luther King whose husband was sitting in an Atlanta jail was sufficient to convince black people that he meant what he said. In one of the closest elections in the entire history of the Presidency, John F. Kennedy won out over Richard M. Nixon, the heavy Democratic black vote being enough to swing the balance in several close states. As the black vote went so went the election.

History has shown that there is quite often a vast difference between the candidate for office and the office holder. Once elected Kennedy was no different from any of his Democratic predecessors. He too was unwilling to "trouble the water" and stir up a hornet's nest within the party on the question of civil rights. Although he had, at the outset, promised to introduce legislation embodying the party's platform position "early" in 1961, he was seen to retreat from this stance during the campaign. Consequently, during his abbreviated term of office no civil rights legislation reached the floor of Congress. The moral commitment he often expressed did not produce legislation. As Arthur Schlesinger explained, it was not that Kennedy was reneging on campaign promises but that he "had a terrible ambivalence about civil rights."[9]

Certainly, if a northern liberal President was hesitant about pressing for civil rights legislation, the southerner who succeeded him was not. Cast from a conservative mold, Lyndon Johnson listed civil rights as the first among the immediate tasks facing him. Throughout the remaining Kennedy Administration and during his four years in office, Johnson became a most outspoken advocate of civil rights. As Senator from Texas he had voted for the milder measures of the Eisenhower Administration

169

on the grounds that they sought "to solve the problems of 1957—not to reopen the wounds of 1865." In his new role as Chief Executive, the farm boy from Texas stated emphatically and without reservation that it was time to produce definitive legislation in the field of civil rights. In the midst of ever-increasing civil rights drives in the South and growing urban unrest in the North that threatened the nation's future, Lyndon Baines Johnson was the right man in the right place at the right time. And he was wise enough to strike while the iron was hot. For the first time in American political history, a Democratic President took the lead in pressing for and obtaining meaningful civil rights legislation.

The civil rights legislation enacted during Johnson's term of office was second only to that of the Reconstruction period. In achieving this monumental task, the thirty-sixth President had bipartisan congressional support. So steadfast was his support—a reaffirmation of Senate Republican leader Everett Dirksen's quote from Victor Hugo that "Stronger than all the armies is an idea whose time has come"—that for the first time in history the Senate cloture rule was adopted during debate on a civil rights bill. The civil rights bills enacted during the Johnson Administration are no small tribute to the quality of Executive leadership that he was able to provide in this vital area during one of the more troubled periods of American histroy.

Greater than any other issue, civil rights has been the major political determinant in the lives of black folks. And during the one hundred year interval between 1868 and 1968, both parties at times considered themselves the champion of black civil rights and made positive contributions. In other areas of political endeavor relating specifically to black advancement, the activities of the two major parties have been dismal failures. What can be said of the Republican instituted Freedmen's Bureau (excluding the educational component) is equally applicable to the Democratic welfare-oriented programs of the New Deal and the Great Society. When the programs had run their course, the negro was substantially no better off economically than he had been before they started. The ingredient needed to make the programs a success was always omitted. If in 1865 the Republicans were willing to forget about the "forty acres and a mule" to appease the southern landowners, in 1965 the Democrats were willing to opt in favor of make-believe, dead-end jobs in so-called anti-poverty programs so as not to offend the party's main ally, organized labor, by tampering with the labor supply balance. As for the Great Society programs, President Nixon exhibited no lack of candor when he stated that "Those who made a profession out of poverty got fat; the taxpayer got stuck with the bill; and the disadvantaged themselves got little but broken promises."[10] However, it should be pointed out that President Nixon's chiding of the Democratic party is mild in comparison with the Democrats' handling of a similar situation. In the Democratic Campaign Text Book of 1880, they were a bit more vituperative in exposing shortcomings of the Republicans relative to programs ostensibly designed to benefit the black man. Based on information presented by Democrats, it was the Republican party that was responsible for the failure of the Freedmen's Bank. In an article entitled "How the Poor Freedmen were Swindled," they accused the G.O.P. of perpetuating the "wickedest and meanest of all frauds." Part of their argument was put into verse which declared that the party of Lincoln was so vile that it would "Cheat the living, rob the dead, and deprive the orphan of his crust of bread."

Listed under the heading of patronage would come the practice of appointing blacks to high-level Federal positions. This policy was first put into practice by President Grant. However, he and Lincoln used Frederick Douglass, a black Republican, as confidential White House adviser. Later, another leading black Republican, Booker T. Washington, served in that same capacity under several Presidents, most notable of whom was Theodore Roosevelt. And although Republican Presidents have always made judicious use of black political patronage, the practice was not instituted under a Democratic Chief Executive until the regime of Franklin Delano Roosevelt. Among the many precedents established within Democratic party ranks during the Administration of Lyndon Baines Johnson was the appointment of the first black to the Supreme Court of the United States and the naming of Robert Weaver to a Cabinet post. However, the numerical record for naming blacks to high-level Federal positions belongs to Richard Nixon. As Chief Executive he made more high-level black appointments and upgraded more blacks in civil service status than any former President.

High-level appointments—those ornamental gewgaws of political life —have been used most effectively by both major parties as an ancillary aid in attracting the attention of the black electorate. Quite often they have been used as a substitute for actual programs and genuine performance. In the main, since blacks have never really achieved a two-party identity, they have served to keep the negro attached almost exclusively to a particular party.

Reviewing the past activity of blacks with respect to the adversary system of American politics, it is evident that historically it has been an either/or situation. As Tables 3 and 14 indicate, either we were Republicans or else we were Democrats. We have not been able to build permanent grass-roots bases within both parties simultaneously. Only during the transition from one party to the other are the superficial aspects of two-party involvement discernible (Table 10). Obviously, given the context of practical American politics, such a one-sided approach suffers from severe limitations. On one hand, any voting bloc attached exclusively to a single party over an extended period of time tends to be taken for granted and gradually loses influence within party councils. On the other hand, belonging exclusively to one party within a two-party system is not "playing the game"—a serious mistake that left uncorrected leads eventually to a form of self-relegated disenfranchisement.

One-party politics in America imposes severe limitations upon its practitioners. As a process, exclusionary, single-party politics is fundamentally antithetical to the practice of American democrary for it eliminates the freedom-of-choice factor. Without freedom of choice it becomes exceedingly difficult to bring about political reform either within or between the two major parties. Consequently, for blacks to register discontent with the practices of a particular party, it has often been necessary to adopt protest methods. Occasionally the techniques employed have included the Primary. But obviously it too has severe limitations. The traditional methods of protest include running third-party candidates, "crossing-over," and boycotting the polls on election day.[11]

Prior to 1936 the negro was a "born" Republican. Robert R. Church, a black National Republican Committeeman from Tennessee, once said that "To the negro, devils and Democrats are the same thing" and that no self-respecting negro should be caught dead pulling the Democratic lever on election day. After the election of Franklin Roosevelt to a second term in 1936, the negro became a "born" Democrat. And during the 1972 Presidential campaign, Democratic Georgia State Legislator Julian Bond labeled any black who would vote for the Republican candidate a "political prostitute." Overlooking the tone of the rhetoric, the lesson that comes through is that the negro is neither a "born" Republican nor a "born" Democrat. It is safe to say, as the historical facts allow, that the black man in America is not genetically predisposed to either of the two major parties. Rather, he has been content to seek political opportunities where they already existed. He has rarely organized and fought on a nationwide scale to create and expand political opportunities where they did not exist.

In looking back after more than one hundred years of active political participation, we discover that our approach to politics has been mainly visceral. Our prime motivation as to party preference has been—and not without justification—to those things that appealed to us emotionally. And so we were Republicans because Lincoln removed our legal shackles and we were Democrats because Roosevelt fed us. However, circumstances do change, and over an extended period of time new approaches must be devised if old problems are to be resolved. Present and future demands of the race require that we expand our political participation in the two-party system. Such demands also require that we increasingly become more cerebral in our approach—that we use our heads as well as our hearts in establishing priorities. In terms of political power, this means that we begin at the beginning—in the urban wards and precincts and in the rural county districts. For it is in these areas that the real political power in the American political system lies. It is at these levels that the black masses, North and South, East and West, can relate to that power. It is at these levels that school commissioners, police commissioners, health commissioners, sheriffs, mayors, city and county and state and federal representatives are chosen. It is at these levels that the real political battle must be waged.

To successfully expand our role in the American political process requires that we adopt a new political relevance. In short, this means that we become involved, at the grass-roots level, in the affairs of both major parties. It also means that we seek after, fight for, and obtain equitable and effective representation at every level in the party councils of both parties, and that we leave no stone unturned in securing our due measure of that political power that has so long eluded us. This approach insures a degree of freedom normally absent in one-party politics. Simply put, a two-party strategem can produce added dividends on which to build a surer and more secure future for our race. Judiciously deployed, two-party politics will enable us to move forward, toward the front of the line. And when we move forward, America moves forward.

* * *

"We ain't what we ought to be; we ain't what we gonna be; but thank God we ain't what we use to be." So goes an old negro saying that grew out of the black man's experience in a strange land governed by people stranger still. Contained in those few lines are all the philosophy that several generations of Heideggers and Kierkegaards could be called upon to try and explain. Contained in these simple lines are the words that gave form to the meaning of being black in America. These words are the foundation on which generations of black people built their hopes for the future. They are the words but express both the dream and the vision.

If, as we have been led to understand, the dream is about freedom, certainly the vision must be of a time and place where that freedom becomes the right of all. Freedom as a right of all is the reason that America exists. It is the guiding principle that determines the Country's future course.

The elliptical phraseology used by the Founders in framing the Constitution relegated millions of African people to an apolitical class of servile "persons." That phraseology had to be corrected by blood in order for America to remain. In each of the centuries spanned by America, the presence of the black man has had a profound effect upon the nation's definition of freedom. It appears, in a sense, as though the black man himself were freedom's definer. His experience in America has certainly put him in a unique position. But America, when it is ultimately defined, will be defined not in terms of black, not in terms of white nor in terms of hybridized yellow. The ultimate definition of America will be made on the basis of the extent to which the American democratic system has been able to permit the full political and economic expression of the America that is black and the America that is white speaking a common language, having a common meaning. This is the *sine qua non* of American existence. This is the end toward which history has pre-determined America's course. There is no turning back the clock.

The principle upon which both the politics and the people depend was once plainly stated by Everett Dirksen: "America grows, America changes." To do otherwise would be fatal. That purpose toward which the nation has evolved must continue.

NOTES

CHAPTER 1: FROM THE BEGINNING

1. Professor Leo Weiner of Harvard pointed out in his three-volume study, *Africa and the Discovery of America,* that it is very likely that blacks from Africa had migrated to the American continent long before the voyage of Columbus. He introduces facts that demonstrate that many of the rites, practices, ceremonies, and words of the aborigines of the West Indian Archipelago came from Africa. Based on his studies he states that many supposedly Indian words such as "canoe" and the appellations for yam and tobacco, "nyambi" and "tubbāq" are of African origin. He also presents evidence to show that tobacco and its smoking were introduced into America from Africa by Guineans who had touched down in the New World long before Columbus.

2. Articles of the Mosaic Code provide that "there shall never be any bond slavery, villeinage, nor captivity among us, unless it be lawful captives, taken in just wars, and such strangers as willingly sell themselves or are sold unto us, and these shall have all the liberties and Christian usages which the law of God established in Israel requires. This exempts none from servitude who shall be judged thereto by authority."

3. Article VI of the Ordinance stated that "there shall be neither slavery nor involuntary servitude in the said territory otherwise than in punishment of crime thereof the parties shall be duly convicted."

4. Motion of James Madison as amended (parenthesis) and finally accepted, "The Legislature of the U.S. whenever two-thirds of both Houses shall deem necessary, or on the application of two-thirds of the Legislatures of the several states, shall propose amendments to this Constitution, which shall be valid to all intents and purposes as part thereof, when the same shall have been ratified by three-fourths at least of the Legislatures of the several states, or by Convention in three-fourths thereof, as one or the other made

of ratification may be proposed by the Legislature of the U.S. (provided that no amendments which may be made prior to the year 1808, shall in any manner affect the 4 and 5 sections of the VII article)."

CHAPTER 2: GROWING PAINS

1. The General Assembly of the Presbyterian Church in America in 1788 issued a pastoral letter recommending the abolition of slavery. In Maryland and Virginia the Methodist Episcopal Church, at one point, disqualified slaveholders from membership. Quaker activity in the abolition movement is well documented.
2. In 1800, of the 893,041 slaves in the United States, the vast majority (345,796) were to be found in Virginia.
3. Henry Adams, *History of the United States,* Vol. I (New York, 1909), p. 391.
4. Adams, *op. cit.,* pp. 20–21.
5. *Annals of the Congress of the United States,* 9 Cong., 2 Sess., (December 17, 1806), p. 167.
6. The first two-party election in the country took place in 1796. It posed Thomas Jefferson (Democrat) against John Adams (Federalist). The Electoral College chose Adams by 3 votes.
7. The election of 1800 was the first to be decided by the House of Representatives. Jefferson finally was elected over Aaron Burr by a vote of 73 to 65, but not before having made a deal with Alexander Hamilton, his long-time opponent.
8. *Annals of the Congress of the United States,* 15 Cong., 2 Sess., (February 16, 1819), pp. 1204–05.
9. A resolution offered by Charles G. Atherton, representative from New Hampshire, was adopted by a vote of 127 to 78. According to this resolution, a formal reception of petitions on the question of slavery was denied although their presentation remained unaffected. This resolution became known as the "Atherton Gag Resolution."

CHAPTER 3: THE ISSUE

1. One southern state from which neither Van Buren nor Harrison received any electoral votes was South Carolina. This state gave its 11 electoral votes (chosen by the State Legislature) to Willie P. Mangum, a states' rights candidate, who ran on the Nullification ticket. According to the South Carolina Legislature, nullification meant that the tariff laws did not operate within their boundaries and the Federal courts lacked jurisdiction to enforce such laws. Furthermore, if the Federal Government did not recognize her sovereign right to take such action she would secede from the Union.
2. *The Congressional Globe,* 27 Cong., 2 Sess., Vol. XI (January 26, 1842), p. 176.

3. The brig *Creole* left Richmond for New Orleans in October 1841 with cargo and about 135 slaves aboard. On November 7 the blacks mutinied and took the ship into port in Nassau where it arrived on November 9. Nineteen of the blacks were accused by the British authorities of mutiny and murder and were therefore imprisoned. Some of the remaining blacks were released and set free beyond the control of the American consul and ship's captain both of whom wanted them returned to the United States. However, before they could be returned to the United States, advice from the British Government was necessary. In the meantime Secretary of State Webster, in a letter dated January 29, 1842, instructed the American minister in London to become involved in the case. His instructions were to present the case to the British Government, "with a distinct declaration, that, if the facts turn out as stated, this government think it a clear case for indemnification." Lord Brougham stated a different point of view before the House of Lords. In his opinion there was no international law by which the United States could claim the parties involved. All agreed, they were subject only to British law which had outlawed all aspects of slavery in 1807. Subsequently, orders were given to free the mutineers and not to surrender the fugitives to the United States Government.

4. According to the Convention rules, a two-thirds vote was required for nomination. He and his backers attempted to rescind this to allow for a simple majority. Their efforts proved fruitless.

5. This quotation is from a letter sent by Secretary Calhoun to William R. King, American Minister at Paris.

6. The Oregon Treaty of 1846, realized during the Polk administration, fixed the boundary between the British and American claims at the 49th parallel west of the Rocky Mountains except at the western terminus of that line where it is to swerve southward around Vancouver Island and out through the Strait of Juan De Fuca. The settlement of this boundary hinged on the two countries settling their differences and initiating mutual tariff policies (Corn Law repeal and Walker Tariff).

7. In 1828, when Andrew Jackson was first elected, a total of 1.2 million popular votes were cast. When Polk ran and won in 1844, 2.7 million voters took part in his election.

8. This was not the first time that gold had been found in America but the impact of its discovery had never been as widespread and never before had it been a factor of such great importance to the expansion of European people. Actually, gold in America was first discovered in 1799 in North Carolina where an industry persisted well into the mid-1820's. In northern Georgia, gold was discovered on Cherokee land in 1829—land which eventually they had to cede for Indian rights became academic in the turbulence of a gold rush.

9. This law allowed any negro suspected of being a runaway slave to be captured and sent south without the opportunity to testify in his own behalf. The case was heard before a commissioner who was amply rewarded if he ruled against the freedom of the person.

10. This was a term used to categorize those whose views on slavery could antagonize no one.

1. Boston politics and society were controlled by northern business-men who did extensive business with their southern counterparts. Boston's imports by sea from New Orleans totaled 3.3 million dollars in 1839. This figure rose steadily. For example, in an eight-month period between September 1, 1841 and May 1, 1842, at least one-fourth of the lard and flour and one-half of the pork and corn that left New Orleans aboard Yankee ships went to Boston and was used to feed factory workers. Cotton, which had re-placed rum and codfish, as the most important cargo for the North-ern maritime industry, was carried to several foreign ports (Flanders, Lancashire, Normandy, Prussia, Alsace, Saxony) from New Orleans by Yankee ships. The men controlling this maritime industry were referred to as Lords of the Long Wharf. Their vessels also carried large quantities of ice from New England ponds to the South, the West Indies, and Orient. Another group of northern businessmen operated in conjunction with southern slaveholders, Lords of the Lash. They were called the Lords of the Loom and every pound of cotton that they received in their New England mills came aboard northern sailing vessels from ports in Savannah, Charleston, Mobile, and New Orleans.

2. This party led by Chase and Sumner was composed of northern Democrats who had left the regular party over the question of slavery. They labeled the Fugitive Slave Act of 1850 "as repug-nant to the Constitution, to the Spirit of Christianity and to the sentiments of the civilized world." Their stated purpose, according to their platform of 1852, was to defeat both the Whig and the "Slave Compromise party"—regular Democrats.

3. Evidence indicates that Douglas' stand was also influenced by the geographical location of the state he represented. In wishing to see Chicago and St. Louis opened to the vast trade of the Mississip-pi Valley and developing West, he aimed to lure Jefferson Davis, then War Department head, away from a plan being developed by the army engineers. The plan proposed by them called for a rail-road linking Memphis and Vicksburg, along an extremely southern route, to Los Angeles and San Francisco. Douglas reasoned that by opening the Nebraska Territory to slavery economic expediency would cause Davis to forego his plan, in which event Douglas' plan would readily be agreed to by the slave interests. It goes without saying that Douglas' proposed railroad route connecting the South and the East with the West coast had Chicago as its focus.

4. A month prior to this meeting an "Appeal of the Independent Democrats in Congress to the people of the United States" written by Salmon P. Chase of Ohio and bearing the signatures of Joshua Giddings, Edward Wade, Gerrit Smith, Charles Sumner, and Preston King, along with other anti-slavery politicians, was published. This "Appeal," as it came to be known, was published to protest the pas-sage of the Kansas—Nebraska Bill which permitted the extension of slavery into areas heretofore denied it by the Missouri Compromise. The "Appeal" contained no mention of any attempt to form a new party.

5. Still more vicious epithets were thrown at the new party by old line Democrats who referred to it as the *black* Republican or nigger-loving party.

6. Although Pierce won an overwhelming majority of the electoral vote, the results indicate that his absolute popular majority was only 46,281. He received a total of 1.6 million votes to 1.4 million for Scott and 156,149 for John P. Hale, the Free Soil candidate. The Native American and Southern Rights Party candidates together received 4,985 votes.

7. The New England Emigrant Aid Society was the brain child of Eli Thayer, a member of Congress from the State of Massachusetts. Its purpose was to make Kansas a free state by actual settlement. Thayer was aided in this venture by Amos A. Lawrence, a millionaire Boston merchant, and J.M.S. Williams and John Carter Brown of Rhode Island. The organization which began in July 1854 set out on the 19th of that month for Kansas with a company of twenty-four. Organizational purpose caused Thayer to remain behind. Based on orders received from Thayer, Charles Brascomb, already in Kansas, selected the site of the present city of Lawrence to begin the Free Soil settlement. The original twenty-four were joined in the space of two weeks by seventy more. Included among the second group were Samuel C. Pomeroy and Dr. Charles Robinson. Future events under the free-state constitution would see these early settlers fulfill prominent roles in the state. Robinson would become the first free-state governor, Pomeroy, a United States Senator.

   The pro-slavery elements in Missouri were not to be found sitting idly by in acquiescence to the anti-slavery elements from the East. When word reached Missouri of the Emigrant Aid Society's plan to settle 20,000 Free Soilers in Kansas, the Missourians were quick to react. They formed an association (Westport, Missouri, July 1854) and resolved to hold themselves in readiness "whenever called upon by any of the citizens of Kansas . . . to assist and remove any and all emigrants who go there under the auspices of the Northern Emigrant Society."

   Organized under such names as the "Blue Lodger," "Social Bands," "Sons of the South," etc., the pro-slavery elements in the struggle for Kansas had the upper hand. They were able to cross their minions over the state line and take immediate possession of the land. At first they were quite successful.

8. During the election for the free-state constitution (December 15, 1855), armed bands of Missourians menaced the resident citizens in an effort to deter their voting. Ballot boxes at Kickapoo, Leavenworth, and several other places were destroyed. When residents from the territory, on instruction of the election inspectors, were told that they would be allowed to cast their ballots in other precincts, bloody encounters between the Missourians and Kansans took place at the ballot boxes. While en route home, the Missourians captured R.P. Brown, member-elect to the Kansas House of Representatives and murdered him.

9. This call was also read and included as part of the Official Proceedings of the Republican National Convention, held as scheduled in Pittsburgh.

10. The so-called manifesto was actually a confidential report to the State Department in which Buchanan, then Minister to England, joined with the American Ministers to France (Mason) and Spain (Soule) in arguing that if Spain were not willing to sell Cuba to the United States for 1,300,000 dollars the American Government (Pierce Administration) could, based on the principles of self-preservation, justifiably "wrest" the land from its owners in order to prevent its being Africanized into a second Santo Domingo (Haiti).

CHAPTER 5: ". . . AS AMERICAN AS CHERRY PIE"

1. *The Congressional Globe*, 34 Cong., 1 Sess., (May 19–20, 1856), pp. 529–44.
2. The name given to the woman of his devotion by Don Quixote in Cervantes' classic novel. She lived in the village adjacent to that of Don Quixote. Her real name was Aldonza Lorenzo. Her father was Lorenzo Corchuelo, and her mother Aldonza Nogales. Quixote chose to call her Dulcinea del Toboso (for she was born at that place) thinking it to be harmonious, uncommon, and significant. Dulcinea is often used synonymously for "sweetheart."
3. A crime against the majesty and sovereignty of the Roman people, i.e., high treason.
4. William Tell is the legendary national hero of Switzerland. Fable has it that he was the champion of the Swiss in the War of Independence against Emperor Albert I of Austria, slain in 1308. Having refused to bow to the hat of the tyrant Gessler set up in the marketplace as a symbol of Austrian domination, Tell was ordered by the imperial governor to shoot an apple off the head of his own son. Tell succeeded in this dangerous trial of skill but in his agitation dropped an arrow from his robe. When queried by Gessler as to the purpose of the second arrow Tell fearlessly replied, "To kill thee had I slain my son." Upon hearing this Gessler ordered him to be carried in chains across the lake to Kursnacht Castle, the home of the imperial governor, and thrown "to the reptiles that lodged there." He was, however, rescued by the peasantry and, having shot Gessler, freed his country from the Austrian yoke.
5. In addition to Keith and Simonton, the attack was witnessed by Senators Douglas, Toombs, Mason, and Slidell of Illinois, Georgia, Virginia, and Louisiana, respectively. It is said that Keith and Henry A. Edmundson, Congressman from Virginia, had advance knowledge of Brooks's plan to chastise Sumner. Keith was later charged with being an accessory to the assault.
6. Wilson, Sumner's colleague in the Senate from Massachusetts, refused the duel on the grounds of barbarity and illegality but in order to protect his manhood reiterated his belief in the doctrine of self-defense. His invoking the self-defense principle caused other Congressmen to arm themselves. A few days after the incident, in order to board a train for New Jersey where he was to make a political speech, Wilson was escorted to the railroad station by several friends whose belts were seen bulging with bowie knives and pistols. Over in the House, Burlingame took personal charge of the affair and accepted Brooks's challenge to duel. In order to avoid arrest

he left for Canada at night. Brooks failed to appear on the grounds that he feared crossing enemy territory to reach Canada.

7. States that held statewide elections in October. In 1856, the Pennsylvania statewide election was held on October 14. Maryland's election of that year, held on the eighth of October, was attended by severe violence. In Baltimore, an eighth ward fight in which the "blackguards" fought the "rip-raps" and the "plug-uglies," ended with four dead and fifty wounded.

8. In 1834, Dred Scott, a black man, was held in slavery by Dr. Emerson, an army surgeon then stationed in Missouri. On his transfer to Rock Island, Illinois, that year the physician took Scott with him. Two years later, the two again accompanied each other to Fort Snelling, in what is now the state of Minnesota. While at Fort Snelling, Dr. Emerson acquired a black woman who was being held as a slave by a Major Taliaferro. With the consent of the former, Scott and the woman, named Harriet, were married. Scott fathered two children by Harriet. One, Eliza, was born on a Mississippi steamboat north of the Missouri line. The other Lizzie, was born at Jefferson Barracks in Missouri. In a later business transaction, John A. Sanford of New York City acquired the entire family. On the basis of the fact that he now resided in "free" territory Scott brought suit for his freedom in the Circuit Court and was overturned by the Missouri Supreme Court whose verdict was eventually sustained by the United States Supreme Court. The Supreme Court based its decision on the opinion that Scott was not a citizen of Missouri in the way the word is used in the United States Constitution. Therefore, the United States Circuit Court had no jurisdiction in the case and could not render a verdict. For want of this jurisdiction, the suit brought by Scott had to be dismissed.

9. Roger B. Taney had been confidential adviser to President Jackson. When his Secretary of the Treasury Duane refused to withdraw the government deposits from the United States Bank, Jackson attempted to name Taney to that post. However, when Congress failed to confirm Taney in the new post, Jackson appointed him to the Supreme Court. He was appointed Chief Justice, against the wishes of Clay and Webster, when Marshall died in 1835.

10. The English compromise offered Kansas immediate admission as a state and a large grant of government land if the people accepted the Lecompton Constitution: If they did not assent to the document, they would be required to remain a territory until they reached a population of 90,000—the numbers required for a congressional district. With this sort of inducement, plus patronage and forgiveness, Buchanan had hoped to bring Douglas and his followers into line and secure passage of the measure. When the entire constitution was submitted to the people of Kansas on August 3, 1858, they voted it down 11,088 to 1,788.

11. According to the rules agreed to by the two men, each contestant was to have a turn at opening the debate. The opening speaker was to be allowed one hour to make his point. Following his speech, the second contestant was permitted an hour and a half in which to build his case and refute the charges made by his opponent. The opening speaker was then permitted one half-hour rebuttal time. Unquestionably, slavery was the main topic of the

debate. Issues, such as unemployment, immigration, the tariff, etc., were all avoided in spite of the fact that the country had just experienced a severe depression in 1857.

12. The book was written by Hinton R. Helper of North Carolina and published in 1857. It did not attract wide attention until 1859. Basically a compilation of facts and figures, its purpose was to show slave labor to be economically non-competitive with free labor.

13. Of the thirty-three delegations at the convention fifteen were slave and eighteen were free. The Pacific coast states, Oregon and California, voted with the South; therefore, the slave states would end up with a majority of one on any purely sectional vote.

14. Norman Judd, a railroad attorney and Illinois Republican State Chairman, had arranged to bring Lincoln's supporters to the con vention gratis from all parts of the state. He had also had duplicate admission tickets printed to be distributed among the Lincoln people who arrived early and took their places inside the auditorium.

15. The majority of the southern electorate did not favor disunion. Breckenridge, the secessionist candidate, fell 135,000-plus votes short of an absolute majority in the southern states.

16. Lincoln chose the following Cabinet: William H. Seward of New York, Secretary of State; Salmon P. Chase of Ohio, Secretary of the Treasury; Simon Cameron of Pennsylvania, Secretary of War; Caleb Smith of Indiana, Secretary of the Interior; Gideon Welles of Connecticut, Secretary of the Navy; Edward Bates of Missouri, Attorney General; Montgomery Blair of Maryland, Postmaster-General.

CHAPTER 6: PACHYDERMS AND PERFORMANCE

1. According to the figures furnished by the Adjutant-General's office, 376,553 died of wounds and disease. Of this number, 242,732 were from the North and 133,821 were from the South. An additional 60,308 (North, 30,156; South, 30,152) died while prisoners.

2. As of June 30, 1860, the national debt was given as 64.8 million dollars. On March 31, 1865, this figure had climbed to 2.4 billion dollars.

3. As of 1860 there were 31.5 million people living in the United States. Of this number 4.4 million, approximately 14 per cent, were negroes and most lived in the South. Among the 4.1 million residing below the Mason–Dixon Line, 3.9 million were classified as slaves. This figure included 411,000 mulattoes. Nationwide there were 488,000 free negroes of which 258,000 lived in the South.

4. Via statutes referred to as Black Codes, every negro was required to be in the service of some white, and to have a lawful residence as well as employment, and to carry an official certificate showing both. Vagrancy penalties were placed on anyone who could not support himself and his dependents who refused to work for usual and common wages. This penalty was strictly enforced for negroes found unlawfully assembling.

5. This Act, passed by the Republican-dominated thirty-ninth Congress on March 2, 1867, twenty-eight days prior to adjournment, provided that the President could not remove any executive official from office without the consent of the Senate. Violation of this Act would be a misdemeanor and would subject him to a fine or imprisonment. It further allowed that orders to the military forces could be issued only through the general in command of the army who could not be assigned away from Washington by the President except by request of the former or through previous Senate approval.

6. Texas, Virginia, and Mississippi were not in the Union in 1868. Louisiana capitulated to the wishes of the Democratic Party, thereby yielding the disputed election to the latter. The Georgia vote was thrown out.

7. California, Colorado, Connecticut, Delaware, Indiana, Kansas, Kentucky, Maryland, Michigan, Nevada, New Jersey, Ohio, Oregon, and Pennsylvania remained unshaken in their restriction of suffrage to white persons. It therefore became necessary, in order to make the provisions of the Fifteenth Amendment effective, for Congress to enact on May 31, 1870, a law declaring: "All citizens of the United States who are or shall be otherwise qualified by law to vote at any election by the people in any state, territory, district, county, city, parish, township, school district, municipality, or other territorial division, shall be entitled and allowed to vote at all such elections without distinction of race, color, or previous condition of servitude, any constitution, law, custom, usage, or regulation in any state, territory or by or under its authority to the contrary not withstanding."

8. Pinckney Benton Stewart Pinchback, in his day, held more offices than most white men and any other negro. Within the Republican party he belonged to the State Executive Committee and was a delegate to several national conventions. At the state level he was elected to the constitutional convention, the legislature, the Lieutenant governorship, and the Senate presidency. His claim to having been elected to the United States Senate in 1872 from Louisiana for a term of six years beginning March 3, 1873, was turned down by that body on March 8, 1876.

9. The President's salary in 1869 was 25,000 dollars per year as established by Congress in 1789.

10. Two schools had not integrated. They were located in counties that had signed long-term government contracts with the Defense Department. However, it was understood that at the expiration date of the contract, the schools would be integrated.

CHAPTER 7: DAWDLING DONKEYS

1. The Democratic Republicans (Jacksonian Democrats) were the immediate partisan predecessors of the Democratic party. Prior to the Democratic Republicans, the party was called the Jeffersonian Republicans. Throughout the text of the book the term Democrat has been applied to the party's political progenitors.

2. The Virginia and Kentucky Resolutions were a series of resolutions adopted by the Virginia and Kentucky legislatures as an expression of opposition to the Alien and Sedition Laws. The Kentucky Resolutions were drafted by Jefferson, then Vice-President, and introduced by John Breckenridge on November 16, 1798. The Virginia Resolutions were drafted by James Madison on December 24, 1798. They asserted that the Constitution was a compact between sovereign states and that it was their right to interpret it and determine the validity of laws passed under its authority. In 1799, the two states passed a second set of resolutions declaring that "the rightful remedy for a state was Nullification" in the event that laws passed by Congress were obnoxious and inimicable to its existence as a sovereign entity.

3. This organization was the forerunner of the National Association for the Advancement of Colored People (N.A.A.C.P.). The N.A.A.C.P. was founded in 1909 by liberal whites and negro intellectuals. Included among the original sponsors of the group were William English Walling, Mary White Ovington, Bishop Alexander Walters, Dr. Henry Moskowitz, John Dewey, Francis J. Grimke, Ida Wells Barnett, Charles Edward Russell, and Dr. W.E.B. Du Bois. At the time of the founding William Trotter dissented and formed the National Equal Rights League.

4. In the election of 1912 there were three major candidates for the office of President. William Howard Taft had the party regulars' nomination and ran on the Republican ticket. Theodore Roosevelt ran on the Progressive slate. Woodrow Wilson was the Democratic party nominee. When the results were in, Wilson polled 6.3 million votes to 4.2 million for Roosevelt and 3.5 million for Taft.

5. Prior to the election of Wilson in 1912, only one Democrat had been elected President since the War of 1860. Grover Cleveland of Buffalo, New York, in his first term of office, appointed James M. Trotter of Boston, Registrar of the Treasury. He raised the ire of Southern Democratic colleagues by inviting Frederick Douglass and his wife to an official White House reception.

6. The political organization that Morton headed was called the United Colored Democracy. Its aim was to control all the black patronage in Harlem.

7. According to the *Chicago Defender* of September 3, 1932, Uvalde, Texas, the home of "Cactus" John Garner, was said to ban the presence of negroes.

8. Arthur M. Schlesinger, Jr., "The Politics of Upheaval," *The Age of Roosevelt*, Vol. 3 (Boston, 1960), p. 431.

9. Foreman's official title was Adviser on the Economic Status of the Negro.

10. This organization was the Political Action Committee of the Congress of Industrial Organizations (CIO). Headed by Sidney Hillman, it ran an intensive drive in the larger industrial cities. Its appeal was to the half million negro members of the CIO and to the average black non-union voters.

11. Henry Lee Moon, *Balance of Power: The Negro Vote* (Garden City, 1948), p. 35–36.

12. Harry Golden, *Mr. Kennedy and the Negro* (Cleveland, 1964), p. 70.
13. In Illinois where 250,000 negroes voted for Kennedy, the Democrats carried the state by a mere 9,000 votes. In Michigan the same pattern prevailed. There, Kennedy's vote margin was 67,000 in a state having an estimated 250,000 black votes cast. Below the Mason–Dixon Line in South Carolina, 40,000 black votes enabled Kennedy to carry the state by a margin of 10,000 votes. These three states alone contributed 55 votes in the Electoral College. Had these electoral votes gone to Nixon, he would have won the Presidency by an electoral vote of 274 to 248. As it was, Kennedy was the winner, 303 to 219.
14. The states directly affected by the law were Alabama, Alaska, Georgia, Louisiana, Mississippi, South Carolina, and Virginia. Thirty-four counties in North Carolina and one county each in Arizona, Idaho, and Maine were also affected.
15. Martin Luther King was assassinated by a sniper's bullet. The murder took place in Memphis, Tennessee, on April 4, 1968. Dr. King had been in Memphis to lead a protest march in support of 1,300 men, mostly black sanitation workers who sought Union recognition and higher wages. As a result of the murder, violence occurred in 125 cities in twenty-eight states. Between April 11 and April 14, forty persons died, 26,000 were injured, and 21,000 were arrested. The estimated damage due to fire and looting was set at 70 million dollars. More than 20,000 troops and 45,000 national guardsmen saw duty in the holocaust.

CHAPTER 8: GET SMART

1. This quote is taken from a letter written to Monsieur De Meusnier in Paris on January 24, 1786. Monsieur De Meusnier was the author of that portion of the *Encyclopedie Politique* entitled "Economic Politique et Diplomatique."
2. The New York *Tribune*, June 16, 1854, Editorial.
3. This quote was taken from a speech delivered by Lincoln on September 16, 1859, in Columbus, Ohio.
4. *Congressional Record*, 56 Cong., 2 Sess., Vol. 34 (January 29, 1901, p. 1633.
5. The Civil Rights Act of 1875 passed by a Republican Congress declared among other things that the negro was not to be discriminated against in theaters, public conveyances, hotels, restaurants, and other places of amusement. On October 15, 1883, the Supreme Court of the United States declared that the Constitution did not give Congress the right to legislate on such matters. True, the Fourteenth Admendment did prohibit a state from denying equal privileges, but it did not apply to individuals. That was a matter of local jurisdiction, i.e., states' rights.
6. *Fifteenth Census of the United States,* "Population," Vol. VII (Government Printing Office, Washington, D.C., 1930).
7. That election pitted Democrat George McGovern against Republican incumbent, Richard Nixon. Edwin T. Sexton, Jr., director of

the black political division of the Republican National Committee "guess-timated" that the Republicans would win 25 per cent of the negro vote in the Presidential election (*Congressional Quarterly*, June 24, 1972, p. 1522). To help increase the Republican share of the black vote, an organization directed by civil rights leader, Floyd B. McKissick, former director of the Congress of Racial Equality (CORE), Sammy Davis, Jr., and other prominent negroes promoted the G.O.P. cause nationally. In spite of their widely heralded appeal to negroes to vote Republican, Nixon garnered only 13 per cent of the black vote—substantially no more than the 12 per cent he had received in 1968.

8. Henry Lee Moon, "Woodrow Wilson—Educated Racist," *The Crisis*, Vol. 77 (1970), pp. 290—93.

9. Arthur Schlesinger, Jr., *A Thousand Days* (Boston, Houghton Mifflin Company, 1965), pp. 930—31.

10. This statement appeared as part of the State of the Union Message (fourth in series) delivered by President Richard M. Nixon on Feburary 24, 1973. Figures supplied in a report prepared by the General Accounting Office tend to verify its accuracy. According to the report concerning fiscal 1971, the Neighborhood Youth Corps had a budget of 59 million dollars for its in-school program. On a nation-wide basis, eligibility was estimated at one million youths. However, only 95,000 "got a taste of the gravy." Furthermore the program fell far short of its stated goals of providing remedial education and "meaningful" job opportunities. Based on data from the three cities studied (Houston, Norfolk, and Washington D.C.) 2,367 youths took part in programs that cost 1,575,000 dollars. Most of the youths were ineligible based on program standards. Only 17 per cent of the eligible students received remedial education. As to "meaningful" job opportunities, most of the boys employed in the program (54 per cent) were employed as assistant janitors. In Washington, D.C., a "courtesy patrol" operated whose duties were "to patrol neighborhood and help elderly people off buses, help remove litter, and maintain general surveillance over neighborhood streets."

11. The history of third parties and blacks is covered in *The Negro and Third Party Politics* by Haynes Walton, Jr. (Dorrance, 1968).

The "crossing-over" technique as a means of registering dissatisfaction was effectively used by blacks in the 1972 Illinois statewide elections. Normally expected to provide the margin of votes necessary for the election of officials running on the Democratic ticket, the heavy black vote in Chicago crossed over and voted for the Republican State Attorney General candidate, William J. Scott. Chicago's black vote coupled with the down-state white Republican vote insured his election over Daley-machine incumbent Edward V. Hanrahan—the man charged by the black community with ordering the death-dealing 1969 raid on Chicago's Black Panther headquarters.

Boycotting the polls on election day was successfully employed by blacks in Rochester, New York, during the 1969, city-wide elections. Generally speaking, wards having black populations greater than 50 per cent demonstrated a marked decrease in voter turn-out. As the result of a campaign carried out by a group of insurgent political activists and coordinated by a black Republican high-school teacher, the total vote from the black wards fell off approximately one-third. Specifically, in the east-side Seventh Ward where the campaign was concentrated, the vote-total was down 4,431 votes when compared with the previous city-wide elections of 1965. The fall-off had the greatest impact on the Democratic party. Seventy per cent of the previous voters who failed to vote came out of the Democratic column. When the final tallies were in, the Republicans had captured control of the city away from the Democrats who had been in power since 1961.

APPENDIX

Table 1

BLACK ANTI-SLAVERY NEWSPAPERS

Name	City	Date of 1st Issue
Freedom's Journal	New York, N.Y.	March 30, 1827
Rights of All	New York, N.Y.	March 28, 1827
The Weekly Advocate	New York, N.Y.	Jan. −, 1837
Colored American	New York, N.Y.	March 4, 1837
National Reformer	Philadelphia, Pa.	Sept. −, 1838
African Methodist Episcopal Church Magazine	Albany, N.Y.	Sept. −, 1841
The Elevator	Philadelphia, Pa.	1842
The National Watchman	Troy, N.Y.	1842
The Clarion	Troy, N.Y.	1842
The Peoples Press	New York, N.Y.	1843
The Northern Star	Philadelphia, Pa.	
The Mystery	Pittsburgh, Pa.	1843
The Genius of Freedom		1845
The Rams Horn	New York, N.Y.	Jan. −, 1847
The North Star	Rochester, N.Y.	Nov. −, 1847
The Impartial Citizen	Boston, Mass.	1848
The Christian Herald	Philadelphia, Pa.	1848
The Colored Man's Journal	New York, N.Y.	1851
The Alienated American	Cleveland, Ohio	1852
The Paladium of Liberty	Columbus, Ohio	
The Disfranchised American	Cincinnati, Ohio	
The Colored Citizen	Cincinnati, Ohio	
The Christian Recorder	Philadelphia, Pa.	1852
The Mirror of the Times	San Francisco, Cal.	1855
The Herald of Freedom	Ohio	1855
The Anglo African	New York, N.Y.	July 23, 1859

Source: *Negro Year Book,* 1925–26, p. 222.

Table 2

MEMBERSHIP OF STATE CONVENTIONS (1867–68)

State	Convention Delegates		Registered Voters (1868)		Admitted To Union
	Black	White	Black	White	
Alabama	18	90	104,518	61,295	June 25, 1868
Arkansas	8	58	66,831*		June 22, 1868
Florida	18	27	16,089	11,914	June 25, 1868
Georgia	33	137	95,168	96,333	June 25, 1868
Louisiana	49	49	84,436	45,218	June 25, 1868
Mississippi	17	83	139,690*		Feb. 22, 1870
N. Carolina	15	118	72,932	106,721	June 25, 1868
S. Carolina	76	48	80,550	46,882	June 25, 1868
Texas	9	81	49,497	59,633	Mar. 30, 1870
Virginia	25	80	105,832	120,101	Jan. 26, 1870

*Totals–not given by race

APPENDIX

Table 3

BLACK MEMBERSHIP IN THE UNITED STATES CONGRESS
(1870–1901)

Year	Name	Party	State
Senate			
1870–71	Hiram R. Revel	Republican	Mississippi
1875–81	Blanche K. Bruce	Republican	Mississippi
House			
1870–79	Joseph H. Rainey	Republican	South Carolina
1870–71	Jefferson F. Long	Republican	Georgia
1871–73	Benjamin S. Turner	Republican	Alabama
1871–73	Robert C. DeLarge	Republican	South Carolina
1871–74	Robert B. Elliot	Republican	South Carolina
1871–76	Josiah T. Walls	Republican	Florida
1873–75 1877–79	Richard H. Cain	Republican	South Carolina
1873–77 1882–83	John R. Lynch	Republican	Mississippi
1873–75	Alonzo J. Ransier	Republican	South Carolina
1873–75	James T. Rapier	Republican	Alabama
1875–77	Jeremiah Haralson	Republican	Alabama
1875–77	John A. Hyman	Republican	North Carolina
1875–79 1882–83 1885–87	Robert Smalls	Republican	South Carolina
1875–77	Charles Nash	Republican	Louisiana
1883–87	James E. O'Hara	Republican	North Carolina
1889–93	Henry P. Cheatham	Republican	North Carolina
1890–91	John M. Langston	Republican	Virginia
1890–91	Thomas E. Miller	Republican	South Carolina
1893–97	George W. Murray	Republican	South Carolina
1897–1901	George H. White	Republican	North Carolina

Table 4

BLACK MEMBERSHIP IN SEVERAL STATE LEGISLATURES

State	1868–69	1870–71	1871–72	1873–74	1874–75	1876
Alabama						
Senate	1(33)*	4(33)	4(33)	4(33)	6(33)	6(33)
House	26(100)	27(100)	14(100)	27(100)	29(100)	23(100)
Arkansas						
Senate	1(24)	2(24)	n.d.	2(24)	n.d.	n.d.
House	7(80)	9(80)	n.d.	9(80)	n.d.	n.d.
Georgia						
Senate	3(44)	2(44)	n.d.	n.d.	n.d.	n.d.
House	31(176)	26(175)	n.d.	n.d.	n.d.	n.d.
Mississippi						
Senate	n.d.	4(33)	n.d.	9(37)	n.d.	5(37)
House	n.d.	31(108)	39(115)	55(116)	n.d.	16(116)
North Carolina						
Senate	3(50)	9(56)	5(50)	4(50)	4(50)	n.d.
House	18(120)	1(102)	12(120)	13(120)	13(120)	7(120)
South Carolina						
Senate	10(31)	12(31)	n.d.	17(31)	17(31)	17(31)
House	82(124)	75(124)	n.d.	61(124)	61(124)	54(124)
Texas						
Senate	n.d.	2(30)	n.d.	n.d.	n.d.	n.d.
House	n.d.	8(90)	n.d.	n.d.	n.d.	n.d.
Virginia						
Senate	6(40)	6(40)	3(40)	3(40)	3(40)	3(40)
House	18(137)	21(137)	14(137)	17(132)	17(129)	13(125)

Source: *Negro Year Book,* 1925–26, p. 239.
*number in parenthesis is the total membership of that body
n.d.—no data available

Table 5

CANDIDATES AND PLATFORM POSITIONS THAT APPLY
PREFERENTIALLY TO STATUS OF BLACKS
(1856–1972)

Election Year	Presidential Candidates	Party Position	
		Democratic	Republican
1856	James C. Buchanan (D)* John C. Fremont (R)	Pro-slavery	Anti-slavery
1860	Stephen A. Douglas (D) John C. Breckinridge (D) Abraham Lincoln (R)*	Pro-slavery	Anti-slavery
1864	George McClellan (D) Abraham Lincoln (R)*	none	Anti-slavery
1868	Horatio Seymour (D) Ulysses S. Grant (R)*	none	Pro-civil rights
1872	Horace Greeley (D) Ulysses S. Grant (R)*	none	Pro-civil rights
1876	Samuel J. Tilden (D) Rutherford B. Hayes (R)*	none	Pro-civil rights
1880	Winfield S. Hancock (D) James A. Garfield (R)*	none	none

*winner

(continued)

193

Table 5 (continued)

Election Year	Presidential Candidates	— — — — — Party Position — — — — —	
		Democratic	Republican
1884	Grover Cleveland (D)* James G. Blaine (R)	none	Anti-disenfranchisement
1888	Grover Cleveland (D) Benjamin Harrison (R)*	none	Anti-disenfranchisement
1892	Grover Cleveland (D)* Benjamin Harrison (R)	none	Anti-disenfranchisement
1896	William J. Bryan (D) William McKinley (R)*	none	Anti-lynching, anti-disenfranchisement
1900	William J. Bryan (D) William McKinley (R)*	none	Anti-disenfranchisement
1904	Alton B. Parker (D) Theodore Roosevelt (R)*	none	Pro-equal protection under law
1908	William J. Bryan (D) William H. Taft (R)*	none	Pro-equal treatment, anti-disenfranchisement
1912	Woodrow Wilson (D)* William H. Taft (R)	none	Anti-lynching
1916	Woodrow Wilson (D)* Charles E. Hughes (R)	none	none
1920	James M. Cox (D) Warren G. Harding (R)*	none	none

(continued)

APPENDIX

Table 5 (continued)

| Election Year | Presidential Candidates | — — — — — Party Position — — — — — | |
		Democratic	Republican
1924	John W. Davis (D) Calvin Coolidge (R)*	none	Anti-lynching
1928	Alfred E. Smith (D) Herbert Hoover (R)*	none	Anti-lynching
1932	Franklin D. Roosevelt (D)* Herbert Hoover (R)	none	Pro-civil liberties
1936	Franklin D. Roosevelt (D)* Alfred Landon (R)	none	Anti-welfarism
1940	Franklin D. Roosevelt (D)* Wendell Wilkie (R)	Anti-discrimination, pro-equal protection under law	Anti-discrimination, anti-disen-franchisement, anti-mob violence
1944	Franklin D. Roosevelt (D)* Thomas E. Dewey (R)	Pro-equal protection under law	Pro-Fair Employment Practices Commission (FEPC), anti-poll tax, anti-lynching
1948	Harry S. Truman (D)* Thomas E. Dewey (R)	Pro-equal treatment under law	Anti-lynching, pro-equal opportunity, anti-poll tax, anti-racial segregation
1952	Adlai Stevenson (D) Dwight D. Eisenhower (R)*	Pro-equal opportunity, anti-dis-crimination, pro-equal treat-ment under law	Anti-bigotry, pro-civil rights, anti-dis-crimination, pro-appointment of blacks to high federal posts, anti-Capital city segregation, anti-poll tax, pro-FEPC

(continued)

Table 5 (continued)

Election Year	Presidential Candidate	Party Position — Democratic	Party Position — Republican
1956	Adlai Stevenson (D) Dwight D. Eisenhower (R)*	Pro-equal opportunity, pro-equal treatment under law, anti-discrimination	Pro-equal opportunity, pro-equal protection under law, pro-Warren court decision
1960	John F. Kennedy (D)* Richard M. Nixon (R)	Pro-equal opportunity, pro-equal protection under law, pro-enforcement of 1957 and 1960 civil rights laws, anti-poll tax, pro-compliance with Warren court decision, pro-FEPC, pro-permanent Commission on Civil Rights, anti-discrimination	Anti-discrimination, pro-compliance with Warren court decision, pro-enforcement of civil rights laws, pro-increased enfranchisement, pro-establishment of Commission on Equal Job Opportunity, pro-Civil Rights Commission, anti-Senate Rule 22
1964	Lyndon B. Johnson (D)* Barry Goldwater (R)	Pro-civil rights	none
1968	Hubert H. Humphrey (D) Richard M. Nixon (R)*	Pro-civil rights	none
1972	George S. McGovern (D) Richard M. Nixon (R)*	Pro-school desegregation, anti-white rule in South Africa, pro-military and economic aid to Africa, anti-military aid to Portugal, pro-United Nations (UN) sanction against Southern Rhodesia, pro-UN assertion in Namibia, anti-tax relief given U.S. companies doing business with white-minority controlled governments in Africa	Pro-equal opportunity, pro-appointment of blacks to high federal posts, pro-voting rights protection, anti-*de jure* school segregation, anti-busing, pro-sovereignty of African states, pro-non-violent, evolutionary change in southern Africa

*winner

APPENDIX

Table 6

HIGH-LEVEL BLACK APPOINTMENTS
OF THE EISENHOWER ADMINISTRATION

Name	*Position*
Marion Anderson	Alternate United Nations Delegate
Consuella C. Young	Librarian, Bombay, India
Samuel R. Pierce Jr.	Special Assistant to Deputy Secretary of Labor; also Associate Counsel to the House Judiciary Subcommittee on Antitrust
Dr. Reginal W. Goff	Consultant to Ministry of Education in Iran, International Cooperation Administration
Gwendolyn Fowler	Assistant Program Analyst, Saigon, Viet Nam International Cooperation Administration
Dr. Francis M. Hammond	Information Specialist, U.S.I.A.; also Cultural Affairs Officer and Cultural Attache, U.S. Embassy in Morocco
John N. Nelson	Chief, General Ledger Section, Post Office Department
Joseph N. Birch II	Attorney, Crime Division, Post Office Department
Dr. John Eubanks	Chief of Rural Improvements Staff, U.S. Operations Mission, ICA
Dr. Felton Clarke	Board of Foreign Scholarships, State Department
George E.C. Hayes	Chairman, Public Utilities Commission
Howard Jenkins	Legislative Attorney, Solicitor's Office, Department of Labor
Ivan McLeod	NLRB, Deputy Assistant General Counsel
William Powell	U.S.I.A. Information Specialist, Liberia
Otto McClarrin	U.S.I.A. Information Specialist, Afghanistan
George L. Holland	Veterans Program, Formosa
J. Ernest Wilkins	Assistant Secretary, Department of Labor
Scovel Richardson	Chairman, Federal Parole Board
E. Frederic Morrow	Administrative Assistant to the President, White House

(continued)

Table 6 (Continued)

Name	Position
Arthur B. McCaw	Chief Field Investigator in Korea, I.C.A.
Joseph Mitchell	Attorney, Corporate Regulations Division Securities and Exchange Commission
John Scott	Attorney, Internal Security, Department of Justice
Carmel Carrington Marr	Area Adviser on Staff of Ambassador Henry Cabot Lodge, Jr., U.S. Mission to United Nations
Ulysses G. Plummer, Jr.	Attorney for Bonneville Power Administration, Oregon
Richard L. Jones	United States Ambassador to Liberia
Walter Gordon	Governor, Virgin Islands
George Reed	Chief of Mission, Monrovia, Liberia, I.C.A.
Alexander Laneuville	Special Assistant in Office of the Administrator, Veterans Administration
L.B. Toomer	Register, United States Treasury
Joseph A. Clarke	Special Assistant to Deputy Postmaster General, Post Office Department
James A. Tillman, Jr.	Assistant Training Officer, Far Eastern Region I.C.A., Djakarta, Indonesia
Archibald J. Carey, Jr.	First Alternate Delegate to United Nations and Vice-Chairman of President's Committee on Employment Policy
Vernon F. Greene	Assistant Chief, Legislative Division, Post Office Department
James M. Nabrit	Member of President's Committee on Government Contracts
Asa T. Spaulding	Member of U.N.E.S.C.O.
Charles B. E. Freeman	Attorney, Tax Division, Justice Department
Joseph R. Ray, Sr.	Special Assistant to the Administrator of Housing and Home Finance Agency
Philip Sadler	Special Assistant to Commissioner of Public Housing on Racial Relations
Lois Lippman	Secretary in the White House
George Maceo Jones	Architectural Adviser, F.O.A.
Mallory C. Walker	Immigration and Naturalization Examiner, Oregon

(continued)

APPENDIX

Table 6 (continued)

Name	Position
Dr. Frank M. Snowden, Jr.	Cultural Attaché, American Embassy in Rome, U.S.I.A.
Joseph H. Douglass	Assistant to Assistant Secretary for Program Analysis, on Problems of Youth, Health, Education and Welfare Department
Leo P. Miller	U.S. District Attorney for the Virgin Islands
Robert Haith	Assistant Director, Veterans Hospital, Tuskegee, Alabama
Dr. J. Max Bond	Chief, Educational Mission, Afghanistan
Frank Walker	Administrative Aide, Postal Transportation System, New Orleans, Louisiana
Charles H. Mahoney	United Nations Delegate
Robert Lee Brokenburr	Alternate United Nations Delegate
Julia Cooper	Attorney (first lady), Criminal Division, Justice Department
Roberta Church	Minorities Consultant, Department of Labor
Jewell Stratford Rogers	Assistant U.S. District Attorney
Franklin H. Williams	Ambassador to the United Nations

Table 7

HIGH-LEVEL BLACK APPOINTMENTS
OF THE NIXON ADMINISTRATION

Name	Position
Elizabeth Koontz	Director Women's Bureau, Department of Labor
Robert Duncan	Judge, United States Court of Appeals
Benjamin Hooks	Member Federal Communication Commission
John Reinhardt	Ambassador to Nigeria
John Powell	General Counsel, U.S. Commission on Civil Rights
Frank Kent	Associate Director for Human Affairs, Office of Economic Opportunity
Patricia King	Deputy Director, Office of Civil Rights, Health, Education and Welfare Department
Arthur Reid	Director of Inter-governmental Relations, Office of Economic Opportunity
Albert E. Hampton	Comptroller, Department of Housing and Urban Development
George Haley	Chief Counsel, Urban Mass Transportation, Department of Transportation
Samuel R. Pierce, Jr.	General Counsel, U.S. Treasury Department
T. M. Alexander, Jr.	Assistant Commissioner for Unsubsidized Insured Housing Programs
Howard Jenkins, Jr.	Member National Labor Relations Board
Samuel C. Adams, Jr.	Assistant Administrator for Africa, Agency for International Development
John L. Costa	Commissioner, Assistance Payments Administration, Health, Education and Welfare Department
Constance Newman	Director of Volunteers in Service to America
Ben Holman	Assistant Attorney General, Community Relations Service, Department of Justice
Samuel Singletary	Director of Minority Affairs, Office of Economic Opportunity

(continued)

APPENDIX

Table 7 (continued)

Name	Position
Chris Roggerson	Director, Office of Voluntary Program, Equal Employment Opportunity Commission
Dr. Alfred L. Edwards	Head of Rural Development and Conservation, Department of Agriculture
Theodore R. Britton Jr.	Deputy Assistant Secretary for Research and Technology
Colston Lewis	Commissioner Equal Employment Opportunities Commission
James Frazier	Director, Office of Civil Rights
Samuel C. Jackson	General Assistant Secretary for Community Planning and Management, Department of Housing and Urban Development
John L. Jenkins	Director of Office of Minority Business Enterprise, Department of Commerce
John L. Blake	Director, Job Corps, Department of Labor
Lutrelle F. Parker	Examiner in Chief, U.S. Patent Office, Department of Commerce
Gloria Toote	Director of Voluntary Action Liaison, ACTION
Samuel J. Simmons	Assistant Secretary for Equal Opportunity, Department of Housing and Urban Development
James E. Johnson	Head of Manpower and Reserve Affairs, Department of the Navy
Calvin Banks	Chief, Community Assistant Division, Department of Transportation
William H. Brown III	Chairman, Equal Employment Opportunity Commission
Stanley B. Thomas, Jr.	Head of Youth and Student Affairs, Health, Education and Welfare Department

Table 8

THE "BLACK CABINET" (F.D.R.)

Name	Position
Mary McLeod Bethune	President, Bethune Cookman College
Edgar Brown	United Government Employees
Dr. Roscoe C. Brown	Public Health Service
Dr. Ambrose Caliver	Department of Interior
Joseph H. Evans	Farm Security Administration
Charles E. Hall	Department of Commerce
William H. Hastie	Dean, Howard University Law School
Dr. Frank S. Horne	Teacher and poet
Joseph R. Houchins	Department of Justice
Henry A. Hunt	Farm Credit Administration
Dewey R. Jones	Department of Interior
Eugene Kinckle Jones	Executive Secretary, National Urban League
Edward H. Lawson Jr.	Works Progress Administration
Ralph E. Mizelle	Post Office Department
Lawrence A. Oxley	Department of Labor
Ted Poston	Office of War Information
J. Parker Prescott	Housing Authority
Alfred E. Smith	Works Progress Administration
Dr. William J. Thompkins	Recorder of Deeds
William J. Trent	Department of Interior
Robert L. Vann	Editor, *Pittsburgh Courier*
Dr. Robert C. Weaver	Department of Interior
Arthur Weiseger	Department of Labor
John W. Whitten	Works Progress Administration

Table 9

RELIEF DATA–SOUTHERN CITIES
AND OTHER IMPORTANT URBAN CENTERS
(MAY, 1934)

Cities	Total Blacks On Relief	Blacks In Domestic Service On Relief	Percentage Domestic Service
Bowling Green, Ky.	130	80	61.5
Biloxi, Miss.	360	217	60.2
Wheeling, W. Va.	438	200	45.6
Lake Charles, La.	886	328	37.0
Houston, Texas	6,839	3,829	56.2
Jackson, Miss.	1,714	964	56.2
Evansville, Ind.	1,647	810	49.2
Lexington, Ky.	1,491	644	43.2
Charlotte, N.C.	3,153	1,778	56.3
Norfolk, Va.	4,943	2,461	49.7
Cincinnati, Ohio	11,669	4,900	43.7
New Orleans, La.	14,749	5,600	38.0
Washington, D.C.	21,315	10,213	48.3
Kansas City, Mo.	4,935	2,807	56.8
Indianapolis, Ind.	8,477	4,263	50.2
St. Louis, Mo.	18,440	7,950	43.1
Wilmington, Del.	2,426	1,090	32.5
Atlanta, Ga.	16,541	10,248	61.9
Gastonia, N.C.	140	69	49.2
Birmingham, Ala.	15,806	7,742	48.9
Oakland, Calif.	735	375	51.0
New York City	58,950	27,330	46.3
Boston, Mass.	2,534	1,232	48.6
Reading, Pa.	483	158	32.8
Rochester, N.Y.	462	203	43.9
Detroit, Mich.	15,070	3,380	22.4
Pittsburgh, Pa.	13,930	5,544	39.8
Akron, Ohio	2,365	995	42.0
Duluth, Minn.	59	15	25.4
Milwaukee, Wis.	1,575	495	31.4
	278,388	121,044	43.4

Source: Robert C. Weaver, *Opportunity: Journal of Negro Life,*
Vol. 13–14, 1935–36, p. 200.

Table 10

MAJOR PARTY VOTE FOR ROOSEVELT
IN 1932, 1936 AND 1940*

City	Ward	1932 %	1936 %	1940 %
Baltimore	5	46.4	64.2	72.1
	14	49.2	54.6	60.7
	17	43.0	46.9	59.6
Chicago	2	25.4	47.9	51.2
	3	20.7	50.1	54.2
Columbus	6	27.9	47.7	50.7
	7	23.2	46.6	57.1
Detroit	3	46.0	71.4	75.3
	5	50.2	75.0	79.2
	7	53.9	79.0	80.0
Kansas City, Kansas	2	41.5	61.3	59.6
Kansas City, Missouri	4	70.8	79.4	66.5
New Haven	9	38.9	61.0	58.7
Pittsburgh	5	53.3	76.6	77.1
Wilmington	6	28.3	40.1	41.5

* Gunnar Myrdal, *An American Dilemma* (New York, 1944), p. 496.

APPENDIX

Table 11

BLACK MEMBERSHIP IN STATE LEGISLATURES
(1935–1941)

Name	State	Party	Legislative Body
C.W. Anderson	Kentucky	Republican	House
W.T. Andrews	New York	Democrat	Assembly
John H. Brigerman	Pennsylvania	Democrat	House
R.L. Brockenbour	Indiana	Republican	Senate
H.S. Brown	Pennsylvania	Democrat	House
Daniel Burrows	New York	Democrat	House
Charles C. Diggs	Michigan	Democrat	House
C.K. Gillespie	Ohio	Republican	House
W.H. Grant	Indiana	Republican	House
E.A. Green	Illinois	Republican	House
A.F. Hawkins	California	Democrat	Assembly
J.S. Hunter	Indiana	Democrat	House
H.E. Jack	New York	Democrat	House
C.J. Jenkins	Illinois	Republican	House
E.F. Thompson	Pennsylvania	Democrat	House
W.H. Towers	Kansas	Republican	House
Rev. D.D. Turpeau	Ohio	Republican	House
W.J. Warfield	Illinois	Republican	House

*Source: *The Negro Handbook*, 1942, p. 178.

Table 12
HIGH-LEVEL BLACK APPOINTMENTS
OF THE ROOSEVELT ADMINISTRATION

Name	Position
Charles L. Franklin	Economist, Social Security Board
Truman K. Gibson	Junior Assistant Civilian Aide of the War Department; also Active Civilian Aide, Secretary of War (1943) and Assistant Executive Secretary, Fair Employment Practices Committee (1944)
Charles M. Handson	Inspector of Wages and Hours Division, Department of Labor
William H. Hastie	Civilian Aide to the Secretary of War
T. Arnold Hill	Assistant Director, Division of Negro Affairs, National Youth Administration; also Special Assistant, Office of Price Administration
Frank S. Horne	Acting Special Assistant, United States Housing Authority
Campbell C. Johnson	Executive Assistant to the Selective Service Director; also Member, Board of Intermediate Sentence and Parole (1942)
Emmer Lancaster	Special Adviser, Commerce Department
Arnett G. Lindsay	Supervisor of Negro Manuscripts, WPA
Ralph E. Mizelle	Attorney, Solicitor's Office, Post Office Department
Pauline Redmond	Assistant Information Specialist, National Youth Administration
Cuthbert P. Spencer	Assistant District Supervisor, 1940–U.S. Census, New York
Channing H. Tobias	Adviser, Selective Service; also Member, Joint Army and Navy Committee on Welfare and Recreation
William H. Trent Jr.	Racial Relations, Personnel Office, Federal Works Agency
Robert C. Weaver	Administrative Assistant, Advisory Committee on National Defense; also Assistant to Director of Operations, War Manpower Commission (1942), and Adviser to War Production Board on Negro Labor (1944)
William D. Alexander	Information Specialist, Office of Facts and Figures
Claude A. Barnett	Special Assistant, Secretary of Agriculture

(continued)

APPENDIX

Table 12 (continued)

Name	Position
Theodore M. Berry	Liaison Officer, Morale Division, Office of Facts and Figures
William M. Cooper, Sr.	Field Representative, Office of War Information
William H. Dean, Jr.	Economic Adviser to the Virgin Islands
W.C. Hueston, Jr.	Deputy Probation Officer
F.D. Patterson	Special Assistant, Secretary of Agriculture
Theodore R. Paston	Information Specialist, Office of War Information
R.W. Ross	Law Examiner, Minerals Division, Department of Interior
S.B. Dabny	U.S. Employment Office, Hawaiian Islands
Joseph H.B. Evans	Associate Regional Director, Region IV, Fair Employment Practice Committee
Thomas C. Hall	Assistant Solicitor, Post Office Department
James W. Johnson	Collector of Internal Revenue, Third New York District
Martin A. Martin	Associate Attorney, Department of Justice
Arthur W. Mitchell	Special Consultant, Secretary of War
Nelson H. Nicholes	Acting Territorial Attorney, Virgin Islands
J. Finley Wilson	Consultant, Interracial Section, War Finance Staff
A.H. Dabney	Assistant to Administrator, WPA (Massachusetts)
Augustes Daly	Deputy Collector of Internal Revenue, Third District, New York
Eugene Davidson	Investigator, Fair Employment Practices Committee
William H. Dean, Jr.	Consultant, National Resources Planning Board
Elmer W. Henderson	Field Representative, Fair Employment Practices Committee
William E. Hill	Special Assistant, U.S. Housing Authority
Earl B. Dickerson	Member, Fair Employment Practices Committee
George M. Johnson	Assistant Executive Secretary, Fair Employment Practices Committee
W. Robert Ming	Staff Member, Office of Price Administration

(continued)

Table 12 (continued)

Name	Position
Curtis P. Mitchell	Junior Attorney, Federal Works Agency
Arthur A. Taylor	Assistant U.S. Attorney, New York
Herman A. Washington	Special Assistant, U.S. Housing Authority
Milton P. Webster	Member, Fair Employment Practices Committee
Ralph J. Bunche	Member, Anglo-American Carribean Commission, State Department
Edward Dudley	Legal Council to Governor of Virgin Islands
Phillip J. Jones	Assistant U.S. Attorney, Brooklyn, New York
John R. Pinckell	Member, Small Business Advisory Committee
Lt. Colonel Marcus H. Ray	Civilian Aide to Secretary of War

APPENDIX

Table 13

HIGH-LEVEL BLACK APPOINTMENTS
OF THE KENNEDY ADMINISTRATION

Name	Position
Howard Jenkins, Jr.	Member, National Labor Relations Board
Ruth H. Jones	U.S. Collector of Customs, Virgin Islands
George L.P. Weaver	Assistant Secretary of Labor
Howard B. Woods	Member, Equal Employment Opportunity Committee
Carl T. Rowan	Ambassador to Finland
Robert C. Weaver	Administrator, Housing and Home Finance Agency
Andrew J. Hatcher	Associate Press Secretary
Patricia R. Harris	Co-Chairman, National Women's Committee for Civil Rights
Spottswood W. Robinson III	U.S. District Court Judge, District of Columbia
Wade H. McCree, Jr.	U.S. District Court Judge, Michigan
Thurgood Marshall	Circuit Judge, Second Circuit
Frank Montero	Adviser, U.S. Mission to the United Nations
Clifford R. Wharton	Ambassador to Norway

Table 14

HIGH-LEVEL BLACK APPOINTMENTS
OF THE JOHNSON ADMINISTRATION

Name	Position
James M. Nabrit	Ambassador to the United Nations
Thurgood Marshall	United States Solicitor General; also Associate-Justice, United States Supreme Court
Patricia R. Harris	Ambassador to Luxembourg
Geraldine D. Whittington	White House Secretary
Robert C. Weaver	Secretary, Department of Housing and Urban Development
Carl T. Rowan	Director, United States Information Agency
Howard B. Woods	Associate Director, United States Information Agency
Chester C. Carter	Deputy Chief of Protocol, State Department
Theodore M. Berry	Director, Community Action, Office of Economic Opportunity
Lisle C. Carter	Assistant Director for Inter-Agency Relations, Office of Economic Opportunity
Arthur Christopher, Jr.	Trial Examiner, National Labor Relations Board
Campbell C. Johnson	Assistant Director, Selective Service
Samuel C. Jackson	Commissioner, Equal Employment Opportunity Commission
Aileen C. Hernandez	Commissioner, Equal Employment Opportunity Commission
Wiley A. Branton	Executive Secretary, President's Council on Equal Opportunity
Joseph H. Douglass	Chief, Office of Inter-Agency Liaison, National Institute of Mental Health
Shelton B. Granger	Deputy Assistant Secretary, Health, Education and Welfare Department
Samuel W. Allen	Legal Counsel, Community Relations Service

(continued)

Table 14 (continued)

Name	*Position*
Samuel D. Proctor	Northeast Regional Director, Office of Economic Opportunity
Bennetta B. Washington	Director, Women's Job Corp, Office of Economic Opportunity
Samuel F. Yette	Special Assistant for Civil Rights, Office of Economic Opportunity
Roger W. Wilkins	Director, Community Relations Service
Andrew F. Brimmer	Assistant Secretary of Commerce
Samuel C. Adams Jr.	Overseas Director, Agency for International Development
Thomas E. Posey	Chief, Labor and Industry Division, Agency for International Development
Charlotte M. Hubbard	Deputy Assistant Secretary of State
Samuel Z. Westerfield	Deputy Assistant Secretary, State Department
Hugh G. Robinson	Military Aide to the President
Clifford Alexander, Jr.	Associate Special Counsel to the President
Walter E. Washington	District Commissioner (Mayor), Washington, D.C.

Table 15

BLACK MEMBERSHIP IN THE UNITED STATES
HOUSE OF REPRESENTATIVES (1973)

Name	Party	State
Ronald V. Dellums	Democrat	California
Augustus F. Hawkins	Democrat	California
Yvonne B. Burke	Democrat	California
Andrew Young	Democrat	Georgia
Ralph H. Metcalfe	Democrat	Illinois
Parren J. Mitchell	Democrat	Illinois
John Conyers, Jr.	Democrat	Michigan
Charles C. Diggs, Jr.	Democrat	Michigan
William Clay	Democrat	Missouri
Shirley Chisholm	Democrat	New York
Charles B. Rangel	Democrat	New York
Louis Stokes	Democrat	Ohio
Robert N.C. Nix	Democrat	Pennsylvania
Barbara C. Jordan	Democrat	Texas
Walter Fauntleroy*	Democrat	Dist. of Columbia

* Non-voting member

Table 16

PORTIONS OF FEDERAL CONSTITUTION
DIRECTLY AFFECTED BY PRESENCE OF NEGRO
(1787)

Preamble: *The term "People" used as collective political*
voice of "Persons" so as not to exclude negroes
from moral consideration as humans

Article	*Section*	*Clause*	*Subject Covered*
1	2	1	Composition and election of members of House of Representatives based upon choice of people
		3	Apportionment of direct taxes and enumeration in the House, distinction among several categories of persons
	9	1	Migration or importation of persons, tax on such importation
4	2	1	Rights of citizens
		3	Return of escaped persons bound to service or labor

Table 17

NUMBER OF BLACKS HELD IN BONDAGE
(1790–1860)

Year	Number
1790	697,897
1800	893,041
1810	1,191,364
1820	1,538,038
1830	2,009,043
1840	2,487,455
1850	3,204,313
1860	3,953,760

Figures taken from U.S. Census Reports for years shown.

SELECT BIBLIOGRAPHY

Adams, Henry. *History of the United States During the First Administration of Thomas Jefferson.* New York: Charles Scribner's Sons, 1931.
Agar, Herbert. *The Price of Union.* Cambridge: The Riverside Press, 1950.
Bunche, Ralph J. *The Political Status of the Negro in the Age of F.D.R.* Dewey W. Grantham, ed., Chicago: University of Chicago Press, 1973.
Curtis, Francis. *The Republican Party 1854-1904.* (2 vols.). New York: G. P. Putnam's Sons, 1904.
De Bow, J. D. B. *The Industrial Resources of the Southern and Western States.* (3 vols.). New Orleans: De Bow's Review, 1852.
Douglass, Frederick. *Life and Times of Frederick Douglass.* Hartford: Park Publishing Company, 1881.
Du Bois, William E. B. *The Negro.* New York: Henry Holt and Company, 1915.
Du Bois, William E. B. *Black Reconstruction.* New York: Harcourt Brace and Company, 1935.
Dubroca, Louis. *La Vie de Toussaint-L'ouverture: Chef des Noirs Insurgés de Saint-Domingue.* Paris: 1802.
Educational Heritage Inc. *Negroes in Public Affairs and Government.* Yonkers: Educational Heritage Inc., 1966.
Foner, Eric. *Free Soil, Free Labor, Free Men: The Ideology of the Republican Party before the Civil War.* New York: Oxford University Press, 1970.
Fortune, Thomas T. *Land, Labor, and Politics in the South.* New York: Fords, Howard and Hulburt, 1884.
Gatewood, Williard B. *Theodore Roosevelt and the Art of Controversy: Episodes of the White House Years.* Baton Rouge: Louisiana State Press, 1970.
Gilpin, Henry D. (ed.). *The Papers of James Madison and His Reports of Debates in the Federal Convention.* New York: J. and H.G. Langley, 1841.

SELECT BIBLIOGRAPHY

Gosnell, Harold. *Negro Politicians: The Rise of Negro Politics in Chicago.* Chicago: University of Chicago Press, 1935.

Helper, Hinton R. *The Impending Crisis of the South.* New York: A. B. Burdick Publisher, 1860.

Herskovits, Melville J. *The Myth of The Negro Past.* New York: Harper and Brothers, 1943.

Hildreth, Richard. *Despotism in America, An Inquiry into the Slave-holding System.* Cleveland: John Jewett and Company, 1854.

Holden, Matthew. *The Divisible Republic.* New York: Abelard-Schuman, 1973.

Kirk, Porter. *The History of Suffrage in the United States.* Chicago: University of Chicago Press, 1918.

Korngold, Ralph. *Citizen Toussaint.* Boston: Little, Brown, and Company, 1944.

Lewison, Paul. *Race, Class and Party: A History of Negro Suffrage and White Politics in the South.* New York: Russell and Russell, 1963.

Logan, Rayford W. *The Betrayal of the Negro: From Rutherford B. Hayes to Woodrow Wilson.* New York: Collier Books, 1965.

Lynch, John R. *Facts on Reconstruction.* Washington, D.C.: Neale Publishing Company, 1924.

Malcolm, X. *The Autobiography of Malcolm X.* New York: Grove Press, 1964.

Meier, August. *Negro Thought in America, 1880-1915: Racial Ideologies in the Age of Booker T. Washington.* Ann Arbor: University of Michigan Press, 1963.

Métral, Antoine. *Historie de L'expédition des Francais a Saint-Domingue: Sous le Consulat de Napoléon Bonaparte.* Paris: Fanjat Ainé, 1825.

Miller, Kelly. *Race Adjustment.* Washington, D.C.: Neale Publishing Company, 1910.

Moon, Henry L. *Balance of Power: The Negro Vote.* Garden City: Doubleday and Company, 1948.

Nowlin, William F. *The Negro in American National Politics (Since 1868).* Boston: Stratford, 1931.

Porter, Kirk H. and Donald Bruce Johnson. *National Party Platforms 1840-1968.* Chicago: University of Illinois Press, 1970.

Schlesinger, Arthur M., Jr. *History of U.S. Political Parties 1789-1972.* (4 vols.). New York: Chelsea House Publishers, 1973.

Seilhamer, George O. *History of the Republican Party.* (2 vols.). New York: Judge Publishing Company, 1899.

Stone, Chuck. *Black Political Power in America.* Indianapolis: Bobbs-Merrill, 1968.

Sundquist, James L. *Politics and Policy: The Eisenhower, Kennedy, and Johnson Years.* Washington, D.C.: The Brookings Institution, 1968.

Tatum, Elbert L. *The Changed Political Thought of the Negro, 1915-1940.* New York: Exposition Press, 1951.

United States Commission on Civil Rights. *Political Participation.* Washington, D.C.: U.S. Government Printing Office, 1968.

Vander, Harry J. III. *The Political and Economic Progress of the American Negro.* Dubuque: Wm. C. Brown Book Company, 1968.

SELECT BIBLIOGRAPHY

Walton, Hanes, Jr. *The Negro in Third Party Politics.* Philadelphia: Dorrance and Company, 1964.

Washington, Booker T. *Up From Slavery: An Autobiography.* Garden City: Doubleday, Page and Company, 1901.

Washington, Booker T. *The Man Farthest Down.* Garden City: Doubleday, Page and Company, 1912.

Weiner, Leo. *Africa and the Discovery of America.* (3 vols.). Philadelphia: Innes and Sons, 1922.

Williams, George W. *History of the Negro Race in America.* New York: G. P. Putnam's Sons, 1883.

Woodson, Carter G. *The Negro in Our History.* Washington, D.C.: Associated Publishers, 1922.

INDEX

INDEX

INDEX

Kansas-Nebraska Territory, 132, 156
Kansas River, 65
Kansas Territory, 64–68, 70, 71, 74,
    75, 76, 77, 80, 86–88, 91, 92
Keating, Kenneth, 167
Keith, Laurence M., 78
Kennedy, John F., 145–146, 147,
    149, 165, 169
Kennedy, Robert, 146
Kentucky and Virginia resolutions, 132
Kierkegaard, Sören, 173
King, John A., 68
King, Martin Luther, 149–150
King, Martin Luther (Mrs.), 169
King, Preston, 83, 103
Knowland, William, 167
"Know-Nothing" Party, 59, 63, 69,
    70, 96
Ku Klux Klan, 161, 163

Lamon, Ward, 106
Lane, Henry S., 70, 71, 100, 101,
    103, 104
Lane, Joseph, 98
Laurens, Henry, 6
Lawrence (Kansas), 65, 66, 67
Leavenworth (Kansas), 65, 67
Le Clerc, Charles, 17, 18, 19
Lecompton Constitution, 87–89, 91, 93
Lee, Robert E., 93, 95, 108
Lewis, Dixon H., 42
Liberator, The, 31
Liberty League, 46
Liberty Party, 34, 40–41, 46
"Lily White," 166
Lincoln, Abraham, 42, 44, 72, 89–92,
    96, 101–103, 104–105, 106, 107,
    108, 109, 110, 111, 115, 137, 138,
    147, 159, 160, 164, 172
Lincoln-Douglas Debates, 91
Linn, Lewis F., 33
"Little Giant," (*see* Douglas, Stephen
    A.)
Livingston, Robert, 18
Lodge, Henry Cabot, 119
Lords of the Lash, 53
Lords of the Loom, 53
Louisiana Purchase, 17, 20, 26
L'Ouverture, Toussaint, 17–20
Lovejoy, Elijah, 31
Lovejoy, Owen, 89, 91
Lynching, 163, 164

Maddox, Lester, 166

Madison, James, 10, 11, 12, 24, 132
Manifest destiny, 20, 51
Mansfield, Mike, 148
Marshall, James W., 47
Marshall, Thomas F., 35
Marshall, Thurgood, 151
Mason-Dixon Line, 69, 80, 81, 82, 84,
    86, 114, 116, 141, 164
Mason, James M., 78, 95
Mauritius, 40
McClellan, George B., 109
McKinley, William E., 120, 123
McLean, John, 72
Meredith, James, 146
Mexican cession, 44
Mexico, 33, 37, 38, 39, 41–42, 43, 44,
    45, 54
Mexico, Gulf of, 17, 37
Migration, 163
Military districts, 111–112
Mississippi River, 18, 20, 26
Mississippi Territory, 15
Missouri, 25–28, 33, 66, 68, 71, 82,
    93, 102, 105
Missouri *Brunswicker,* 65
Missouri Compromise, 28, 33, 43, 49,
    54, 55, 56, 57, 58, 59, 70, 71, 75,
    84, 85, 89, 102, 154, 156
Mitchell, Arthur, 140, 141
Mitchell, Charles L., 114
Monroe, James, 24, 25, 28
Montgomery (Alabama), 113, 167
Moon, Henry Lee, 143–144, 166
Morgan, Edwin D., 92, 99, 103
"Morgan's Forty," 62
Morrill, Lot M., 92
Morris, Gouverneur, 9
Morton, Oliver P., 80
Mosaic Law, 3, 4
Mulattoes, 18

Napoleon, 17–20
Narvaéz, 3
National Anti-Slavery Society, 31
National Association for the Advance-
    ment of Colored People (NAACP),
    134, 135, 138, 140, 143, 146, 168
National Colored Democratic League,
    134
National Independent Political League,
    134
National Negro Democratic Convention,
    133
National Republicans, 25

222

INDEX